Bill 'Swampy' Marsh is an award-winning writer/performer of stories, songs and plays. He spent most of his youth in rural south-western New South Wales. Bill was forced to give up any idea he had of a 'career' as a cricketer when a stint at agricultural college was curtailed because of illness, and so began his hobby of writing. After backpacking through three continents and working in the wine industry, his writing hobby blossomed into a career.

His first collection of short stories, *Beckom Pop. 64,* was published in 1988, his second, *Old Yanconian Daze*, in 1995 and his third, *Looking for Dad*, in 1998. During 1999 Bill released *Australia*, a CD of his songs and stories. That was followed in 2002 by *A Drover's Wife* and *Glory, Glory: A Tribute to the Royal Flying Doctor Service* in 2008. He has written soundtrack songs and music for the television documentaries *The Last Mail from Birdsville: The Story of Tom Kruse*, *Source to Sea: The Story of the Murray Riverboats* and the German travel documentaries *Traumzeit auf dem Stuart Highway*, *Clinic Flights (Tilpa & Marble Bar)*, *Traumzeit in den Kimberleys* and *Einsatz von Port Hedland nach Marble Bar*.

Bill runs writing workshops throughout Australia and is a teacher of short-story writing within the Adelaide Institute of TAFE's Professional Writing Unit. He has won and judged many nationwide short-story writing and song-writing competitions and short-film awards.

*Great Australian Outback Police Stories* is part of a very successful series of 'Great Australian' stories including: *Amazing Grace: Stories of faith and friendship from outback Australia* (2014), *The Complete Book of Australian Flying Doctor Stories* and *Great Australian Outback School Stories* (2013), *Great Australian Country Women's Association Stories* (2011), *New Great Australian Flying Doctor Stories* and *The ABC Book of Great Aussie Stories for Young People* (2010), *Great Australian Stories: Outback Towns and Pubs* (2009), *More Great Australian Flying Doctor Stories* (2007), *Great Australian Railway Stories* (2005), *Great Australian Droving Stories* (2003), *Great Australian Shearing Stories* (2001) and *Great Australian Flying Doctor Stories* (1999). Bill's story of *Goldie: Adventures in a vanishing Australia* was published in 2008 and his semi-autobiographical collection *Swampy: Tall tales and true from boyhood and beyond* was published in 2012.

More information about the author can be found at
www.billswampymarsh.com

# GREAT AUSTRALIAN OUTBACK POLICE STORIES

BILL 'SWAMPY' MARSH

ABC Books

'Stan the Shearer' has been adapted from R. Paul Brady's self-published book *Don't Go Down the Mine Daddy* (2004).
'The Big Hit' has been adapted from Bill's book *Goldie: Adventures in a vanishing Australia* (2008).

ABC Books

The ABC 'Wave' device is a trademark of the Australian Broadcasting Corporation and is used under licence by HarperCollins*Publishers* Australia.

First published in Australia in 2015
by HarperCollins*Publishers* Australia Pty Limited
ABN 36 009 913 517
harpercollins.com.au



**HarperCollins*Publishers***
Level 13, 201 Elizabeth Street, Sydney NSW 2000, Australia
Unit D1, 63 Apollo Drive, Rosedale, Auckland 0632, New Zealand
A 53, Sector 57, Noida, UP, India
1 London Bridge Street, London SE1 9GF, United Kingdom
2 Bloor Street East, 20th floor, Toronto, Ontario M4W 1A8, Canada
195 Broadway, New York, NY 10007, USA

National Library of Australia Cataloguing-in-Publication data:

Marsh, Bill, 1950– author.
Great Australian outback police stories / Bill 'Swampy' Marsh.
978 0 7333 3314 9 (paperback)
978 1 4607 0210 9 (ebook)
Series: Marsh, Bill, 1950– Great Australian stories.
Police, Rural — Australia — Anecdotes.
Australia — Social life and customs.
363.20994

Cover design by Hazel Lam, HarperCollins Design Studio
Cover image courtesy of Alice Springs Collection, Northern Territory Library (PH0034/0068)
Author photo by Chris Carter
Typeset in 10/15pt ITC Bookman by Kelli Lonergan
Printed and bound in Australia by Griffin Press
The papers used by HarperCollins in the manufacture of this book are a natural, recyclable product made from wood grown in sustainable plantation forests. The fibre source and manufacturing processes meet recognised international environmental standards, and carry certification.

Dedicated to R. Paul Brady —
a true mate

**Warning:** This book may contain the names of Aboriginal and Torres Strait Islander people now deceased.

The stories contained in this compilation are derived from interviews. In order to preserve the authenticity of these oral accounts the language used and the views expressed are faithful to the original story-telling. The publisher acknowledges that some of the language used and the views expressed in relation to Indigenous people and the Stolen Generations may be harmful or cause offence to some readers.

**Publisher's note:** The publisher does not necessarily endorse the views expressed or the language used in any of the stories.

Special thanks to Brigitta Doyle and the editing and promotions staff at ABC Books–HarperCollins Australia without whose support these stories may never have seen the light of day; and to my precious support crew of Chris Collins, Kath Beauchamp, David Hansford, Craig Langley, Margaret Loveday and Margaret Worth.

Thanks also to Sunil Badami and Mark Sutton from the *Overnights* programme on ABC Local Radio, and programme director Angie Nelson-Trivisonno, for their support in helping get the word out about my seeking people to interview for these stories.

In 2014 I was involved as Writer-in-Residence for the Festival of a Thousand Stories, a celebration of storytelling, art, poetry and music at Bourke, on the banks of the Darling River. During my time there I met many wonderful people, all with a story or three to tell. In particular I'd like to thank the organisers of the festival and of the Poets Trek where we spent two days journeying across the 'grey plains and red mulga paddocks' in the footsteps of Henry Lawson, Will Ogilvie and Harry 'Breaker' Morant. As Henry Lawson wrote in 1892 when he was in Bourke: 'If you know Bourke, you know Australia'.

During the research process of this book, my partner, Margaret Worth, and I went on a 11,000-kilometre, six-week trip from Adelaide, through the west coast of South Australia, then across the Nullarbor Plain, up to Kalgoorlie, Meekatharra, Newman, Tom Price, Karratha, Port Hedland, Broome, then across the Gibb River Road before branching north up to Mitchell Falls, then back to Kununurra, on to Katherine and home down the Stuart Highway. During that time I interviewed many, many people not only for this book but for future books to come. I'd like to thank those who looked after us during the trip and in particular a big thanks to the Western Australian Police network, who provided me with so many contacts.

It was a very special trip. I know that travel in Australia is expensive and, because of our vast distances, it's time consuming. Yet, while it may be more 'relaxing' and 'cheaper' to pop over to neighbouring places, when you visit some of our natural wonders like Karajini National Park, in the Pilbara region of Western Australia, and the Bungle Bungles and Mitchell Falls, up in the Kimberleys, it does make the effort and expense worthwhile ... and it is our country — our own backyard. This is where our stories are. This is where we learn about our past, where we walk and talk about our present and where we can look into our future.

We are one of the greatest countries in the world and, if we care for it, we have the greatest potential in the world. So, if you do get the time, travel Australia. I'd love to see you out on the road, somewhere.

# Contents


| | |
|---|---|
| Contributors | xi |
| A Policeman's Wife | 1 |
| A Real Education | 6 |
| A Satisfying Result | 11 |
| Aboriginal Police Aides | 17 |
| About Stanley | 22 |
| Airborne | 26 |
| Alf and the Demolition Squad | 31 |
| An Interesting Place | 36 |
| As it Happened | 40 |
| Batman | 45 |
| Beady Eyes | 48 |
| Biggest Beat in the World | 52 |
| Caring | 57 |
| Collar and Tie | 61 |
| Derby | 64 |
| Dinky-di | 68 |
| Dope | 73 |
| Drunks' Assessment Form | 81 |
| Emoluments | 82 |
| Enterprising | 86 |
| Evacuation | 89 |
| Exemplary: Yalgoo's Bush Copper | 94 |
| Eye-opener | 99 |
| Forty-five Minutes | 104 |
| Good Friends | 112 |
| Green | 120 |
| Guilty? | 125 |
| Gutted | 131 |
| Indicators | 135 |
| Kip and Me | 139 |

| | |
|---|---|
| Lame Dick | 142 |
| Malachi Martin | 145 |
| Memories of Maffra | 150 |
| My Grandfather, Tracker Williams | 155 |
| No Power | 161 |
| Not a Wink | 165 |
| Nowhere to Hide | 170 |
| Nullarbor Highway Patrol | 174 |
| Once Was Lost | 180 |
| Over the Moon | 188 |
| People of the Outback | 193 |
| Policeman-the-Bastard | 197 |
| Policing 'The Coen' | 204 |
| Regret Jobs | 208 |
| Scary | 214 |
| Sequel | 219 |
| Speeding | 227 |
| Stan the Shearer | 232 |
| Stunning | 236 |
| The Big Hit | 241 |
| The Captain's Lady — Ballad of Mary Ann Bugg | 248 |
| The First Wife | 250 |
| The Plunkett Shield | 253 |
| The Poetic Policeman | 258 |
| The Shirt off his Back | 260 |
| The Sundown Murders | 265 |
| The Trailer | 269 |
| Visa | 275 |
| Wife-to-be | 281 |
| Wild West | 285 |

# Contributors

The stories contained in this book are written from interviews recorded by Bill 'Swampy' Marsh. The contributors are:

Larry Adams
Bernard & Kay Arrantash
Kath & Noel Beauchamp
Georgia Banks
Rod Boehm
R. Paul Brady
Ray Briggs
Malcolm and Sandra Cole
Chris Collins
John Denham
Brian Eddy
Bruce & Patricia Evans
Jack Goldsmith
Rob & Pat Greenhill
Tiffany Greig
Judy Harland
David & Christine Harris
Matt Hartfield
Garry Hera-Singh
Tim Jennings
Greg Johns
Kevin Jones
Peter Joyce
Roman Kulkewycz
Craig Langley
George A Lee
David Arthur Lindner
Margaret Loveday
Jock MacDonald
Jeanette Mann
Darryl 'Dmac' McCormack
Dan McIntosh
Ian 'Mac' McKechnie
Barb Meredith
Bev Mezzen
Larry Morgan
Kevin 'Kev' Murphy
Roger Parker
Frank and Marie Partington
Allan Peters
Garry 'Gazza' & Pol Purcell
Paul Roe
Jenny Scott
Darren Seivwright
Peter Stephen
Mark Sutton
James Sykes
Peter and Yvonne Threlfall
Margaret Williams

Plus many, many more ...

# A Policeman's Wife

I met my wife twenty-one years ago. It was the night before I did the senior constable exam and a few of us police officers were staying at the Flinders Hotel in Port Augusta. Her parents owned the pub and she was there with a couple of her girlfriends. We met in the bar and we just started chatting.

In outback South Australia, traditionally, the June long weekend is when they hold the Marree races. At that stage I was stationed up at Leigh Creek and the girls asked if we were going to go to the races. I told them yes and that I'd been rostered on duty for the weekend and they said, in a friendly sort of way, 'Oh well, we might see you there.' And that was it.

On the Friday night before the races I was driving to Marree. I was by myself, in a police car, in uniform. From Leigh Creek to Marree was about a hundred and twenty kilometres. In those days it was bitumen as far as Lyndhurst then dirt for the remaining eighty kilometres to Marree. After I went through Lyndhurst a car pulled in behind me, from the Strzelecki Track. Its lights were on high beam and so I'm thinking, You beauty, I'm a young officious copper, I've got myself a drink-driver here. So I stopped and I got out and I pulled this car over. It was a Falcon utility, the type that had a bench seat with a fold-down armrest. There were three girls in the front and, as it turned out, the driver was sober.

As I said, it was dark and so while I'm talking to the driver, unbeknown to me, the girl on the far side of the front passenger seat, she's slipped out of the ute. Anyhow I said, 'See you later,' to the female driver and when I got back to my car there's this girl sitting there; the very same one I'd been chatting to at the hotel in Port Augusta. In those days rum and Coca-Cola was the drink of choice and she'd obviously had a few of those and the last thing I wanted was to turn up in Marree with a girl who'd been drinking. So, about five kilometres out of town, I made her get out of the car. I said, 'You just wait here. Your friends are right behind us. They'll pick you up and take you into town.'

So the story is, I was on duty and my wife-to-be picked me up in my own police car. That's what I say anyway. At that time she was governessing out at Innamincka Station and she was on her way to Marree to catch up with friends for the races. That's when we got together. The following year she was 'belle of the ball' at the Marree races, and I proposed to her. She accepted and eighteen months later we married and we went on to live in a number of outback towns, during which time we had two children. On both those occasions my wife was flown out to Adelaide because they don't like ladies having babies in the bush, just in case of complications.

But back then it was a real team effort for a married couple to go and live in the bush. There was an expectation, especially in the small one-man police stations, that the policeman's wife would step in and look after things when you weren't available. I never worked in a one-man station but in the stations I did work in, my wife had as important a role as I had. If we were out on patrol and a telephone call came in while the other police officers were busy somewhere else, my wife would have to be on hand to answer the call. Same thing: if the station was vacant and someone came in wanting to know some information, she'd have to be available and able to answer their questions. She became as much a part of the social fabric of the town as a police officer was expected to be.

One time we were stationed in the outback. I won't mention the name of the town nor will I mention the names of any of the people who were involved. By that stage our first child wasn't much more than a toddler and the second wasn't even a year old. On this particular day there was only me and an Indigenous community constable on duty. That left me as officer-in-charge.

One of my best mates in town was the local publican and we kind of had a bit of fun-type banter going between us. There'd been a bit of rain around of late and I decided to ring the publican to fill him in on the state of the roads so that he could pass on the information to any tourists who may have been passing through. The instant he heard my voice, he said, 'A guy's in the pub shooting.'

I kind of didn't believe him to start with. I thought he was pulling my leg.

'You're kidding me,' I said.

'No,' he replied, 'I'm fair dinkum.'

As it turned out this bloke had arrived in town with an Aboriginal woman and her two children and he'd just fired a shot down at the hotel. Anyhow I put on my gun belt and grabbed a shotgun. By the time my constable and I got to the hotel there was a man standing outside, in an agitated state, holding a rifle. My offsider had had some trouble with his accoutrement belt so I gave him my revolver and we walked towards the man, all the time asking him to put down the gun. As we did he lifted his rifle and pointed it at us. We then headed to the hotel for cover.

'Put the gun down,' I kept yelling. 'Just put the gun down and let's talk.'

And that's when he fired the first shot at me.

By now he's extremely agitated and he fired a second shot at me. I ducked behind some shelter and he went behind a fence at the hotel. At that point a local woman walked between us and I told her in no uncertain terms to get out of the way. No sooner had she moved than a group of tourists drove down the main street and so I motioned for them to get out of the way as well.

It was about that same time that the man noticed my community constable. 'Is that cop Aboriginal?' he asked. When I told him that he was, he said, 'I want to speak to him.'

I said, 'Mate, we can organise something but put the gun down first.'

Which he didn't. He began walking towards us. Then when he was barely ten metres away, he stopped. At that stage we were pretty much trapped. He then aimed his rifle at me. I aimed my shotgun at him and asked him once more to put the gun down.

'Put the gun down. Put the gun down.'

When he didn't, I pulled the trigger.

But nothing happened.

The safety was still on the shotgun. I then released the safety and asked him one last time to put the gun down. When he didn't, I fired three shots. During the firing of those three shots, he fired at me. I felt the bullet pass just above my head. I later found out that it went through the window of the hotel, ricocheted around the front bar and ended up in a mural on the wall.

The long and short of it was that I fatally shot the man. It's all on record. There were inquiries and so forth and the coroner's report is there for all to see, and I was exonerated.

But probably the main point I'd like to get across is that all during this time my wife was manning the communications over in the police station. Now, if you can imagine: there she is caring for our two very young children. While she's trying to keep them calm, she's also desperately trying to get through to a much larger centre in an attempt to get help. And that's all going on while her husband's out on the street being shot at.

What made matters worse was that someone in town had a young relative working as a journalist on a city newspaper. And when he saw what was going on, he got in touch with her so that she could be the first to break the news. Next thing, there's a newsflash all over the state about how there's been a police shooting up at this particular town. So now there's worried parents and so forth trying to get in touch with my wife, thinking that I might've been the one who'd been shot.

So it was a very tense time; a time in which I carried out my duty in the manner I was trained and paid to do as a member of the police force. But like I said, back in those days it was just an expectation that a policeman's wife took on that type of role willingly, to be supportive of the spouse and to help develop their spouse's career. Back in those days there was no pay for doing that — none at all — and there has never been any official recognition for the part my wife played in the incident. And I reckon she, as do many a police officer's partner, deserves a hell of a lot of recognition.

# A Real Education

I was born in 1925, at a town called Cleve, which is over on the Eyre Peninsula of South Australia. My father was a World War One ex-serviceman and he applied for and got a 1400-acre wheat and sheep block, six mile west of town. Then in 1933 one of my sisters developed very severe polio and my parents decided to move nearer to Adelaide where she'd be closer to medical help. So they sold up and bought a twenty-acre block near Salisbury where they went into dairy farming.

Dairy farming wasn't for me. My mother always wanted me to be either a school teacher or a policeman and I wasn't sure I'd be able to handle classrooms full of kids for the rest of my life so I decided on the police force. Back then you had to be sixteen before you joined and I didn't waste time. I turned sixteen on the 4th of October '41 and I joined the force as a junior constable two days later. We did our training down at the old Port Adelaide encampment. It had originally been set up to help keep things under control after they'd had riots down there during the Depression. Later on, of course, we were shifted from Port Adelaide up to the new Thebarton Police Barracks. That was in about 1943.

So I finished my training and all of that then, in 1945, when the war was in its finishing stages, the Northern Territory Police wanted to get a few of us young fellers on deck for when the army left. Five of us were selected and we were transferred to the Northern Territory Police for two years. We went to Darwin for a start. Darwin was the main naval base for the Americans so it was a pretty lively place to be, then I was sent down to the Daly River.

Daly River's about a hundred and fifty mile due south of Darwin. There was no town there as such, just a very small settlement with a police station set in amongst virgin country. As far as the police force went in Daly River there was only me and old Taz Fister; just the two of us, that's all. Taz was one of them real old-time Territory policemen. He had a wealth of knowledge of the outback and of Aboriginals. In fact, back in the 1930s, when he'd been stationed up at Timber Creek, he became well-known for tracking down and arresting the Aboriginal murderer Nemarluk.

Nemarluk was a local warrior who'd vowed to kill anyone who intruded on his country. To that end he and some of his mates murdered three Japanese fishermen by luring them in with some of his Aboriginal women. Nemarluk and his mates were duly arrested and taken to Darwin where they were found guilty and sentenced to death. But before the sentence could be carried out, Nemarluk made his escape by swimming across Darwin Harbour. Mind you, that was some sort of a feat because it's swimming something like five miles against some pretty strong rips and he did it without running into any of the local crocodiles. He then remained at large for another six months or so until Fitz, another constable by the name of Birt, plus four black trackers, including the equally legendary Bul Bul, eventually recaptured Nemarluk on Legune Station, near the mouth of the Victoria River.

But something that was very interesting to me was when Taz would take me out on patrol throughout the Daly River police district. These patrols were done entirely on horseback. They happened every six months or so and they lasted for a few weeks. It was quite a trip. Old Taz and I and two black trackers would take off with something like twenty horses. Each bloke had two horses for riding, then there were the packhorses who carried all your swags and your cooking gear and lots of tinned food and anything else you needed. At night you'd hobble the horses then light a fire and have a bit of tucker and sleep out in your swag.

Along the way we'd check all the Aboriginal settlements — well, when I say settlements, the Aboriginals in those days in the inner parts of Australia were pretty much still living in their traditional way; just more or less roaming the country day by day. Our main objective was to show them that the police were interested in their welfare. We also visited the various cattle stations to see how things were going there and to check that they were looking after their Aboriginal people okay. Because it was such an isolated area, and not many white people passed through, we were always much welcomed by the station people. They'd even supply us with some salted meat to take along. Salted meat was the prime thing in those days. With no refrigeration, fresh meat would only keep for a few days so, when you killed a beast, you ate what you could fresh, then you salted the rest. I think we ended up living on salted beef and tinned tucker for the entire time we were out on patrol. We hardly had any fresh vegetables at all, not that I can remember anyway.

After Daly River I was transferred to Alice Springs. That was in 1946 when the army was just being let go. Alice Springs wasn't a very big place in those days. I remember there was still a team of Americans out at the aerodrome. They were piloting the big planes. The armed forces used to look after their own people pretty much, but some of the young outback fellers, what we used to call 'ringers', would come into town every three months or so. There were only two hotels in the Alice back then and they'd be bulging at the seams, so she'd be a lively place.

I then came back to South Australia and I went into the Mounted Police. Sometimes, if a country policeman was going on holidays, I'd also go out on relief. I was sent out to Fink one time. Fink's just over the South Australian border, into the Northern Territory. Fink was a railway town. There were five or six permanent homes there for the fettlers and the like, then there was a police station and a telegraph operator. That was the basis of the town. Not much else was there. They didn't even have a pub in those days.

A man named Ron Brown — Brownie — was the policeman at Fink and, when we went out on patrol, because of the desert country that ran all through that area, horses weren't much good, so this time it was on camels. And if you've ever tried riding a camel, it's certainly a different kettle of fish to riding a horse. At least a horse has some sort of a rhythm whereas a camel has a rhythm all of its own. But you get used to it. You had to, and you had enough time to, because the Fink camel patrol covered a huge area. Back in those days it was reckoned to be the world's largest police beat. It took in Mount Dare Station, in the far north of South Australia, then up to Alice Springs, over through the Olgas, Ayers Rock, Lake Amadeus and right over to Mount Gosse in Western Australia

Again it was a similar sort of patrol. There was quite an Aboriginal population that worked on the cattle stations so you had to make sure that everything was going okay there. Actually I had the utmost respect for those Aboriginal stockmen. They kept the whole show together in many ways. And if you were an Aboriginal stockman, working on a cattle station, one of the benefits was that your wife and kids could also live on the station and they were looked after by the station people as well. Many of these places were like little communities. So you'd check on their welfare and make sure they were being treated okay.

As far as the station people went, in those days they were very much pioneering folk. Hard as nails most of them, and I'd say pretty well all of them realised just how tough it'd be trying to make a go of it out there without Aboriginal help. For that reason they used to treat their Aboriginal people reasonably good. Actually it worked very well; that was right up until a few years ago when the laws were changed and the station owners had to pay the Aboriginal stockmen and so forth the proper wage.

In many ways you could say that that's when things started to fall down, because the station people couldn't afford to pay the Aboriginals the proper wage and, without any work, that's when they started drifting into the towns and onto reserves and that.

But that early part of my life in the police force was a real education for me. At that age you're receptive to anything that goes on and so I learnt a lot about the outback and the people who lived out there, both black and white.

# A Satisfying Result

My name is Jim Sykes. I retired from the South Australian Police Force back in 1984 after forty-two years of service. During that time I spent quite a few years in the bush. But being the only policeman in a small country town is not as easy as it may sound. In 1956 I was transferred to Marree — a small town in the far north of South Australia, at the head of the Birdsville Track — where the district I was responsible for was roughly three hundred miles by four hundred miles. In other words, 120,000 square miles.

Apart from those who were employed by the Commonwealth Government like the roadmaster, the stationmaster and the postmaster, there were no other officials in town, other than the Justices of the Peace and myself. The roadmaster was the person who took on the responsibility of looking after all the rolling stock and the upkeep of the rail tracks. That included the maintenance crews who were stationed out in fettlers' camps, which were set about thirty miles or so apart along the rail line. The stationmaster, on the other hand, managed the movement of all the goods and passenger trains. The postmaster looked after the reception and delivery of all postal articles. He was also responsible for manning the switchboard, which controlled all the telephone connections within the town. Back in '56 only nine places in Marree were on the telephone system: the police station, the District and Bush Nursing Hospital, the railway station, the general store, the butcher's shop, Marree Hotel, the school headmaster's house and two private residences.

As the only policeman in town I was soon made aware that I was expected to represent many local organisations and other government departments. On my first day I was informed that I'd been appointed secretary to the District and Bush Nursing Hospital; a job that included being coordinator to the Broken Hill base of the Royal Flying Doctor Service. As we had no resident doctor, Broken Hill, in far-western New South Wales, was our closest medical service. State government department responsibilities included clerk of the local court, local court bailiff, clerk of the police court, police prosecutor, court orderly, commissioner for taking affidavits in and for the Supreme Court of South Australia as well as coroner's constable, to name just a few.

I was also expected to prepare documents for prosecution purposes, type up any evidence and, as arresting officer, give evidence relevant to the particular charge. In addition I was appointed keeper of Marree Commonage as well as stock and health inspector. Then there was assistant protector of Aborigines, which included being the official issuer of food vouchers and blankets, assisting with medical attention to the Aboriginal inhabitants who numbered forty in the town and about four hundred at the Finniss Springs Mission and other outlying districts. I was also issuer of gun licences, collector of dog scalps and was expected to collect monies outstanding for other various government departments as well as carrying out all my general duties in relation to crime and minor traffic matters.

On top of all that, my tasks and responsibilities for policing the cattle industry were enormous in as much as a great deal of my work was spent checking the shipment of the cattle. At that time Marree was where the narrow-gauge railway line from the north met the standard-gauge line heading south. So the cattle that had been railed down from Alice Springs and beyond — which could've meant a journey of anything up to five days and, in isolated cases, without water or food — were unloaded from the narrow gauge, into spelling yards where they were fed and rested. After recovering, they were then reloaded into standard-gauge trucks and sent south to the Adelaide markets.

I well remember a trainload of 'store' cattle arriving from the north. Because of drought, they were in very weak condition. The intention was for them to be transhipped south where they were to be sold and fattened for market. As I watched the cattle being unloaded down a race into the spelling yards, I noticed that many had serious leg injuries so I instructed that they be placed in a separate yard. Worse still, when I inspected the rail trucks I found quite a few cattle who were unable to stand or move. I then ordered the train drover — the person in charge of the stock while they were being transported — to offload those animals. As it's impossible to lift a full-grown bullock, the poor beasts had to be tied by rope and dragged out of the rail truck by the brute strength of a number of men, sometimes with the help of a stockhorse. It was then my duty to dispose of those animals. From memory, I shot about thirty head.

The train drover then had to arrange for the carcasses to be taken to a place just west of town where he had to set fire to them and maintain that fire until they were totally destroyed. In all, this took about three days. As luck would have it, the prevailing winds were not westerlies so the township avoided the horrible stench of the burning carcasses. As I was also the enforcer of the Prevention of Cruelty to Animals Act, I then had to ensure that there was no neglect on the part of the train drover. This was a very difficult task and, although I spent many hours investigating the matter, I was never able to obtain sufficient evidence for a prosecution.

Of course then there were the drovers on horseback who brought mobs of up to three thousand head of cattle, down from south-western Queensland, to the rail head at Marree. This meant a walk of near on five hundred miles down the Birdsville Track and, as cattle can only be moved a few miles a day, the drover, his men and his stock could be on the road for up to several months. During that time they'd pass through a number of station properties, and it was the drover's job to make sure that any cattle belonging to the landowners did not join his herd. To that end I had to keep a wary eye out for any thefts of stock that may have occurred along the way.

The nearest police station north of Marree was Birdsville, in Queensland, and the only communication we had was over the Flying Doctor's network. So any messages to and from Birdsville had to be done via the RFDS radio frequency during a timeslot known as the 'Galah Sessions'. These Galah Sessions also provided the only means by which the cattle station people could talk to one another and have any telegrams read out. In doing so, all voice and telegram transmissions could be overheard by everyone else throughout the network, meaning that everyone got to know everyone else's business — thus the term 'Galah Sessions'.

There were good drovers and bad drovers both on the trains and also of those coming down the Birdsville Track. Anyhow, one day my Aboriginal tracker, Micky, informed me that some stolen cattle were coming down the Track with a drover we'll name Bill Thomas. Now how he got the message I will never understand. There'd been no movements up or down the Track for several weeks and Micky had no form of communication other than perhaps that mysterious way the natives seem to be able to communicate with each other, and often from hundreds of miles apart. Anyhow Micky told me that Bill Thomas was on his way to Marree with three thousand head of cattle and that he'd already stolen about thirty-five head while crossing through other people's properties.

I knew this particular drover well and I'd had my suspicions about him for a long time. It was my opinion that this Bill Thomas had an ongoing arrangement with a particular train drover to rail the stolen stock down south to Adelaide and link up with another accomplice who'd then sell the stolen cattle on. The thing was, I'd never been able to catch this Bill Thomas in the act or in possession of any stolen cattle. But this time I was determined that I would. So I then sought the advice of George Crombie.

George was a well-respected Maree local who'd once owned land and he'd also done a lot of droving in his time. When I first asked George if he'd assist me, he told me that I'd need at least twenty men with horses to ride the forty miles or so up along the Birdsville Track to inspect the herd and to then 'cut out' — separate — the cattle he'd stolen.

'I'm getting too old for that sort of work,' George replied, 'and anyway I probably wouldn't be able to find enough men around here to do the job. And even if I did, Jim,' he added, 'you'd need to pay them all' ... which I couldn't. He also said that if I were to wait in Marree and inspect the cattle while they were being loaded into the rail trucks I'd need to understand every brand on the cattle waybill ... which I didn't.

So I went back to the police station to have a good think about it and that's when I hatched a plan.

That afternoon I returned to George and asked if he'd be prepared to manage the stolen cattle if I could arrange for them to be separated from the herd while they were still out on the Birdsville Track.

'Okay,' he said, 'if you do that I'm prepared to bring them into Marree, identify each of the owners' brands, then have the cattle trucked down to Adelaide and the various owners will be paid for the cattle sold in their name.'

'Okay,' I said, 'you're on.'

I then went to the post office and I sent a telegram to the police officer up at Birdsville:

> *Understand Bill Thomas has a mob of cattle just outside of Marree. Believe that about 35 head of those have been stolen or unlawfully obtained. Have you received reports of any cattle stolen in your area? If so please advise me accordingly as I propose going through the cattle as they are being loaded in Marree. This time Bill Thomas is not going to get away with it.*

Of course, with all the telegrams being read out over the Flying Doctor's radio during the daily Galah Session, I was relying on the telegram being overheard by someone who, in turn, would inform Bill Thomas as to what was going on.

Anyhow, Bill Thomas was due in Marree on the coming Friday. When he didn't arrive I knew my plan had worked. So I sent Micky up the Track to find out where Bill Thomas had 'cut out' the stolen cattle. When Micky returned he said that he'd followed cattle tracks through to Mundowdna Station, where the fence had been cut and cattle had been pushed through. He also advised me that there were thirty-eight head around a waterhole.

'Good,' I said.

I then told George what I'd done and I arranged for him and Micky to go into Mundowdna Station and bring the thirty-eight head of stolen cattle into town.

When Bill Thomas arrived in town the following Tuesday, minus the cattle he'd stolen, I went over to the transhipping yards to confront him. And didn't I give him a thorough dressing down. I said, 'Look, I know you're a cattle thief. Oh, and by the way, thanks very much for cutting out the stolen cattle for us.' I also told him that I'd let the cattle station owners know what he'd done and I'd see that they were paid for the stock he'd stolen. Finally I added, 'What's more, I don't ever want to see you around Marree again.'

And that was that. George and Micky duly brought the thirty-eight head of cattle into town where they were railed down to Adelaide and sold on behalf of their respective owners. For his efforts, George Crombie received a handsome bonus from the selling agents. Micky somehow received a new pair of riding boots and trousers, and one morning I found a carton of beer at the back door of the police station. To the best of my knowledge Bill Thomas never got another droving job.

# Aboriginal Police Aides

Back in my early policing days, the remote north of Western Australia was a different world from anything I'd previously experienced. It was almost like you'd imagine the old American Wild West to be, and at times it felt like it. Most of your work was centred around Indigenous people and until then my only real involvement with Aboriginals was playing footy with or against them when I was down south. Funnily enough, when I got up here, I just happened to get on really well with them. Loved it, actually.

What helped was that I was lucky to have spent quite a bit of time with a few excellent police aides or Aboriginal police liaison officers, as they're now known. To be honest, in those old days, they were sort of used more as policemen, whereas their true role was supposed to be as a liaison in helping bridge the gap between white man's way of law and their Aboriginal culture.

One fella I worked with in the Pilbara region of WA was Ian Tullock; or Uncle Ian as he was more commonly known amongst his people. Ian was great to work with. He'd been in the job for a number of years and he had a very dry and sharp sense of humour. When we'd go out on patrols he'd always try to teach me some basics of their language: phrases like '*bugalah, bugalah*', which means 'hurry up, get up'. And you had to know that one because, as a policeman, you'd often be having to tell some mob or other to hurry up and move on. Then there's cultural things like where they won't speak the name of someone who's passed away. Instead, they referred to them as *naveroo* or *naberoo*.

When I'd do a remote police patrol, Ian would often be both my partner and guide and luckily too, because a lot of the time I had no idea where we were going; didn't have a clue. I'd be driving along out in the middle of nowhere and Ian would be saying, 'Turn left here. Turn right here. Go down over that way.'

'Oh, okay then. Are you sure?'

'Yep.'

And he'd be right.

First we'd head out towards Marble Bar. Marble Bar has the reputation of being the hottest place in Australia, yet, surprisingly enough, there's some very pretty country out that way. It's quite historic too. Apart from the mining, you've got the old American World War Two airfield out on nearby Corunna Downs. That's where the Aussie and American bombers used to take off on sorties into New Guinea and through the Pacific. During the war the Japs apparently spent a lot of time trying to find that base but they never did because, being situated where it was, it was too well hidden.

From Marble Bar we'd cut down through a property that was owned by the Strelley Pastoral Company. Strelley's known to have the oldest operating independent Aboriginal community school in Australia. There were also a couple of abandoned station properties down there. Mind you, some of these communities only had around forty people. One was called Abydos, which some of your readers may know contains a rock formation known as China Wall. Then there's Lalla Rookh, an old goldmining place. Lalla Rookh had been abandoned by that stage. I doubt that much gold was ever found there anyway. It's pretty inhospitable country. They reckon the only surprising discovery the miners came across at Lalla Rookh were the death adders that inhabited the area. Another story goes, it'd get so hot out at Lalla Rookh that the miners used to head into Marble Bar for a cool change and a beer or three at the iconic Ironclad Hotel. And I've already told you how hot Marble Bar gets.

So we'd keep cutting down through that country, heading towards the mining town of Newman. Then we'd somehow end up at Yandeyarra, which had once been a pastoral company's outstation and was now a small Aboriginal community. It was all amazing country, and they were good people too. They were fun to be around. The Aboriginal women in particular were great. They'd always be up for a bit of a laugh. From there we'd cut across country to Mallina Station and from Mallina we'd head back home along the North West Coastal Highway. So that was one of the patrols I used to do with Ian Tullock.

I also came into contact with some other memorable Aboriginal police aides after I'd been transferred up into the Kimberley. We used to do three-day patrols up the Dampier Peninsula and again I was lucky enough to have had a couple of crusty old police aides with me; one by the name of George 'Jalba' Dann and the other was Damian Manado. That was an interesting patrol too because each of the communities up along the peninsula was subject to their own Aboriginal by-laws: for example, not being allowed to consume alcohol on their land. Most of these communities had their own wardens and if someone transgressed those by-laws, when we got there, the warden would tell us about it and we'd charge the offender under the by-laws. So say if we were at Beagle Bay we'd then convene a hearing — Beagle Bay Court of Petty Sessions it used to be called — and we'd also do the same at other places along the way like Lombadina and right up the top at One Arm Point.

Most of the time we'd hold the hearing in the general office area with two Justices of the Peace in attendance. These JPs would always be elders in the community. On occasions we'd have to offer advice on what the penalties should be; hence the reason some described it as being a 'kangaroo court'. But it worked well and it showed the local people that the wardens were there for a reason and how there'd be consequences if anyone misbehaved or ran amok. So we'd prosecute the particular case, then the two JPs would administer whatever fine was to be imposed and all the money from the fine would go back into the community.

If there were more grave matters that needed addressing, say like state law issues such as damage offences, assault offences and whatever, a magistrate would fly up and convene a proper court. Again it was run along the same sort of lines, but with the magistrate dealing out whatever punishment he deemed was necessary. So I did a lot of patrol work up that way with both George and Damian and along the way they showed me through some beautiful places; some best known to only the local Aboriginals.

I also worked with another police aide, Greg Tait. Greg's not in the force any more. These days he's out at Halls Creek. He was and still is a real character. I don't know if you've ever seen the movie *Mad Bastards*. It's set in a fictional town called Five Rivers, which is obviously Wyndham as it shows the Five Rivers lookout. It's about a fella from down south called TJ who'd abandoned his son, Bullet, at an early age and he comes back up to Five Rivers to face his demons. The only trouble is, TJ's got a couple of weaknesses — alcohol and a habit of getting into fights. To make matters worse, Bullet, who's now a teenager, has developed a few faults of his own. Into this mess steps Bullet's uncle Texas, with the aim of trying to sort things out. In the movie Uncle Texas is played by Greg Tait and, I can tell you, I worked closely with Greg for three years and he did not have to do one single piece of acting in that movie. He just played himself.

While Greg was working with me as a police aide he taught me some of the local terms of the area, like 'knock-'em-down rain'. A local band, the Pigram Brothers, wrote a song about it. Knock-'em-down rain is the last big rain before the dry season sets in and it's so fierce that it flattens — knocks down — all the pampas grass.

Greg also introduced me to the term 'sheep-eaters'. It's probably a bit of a derogatory term, but if the Aboriginals use it then I guess it must be okay. In actual fact it's used in the movie *Mad Bastards* and I wouldn't be at all surprised if it wasn't Greg who got it written into the script.

When I first heard him mention the term, I said, 'Hey, Greg, what do you mean sheep-eaters?'

'They're Noongar Aboriginals. Not locals. They're from anywhere down south of Carnarvon.'

That all came about because the southern Aboriginals live mainly in sheep country, while up north it's mainly cattle country. So then because Greg's a Halls Creek boy I said, 'Well, what do you, as a northern Aboriginal, describe yourself as?'

He said, 'I'm a bull-jumper.'

And I still call him Bull-jumper. In actual fact I got in touch with him just yesterday when I was heading out that way and I said, 'Hey, Bull-jumper, are you around for a cuppa?'

Yes, so I've been very lucky to have worked with some great Aboriginal police aides and I think that's all helped in me landing the inspector's job I have now. I'm currently looking after the East Kimberley region, which consists of three police stations: Halls Creek, Kununurra and Wyndham. Then I've got three multifunctional communities. There's Warmun, which most of the old blackfellas still call Turkey Creek; then there's Kalumburu, which is right up the top of WA; and the third one's Balgo, out on the Tanami Road. Really you could say I've got the job I've always wanted. I enjoy the remote experience and I like dealing with the Aboriginal people.

# About Stanley

The Aboriginal community of Amata is over in the western corner of South Australia; a couple of hundred kilometres east of the Western Australian border and about twenty or so k's south of Cave Hill, which is on the Northern Territory border. When I first went to have a look at the place I flew up there with my boss at the time and I asked him, 'So what's the petrol sniffing like up here?'

And he's, like, trying to sell me the place, see, so he goes, 'Oh, I doubt if you'll even see one while you're up here.'

Anyway we get off the plane and there's an Aboriginal bloke I knew, Stanley. So I go, 'Hey, Stanley, how many petrol sniffers you got here?' and Stanley goes, 'Oh we got hundreds here, Darr'l. We got hundreds. I's a real big problem.'

How my working there came about was that back in 1985 the South Australian government decided to introduce the Community Police Aide Scheme. The initial concept was to train Aboriginal people up to be able to police their own communities. To start with they put a white copper in with two police aides at communities like Indulkana, Fregon, Ernabella and at Amata. Anyway, the white police officers did twelve months out in each of these communities before they were pulled out and then it was left to the Aboriginal police aides to take over and police their community.

But it wasn't working. It was all far too complex, especially when it came to internal community issues of family business and that. They had to have constant supervision. So in 1988 I got the position out there as police aide supervisor. I was centred at Amata, where I had two police aides. I also supervised the two police aides at Ernabella and the two at Fregon. Then there was one at Mimili and also later on I had one at Pipalyatjara. Pipalyatjara's right over in the corner of the Western Australian, Northern Territory and South Australian borders. So I moved all over through these various communities where I'd sit down and try to educate the various police aides about police issues and how to go about them. One month there I drove something like twelve thousand kilometres.

While I was at Amata, one of my police aides was the fella I previously mentioned, Stanley. Stanley was my partner and he was a beautiful old man. An elder. He was custodian of the Seven Sisters out at Cave Hill. But anyway, at the place where I'd been working before I went out to Amata, it was like, if you weren't on the job, you were on the grog, socialising. There was nothing else to do. Amata, on the other hand, was dry — well, it was meant to be — so at my farewell party, before I left to go to Amata, everyone's going, 'Ah, you won't make it. You won't make it.' They even gave me a carton of Birell non-alcoholic beer as a farewell present plus a huge dummy about this big. They said, 'You'll spit the dummy and you'll be drinking that non-alcoholic stuff.' Anyway, it didn't happen.

I'd been up there for about three months and things were out of control. There was massive grog-running; massive. Curtin Springs was the nearest liquor outlet and, with Amata being the closest community on the way to Curtin Springs, we had immense problems because the grog runners from all the other communities were coming through Amata to get to Curtin Springs. Then, when they'd got their grog, they'd come back via Amata fully loaded. It was just unbelievable; they were buying five-litre casks and we'd be seizing something like fifty of them at a time — that's two hundred and fifty litres in every vehicle.

Well, I'd really been getting stuck into these grog runners. Then one day Stanley goes, 'Eh, Darr'l, we gotta go to Kulgera tonight.' Kulgera was a couple of hundred k's away, just over into the Northern Territory. Pretty much dirt all the way.

I said, 'Nah, Stanley, we gotta get that mob coming through from Curtin Springs. We gotta get them and we gonna sort them out real good.'

And Stanley goes, 'Nah, nah, Darr'l, we goin' to Kulgera.'

'No,' I said, 'we're not going to bloody Kulgera. We gotta sort these fellas out.'

'Nah,' he says, 'we're going to Kulgera.'

I said, 'Why?'

He said, 'Darr'l, you bin' here t'ree months and you need a drink. You're startin' to hit these fellas too hard.'

Anyhow, unbeknown to me, we get to Kulgera and there's a big party at the police station with all the station property people and that there. As I said, by then I hadn't had a drink for three months and by the time I'd had three cans I'd gone light-headed and wobbly legged. It hit me like a brick, so much so that everyone's going, 'Who's this dickhead?'

But Stanley, he knew I needed to get out of Amata. It was getting to me, and I was hitting them a bit too hard too. I needed a release and so he's telling me I need a drink, and he was right.

And that was Stanley. I don't know what I would've done without him. In his time he'd done lots of things. He'd also been a drover and, like a lot of those blackfellas, he had a great sense of horsemanship. And Stanley was brilliant with horses. One time we got in a real big, wild brumby. You couldn't go near him and within three days Stanley had him broken in, perfect. It was unbelievable.

He was also pretty handy with the whip, too. I was the only white copper out on the APY — Anangu Pitjantjatjara Yankunytjatjara — Lands at that time and one particular night the petrol sniffers went crazy and they started lighting up car tyres and throwing them under the school buildings. Stanley and me, we were trying our best to catch them but, as soon as they'd see us coming, they'd bolt. Anyway, there was a breezeway that came out between the school buildings and Stanley says, 'Darr'l, you go round dat way 'n herd 'em through the guts of the school 'n I'll go round the other end 'n wait for 'em.'

So I've gone out around the other side and I'm chasing these sniffers up through the breezeway, just like drafting sheep. And there's Stanley, he's at the other end and as they go past, he's got his whip and he goes like that with his whip and wraps it around them. Oh I wish I had it down on video because, when Stanley pulled back on the whip, their legs would just shoot straight up in the air in front of them; then, *bang*, down they'd come, on the flat of their arses. God it was funny. And everyone's going, 'Hey, you can't treat 'em like cattle.' And I was saying, 'Well, stop them from lighting up the school then.'

But, oh, I had some great moments out there. I was there for two and a bit years and the country — mate, if they ever open up that country to tourism it'd kill Ayers Rock. There's places like Amata Rock Hole that are just beautiful, then there's Tupul and all those places — again, just absolutely beautiful.

# Airborne

I was born in the little Western Australian Wheatbelt town of Kondinin, which is a hundred and seventy-three miles east of Perth. My parents were mixed farmers — wheat and sheep. They were there for many years, just east of Kondinin. I went to primary school at a small place close by called Pingaring. There were forty-two children when I started school and when I left seven years later there were forty-three. As you can see, there was no great population explosion over that time, and probably less since. By the time I'd finished primary school my parents had moved to Narrogin, so that's where I went to high school. But to be honest, I couldn't get out of the place fast enough. So I did. Of course, looking back now, I wish I had stayed on and tried harder, but it just wasn't for me.

I actually joined the police force by accident. After I left school I wanted to be lots of things, as you did in those days. I wanted to be a farmer. I wanted to join the army. I wanted to join the navy. I wanted to do this and I wanted to do that. In the meanwhile I ended up working in a flour mill in Narrogin. Everything was going all right. Things were good. Then I was working the night shift one time and the thought suddenly struck me: There must be something better than this.

I was still living with Mum and Dad at the time so when I got home earlier that morning I had a shower and a shave, got into some good clothes; all dressed up. Mum was in the kitchen, cooking breakfast, and when she saw me all done up, she said, 'Where are you going?'

I said, 'Down the police station.'

She said, 'Are you in strife again?'

'No, no,' I said, 'I'm not in trouble. I'm just going down there to ask them how you go about becoming a policeman.'

She looked at me; up and down, checking me out. She's still cooking breakfast. She said, 'You're wasting your time you know.'

'Why's that?'

She said, 'You're too bloody short.'

As you can see I am a bit on the short side but, being undeterred, I said, 'Oh well, I'll just go and see them anyway. If they tell me I'm too short, then that'll be it. I'm too short.'

So I went down to the police station, all done up. There was a constable there that I knew and I told him what I was there for. He said, 'Hang on a tick. Just bear with me a moment,' and he went into the shift sergeant's office. Next thing, he comes back and he says, 'When do you want to fill out the application?'

I said, 'Well, I've got nothing else to do.'

So I filled out the application and six weeks later, on the 2nd April 1973, I started at the Police Academy in Perth. It was a ninety-one-day course back then; similar to recruit training in the army and the navy, though not as rigid. But they tried to teach those who'd never marched how to march in step. We also did first aid and everything else that's supposed to prepare you for life in the police force. From there, after recruit training, I went to Central. Then one afternoon I was asked by an old sergeant if I wanted a transfer.

I'd been around a bit by then so I said, 'Where to?' My thinking was that, until he told me where the vacancy was, I wasn't going to jump in and commit myself by saying, 'I do.'

So I was a bit evasive and he was just as evasive. He said, 'Well do you want a transfer or don't you want a transfer?'

I said, 'You tell me where the vacancy is and I'll give you an answer.'

He said, 'There's three places and one of those you definitely won't like.'

'Well, okay,' I said, 'tell me the other two.'

He said, 'One's Narrogin.'

I wasn't going back to my home area straight away so I said, 'No, I don't want that. I don't want Narrogin.'

He said, 'The other one's Bunbury.'

Bunbury's down south; a hundred and ten miles from Perth. I said, 'I don't want to go there either. I've got too many long-lost relatives down in that corner of the world.'

He said, 'Okay, well, that only leaves the one that no one wants.'

'Where's that?'

'Kalgoorlie,' he said.

I said, 'Well, I'll go to Kalgoorlie then.'

He said, 'How soon can you get there?'

I said, 'Well, I'm single.' I said, 'I could be there in forty-eight hours.'

He said, 'Good. You've got a job.'

So on the 3rd November 1973 I started as a constable in Kalgoorlie. Kalgoorlie's a big goldmining town, three hundred and sixty miles east of Perth. There was a downturn in mining at that point. It was all underground. The companies were doing it hard and, because of all the uncertainty, the miners were doing it hard as well. But Kalgoorlie was Kalgoorlie. Back then it was a place where anything and everything goes. Wild times were had by many. But for a young bloke policing, I think it was probably the best thing I ever did. Yes, it was a tough environment but, if you were prepared to pitch in, it was a great learning experience.

What also helped was that I had a good group of sergeants and a good boss. There were thirty-four of us police officers back then. All bar three were Freemasons; me and two other junior officers. I remember one night when they had a Freemasons' meeting and the three of us new ones were left to cover the police station. As it happened, it turned out to be a very uneventful night, which was pretty rare for Kalgoorlie, and so when everyone turned up for work the next day, they said, 'Well, maybe we should have a Freemasons' meeting every night.'

But the connection between the police and Freemasons has always been very strong. We have a standing joke about how the power base of the police force is either the Masons or the Catholics. I think that's true in other states as well. It was more Freemason when I started, then a number of years later the Catholics became more predominant. In WA especially there's a very strong link to Irish Catholicism. Some of our first commissioners of police were Irish Catholics and they achieved great things. Whichever way it goes it doesn't make much of a difference; the ideals are all the same. It's all about your fellow man.

I have fond memories of Kalgoorlie. I remember my second day at work there. This local fellow went out on his first solo flight in the Kalgoorlie Aero Club's little trainer. It was early in the morning when he set off and everything was good. All was going well. Next thing heavy cloud came over and he had no idea where he was. We then get the call: 'There's an aviator on his first solo flight and he's out there somewhere, lost.'

Being new — second day at work — someone in their wisdom decided, 'Well, let's send the young bloke on the search.'

So then I'm out at the airport, thinking, Well, I've never been in an aeroplane before. This could be a complete disaster. I'll probably be as sick as a dog.

Anyhow, up we go. Airborne. There was just the pilot, a co-pilot and myself. We were in a little twin-engine aircraft. We were able to communicate with the fellow by radio but he's out there somewhere, stuck in cloud, and he's still lost. He doesn't know where he is. Our pilot says, 'Can you see a pipeline?' That's the Perth to Kalgoorlie pipeline.

He could just make that out. 'Yes,' he said.

'Well, just keep following that and you'll eventually come to a town.'

'Okay.' So he followed the pipeline and followed the pipeline, then he radioed back, 'I think I've found Southern Cross.' Southern Cross is a hundred and twenty miles west of Kalgoorlie.

So our pilot said, 'Okay, just get in a circling pattern and fly around Southern Cross.' Then he asked a few questions about the cloud conditions and all the rest of it.

Anyhow, we eventually located this aircraft and a few minutes later we've caught up with him. He's still flying perfectly normal. Everything seems to be okay, but I'm thinking, Well, if he's never landed a plane on his own before, anything could happen. I mean, he'd obviously landed a plane during his training but he'd always had an instructor sitting beside him. This was the first time he was cut loose so I'm thinking, If this doesn't work, he's going to go straight into the ground and it's going to be my job to pick up the pieces and sort out the coroner's report.

I was pretty much on edge by this time. Then our pilot started talking him down. You know, 'Do this. Do that.' And I felt almost like I was in the cockpit with the fellow; almost like I'm holding the joystick or whatever it's called. Down he comes, nice and slow. Little by little. Our pilot's still talking to him. 'You're doing well. Gently. Gently.'

By now I'm thinking the worst. I'm breaking out into a sweat. I'm having all sorts of visions of him panicking and getting the plane out of whack and then *bang* — him hitting the ground.

'Down you come. Take it easy.'

'Okay. Okay.' He's following our pilot's instructions to a tee. Everything was going perfectly. Everything was working out. 'Down. Down. Nice and easy.' I'm riding him every inch of the way and when he touched the plane down on the airstrip I think I let out a greater sigh of relief than anyone else did; that's including the lost pilot. What's more, due to the tension of it all I'd completely forgotten about being airsick. I hadn't even given it a thought. That's how intense it all was. It went from deep trepidation to the sheer exhilaration of seeing him landing the plane perfectly. It was an amazing feeling. One I'll never ever forget.

# Alf and the Demolition Squad

One time there was a policeman up here in Hungerford, a feller by the name of Alf Gray. Hungerford being a border town in south-western Queensland, just up the road from Bourke, New South Wales. Anyway, this Alf Gray was here back in — let me think. Oh Jesus, it's a long time ago now. Well, I came out this way in '51 and I worked on some properties as an overseer before I moved into town. So it would've been somewhere around '56 when Alf was at Hungerford.

The area Alf took in would've gone right out to Cameron Corner, which is on the Queensland, South Australian and New South Wales borders. Then it'd go nearly over to Innamincka, which is just inside the South Australian border. I don't think he would've taken in Thargomindah because there was already a couple of coppers up there. Hungerford and Thargomindah's in the same shire; the Bulloo Shire.

Actually there's only about four hundred of us that live in the whole of the Bulloo Shire these days and most of them live in Thargomindah. There's only about ten of us in Hungerford now. There's four of us old pensioners and I'm not going too well myself. I'm eighty-seven and I've got a few health problems and that. Then there's the publican and he's got a woman working for him because he's also got the mail run and he does that twice a week, Tuesdays and Fridays. Then I do what I call the 'cake run' where I take the mail out the hundred and twenty k's there and back to Moombidary Station on the Wednesday and the Saturday to help him out a bit. Why I call it the 'cake run' is that the station manager's wife, Helen, always makes me these cakes with cream on them for when I come out there. They're freshly baked too, a lot of them. Helen's an English woman and she married Scott, the manager. Many years ago the manager's family were well-known drovers and that down around the Bourke area.

So that's what I do to help out the publican and he does the run up and back to Cunnamulla and, oh, she's a big mail run all right. Well, to start with; see, the mail comes out from Brisbane to Charleville. It's sorted in Charleville, then early the next morning a courier brings it down from Charleville and it gets into Cunnamulla at around 11 o'clock. I used to do the mail run for the previous publican, occasionally. It's a round trip of about six hundred kilometres for the day and she's not an easy drive because it's a hundred and eighty-eight k's from Hungerford to Cunnamulla and about a hundred of that's all dirt and corrugations.

The thing is, you leave here at about six in the morning and you go straight up to Cunnamulla with whatever mail you've got. Drop that off. Seeing as you're in town you have to fuel up, then you go around to the chemist and drop everyone's scripts off, then you go around to all the businesses to get stuff from them or drop stuff off to be picked up later on that day or on the next trip. Then you have to go back to the chemist and pick up the scripts, then you go back to the post office and get the mail, once it's sorted. And you have to do all that before you head back home again.

One time I was in Cunnamulla I counted twenty-two different stops I had to make before I headed back to Hungerford. And mind you, on your way back home you have to call into all the stations along the way to deliver and pick up their mail. So you might get back at around 5 or 6 o'clock at night. That's if you're lucky. So she's a hell of a trip, and you do that two times a week.

Yes, so that's about the population of Hungerford as it stands at the present, then we're just about to get a new policewoman.

She's starting maybe next week. We haven't met her yet but apparently she was married and now she's single.

Anyhow, that Alf Gray I was telling you about, he was the first one out here to have a police vehicle. Oh no, sorry — that's wrong — it was the feller after him who was the first one who had a police vehicle. I'm getting a bit mixed up because, see, there was two police fellers by the name of Gray. No relation, but one came after the other. Alf was the first Gray that came to Hungerford then following him was Arthur Gray and it was Arthur who had the first police vehicle in Hungerford. Up until then police work was either done on a horse or, if they didn't have a horse, they usually got compensated for using their own vehicle.

But Alf Gray is the bloke I'm going to tell you about. Alf was the feller who didn't have a police vehicle. Well, not officially he didn't, but he kind of inadvertently acquired a permanent sort of one. Because when Alf was here, a bloke died out on the Dog Fence somewhere and the dead-Dog-Fence feller had an old Nissan or something. Apparently the dead-Dog-Fence feller had no family or anything, because, when Alf drove his Nissan up to Cunnamulla for the funeral, nobody else turned up to see him buried, so that's when Alf decided to snaffle his vehicle.

Anyway, Alf and his missus, they had three little kids. Around town they were known as the 'Demolition Squad' because of all the trouble they used to get into. There was a boy and two girls. Geoffrey was the boy. He was the eldest. He was probably about seven and the youngest, her name was Debbie. Debbie would've only been about three or so; just a little tacker. I can't remember the name of the other girl just now; the middle one.

Anyhow, these three kids, they used to run around the place pretty much wild. The mother didn't seem to worry about it. They were a very casual family, but those kids were always getting up to some strife or other. Now, do you remember the police station from when you were up here? It was over the way a bit from the pub. Well, it was new back then and a few of us were having a drink in the pub one day when we hear this kid screaming. So we all went outside to see what's going on. Trouble was, we didn't know where the hell the screaming was coming from until someone looked up and there's this kid, young Geoffrey, he's stuck right up on the top of the roof of the new police station. How the hell he got there I wouldn't have a clue, but it took us a good while to get him back down, I can tell you.

Another time they shorted out the generator at the pub. Blowed if I know how they did that either, but you can imagine just how well that went down, especially in the middle of summer. Then there was a bloke, he was a roo shooter. He was running a portable cool room where he stuck the dead kangaroos into — a roo chiller. Him and his missus were living in a caravan down near the town's water supply. It was just like a big open dam and the roo hunter's wife, she was forever hunting those three kids back from there because one slip and they could've easily drowned.

Another time we were putting in the golf course a good way out of town and we found them wandering around in the scrub. They'd been down the rubbish dump drinking all the dregs out of the empty longneck beer bottles that'd been dropped off from the pub. Oh, I tell you, there would've been cigarette stubs and ash in the bottom of a lot of those bottles too.

Then there was the time the roads people were putting in the new river crossing at Hungerford. That was across the Paroo, out on the road to Eulo. The roads people also did a lot of other things around town at that time; like they put down a bit of bitumen in the street, just outside the front of the pub. So they must've thought that Hungerford was on the way up, ay? Actually, while we're talking about 'on the way up', many years ago there was supposed to be a railway line go through Hungerford, but it only got as far as Bourke.

Anyhow, before the roads people put in the new river crossing there was just a dirt channel running through it and so, if there was any water in the Paroo and you wanted to get across to Hungerford, there was a telephone tied to a tree over the other side and they had a line running from the tree to the post office. So you'd ring up the post office and they'd get the boat out and come and get you.

Now I just don't know why, but one time these roads fellers left a half-full forty-four-gallon drum of tar lying around with the top cut off it. Then one day somebody came across the Demolition Squad playing down by the river and that little Debbie I was telling you about, the youngest one, she'd somehow got into the drum and there she was, stuck up to her neck in the tar. That's a true story. Blowed if I know how they got her out, and blowed if I know how they got all the tar off her either. It's got me stumped. Kerosene would be the only thing that'd take tar off but it'd burn the hell out of you, especially a little kid. So those kids, it's amazing how they survived.

Then Alf Gray, the policeman and father of the Demolition Squad, he ended up going from here and he joined the Stock Squad over at Mareeba, in Far North Queensland, near Cairns. Then not long after that, he ended up dying. But everyone knew him. He was a real character of a bloke. I remember back when he was here in Hungerford, it was the time when you weren't allowed to drink in a hotel on a Sunday unless you were booked in to stay at that hotel. Like, it was in the law that you had to prove you were a bona-fide traveller who was staying over for the night or whatever. So what we used to do, we'd get together and we'd book a room in at the pub for the Sunday and say we were going to have a birthday party there. That's how we got around that law. Mind you, I don't know how many birthday parties some of us had in the one year but, with only the ten of us in town and two of those already living in the pub, I reckon we would've chalked up quite a few.

## An Interesting Place

We spent five and a half years in the police force up at South Hedland, in the north of Western Australia, and my wife and I, we thoroughly enjoyed it. It was an interesting place in as much as it was there to service the nearby seaport of Port Hedland. Port Hedland's where they ship out all the ore that's been railed in from throughout the Pilbara region. But because it's on a peninsula, land was quite limited and so South Hedland was built to house a lot of those who were associated with the mining industry.

In fact we had quite a welcoming to South Hedland. A cyclone had hit. We had three children by then and I'd just bought my first big four-wheel drive. In fact I think I might've only got it the day before we headed north, and just as well too, because we had to negotiate our way through quite a few floodways and so forth along the way.

Finally we decided that it might be better if we sat out the cyclone a couple of hundred kilometres south, at Karratha. We booked into a hotel there. Nothing in the town was open. Everyone had battened down due to the cyclone, but the people at the hotel were very helpful. Because we couldn't buy food anywhere they gave us a little 'cyclone pack', which contained sandwiches and drinks and so forth. Then the next day, when we heard that the cyclone had travelled further inland, we said, 'All right, the worst is over so let's go on to South Hedland.'

Things were still pretty bad, though. If you're ever going up that way, about twenty kilometres from South Hedland you'll come across the Turner River. It's always dry — well, almost always dry, because when we crossed over it there was water rushing through only a couple of metres under the bridge. That might give you some idea as to how much floodwater was coming down and that was in just the one spot. Anyhow, we continued on and when we drove into town my wife and I just looked at each other and said, 'What have we done?' There were trees down everywhere. Everything was covered in debris and mud. Rubbish was strewn all over the place.

The place we had was what they called 'government employee housing'. It was a three-bedroom, one-bathroom, brick-and-tile house. Due to the cyclone, the backyard was about four inches deep in water and we had no power for two days. With my wife being one of those who needs to get things done right there and then, I went and saw my officer-in-charge and said, 'Have you got a gas lantern? My wife wants to get unpacked.'

'What, right now?' he said.

'Yep,' and so by the time removalists arrived we had a gas lamp. Mind you, this was in January when it's extremely hot and humid, and we'd come from one of the coldest areas of Western Australia up into one of the warmest, which was yet another real shock, I can assure you. Plus there was no air conditioning in the house. All it had was a window at either end, so we opened those up in an attempt to get some air flowing through and we all bunked down in the lounge room. Anyhow, it was all go and, within two days of arriving in South Hedland, we were unpacked and virtually settled in.

But that was life in South Hedland, or anywhere else along that northern coastline for that matter. In any one season you could get anywhere from one to five cyclones. Mind you, they might not all hit the town. Some might come through a hundred kilometres off the coast and so you'll just get high winds and rain. Or they might pass by and drop a lot of water further inland and then you'll get a lot of floodwater coming down the rivers, like what happened in the Turner River when we'd arrived.

As far as policing goes, in the case of a cyclone, you've got your blue, yellow and red alerts, and once you go on to red alert, that's it, you batten down. No one's supposed to be out in the streets so we'll do one last patrol with the sirens on to warn everyone to go indoors. After that we only respond to emergencies. Of course, with me having to be in the office, ready to respond to any emergencies, quite often when there was a cyclone my wife would be left at home with the kids to fend for themselves. Though I remember when our first big cyclone was heading towards town, a few of the police officers became so worried that their houses wouldn't survive a direct hit that they brought their families into the station and set them up in the strongest part of the building, which was the lockup.

So yes, it was an interesting place, South Hedland. It was just unbelievable. With so many workers involved in the mining industry it was a very busy town, with a lot of money floating around at certain times. Just a trades assistant, for example, could bring home a couple of hundred bucks a day, cash. That was excellent money back then. My wife worked in a local restaurant for a while and it wasn't unusual for everyone on the table to tip her fifty bucks, each. And that's a lot of money.

Policing was totally different too. Being involved in the mining industry it was a rough sort of town in many ways, with quite a transient population. We also had a lot of issues relating to alcoholism and the associated violence it involves, including domestic violence and things like that. It was always busy and, with the Aboriginal population, there were quite a few itinerant people. From what I believe, South Hedland's on a traditional south–north Indigenous walkway known as the Warlu Way. So that population would be passing through and then you'd get the people coming in from the Little Sandy Desert, from Well 33 and Jigalong and places like that.

Even to this day you can go up behind the shopping centre, in an area they call Two Mile, and you'll see all the itinerant people camping under trees. Some of them have lived there from as far back as when I first arrived. It's a sad thing, I know, but they leave their communities, quite often for a good reason, such as a funeral or law or something like that. But then, when they get to South Hedland, they get dragged into the alcohol cycle and that's it. What starts off to be a trip for a cultural reason, ends up with them staying on.

Along with that you get the flow-on problems, like the kids roaming the streets at night. Whenever we were out on patrol and we saw kids roaming about, we'd pick them up and take them home and that was it. The best we could do was to try to get them involved in positive things like sporting activities and things like that. We got the PCYC — Police and Youth Citizens Club — up and running. That was very successful. Then there were a lot of other good things happening in association within the shire. While I was there I got a truancy patrol started. That's where we'd get the Aboriginal and Islander education workers on a bus along with the Aboriginal police liaison officers and they'd look out for any problems and they'd step in and help wherever possible. We also had someone from the Department of Child Protection out on patrol, keeping an eye out. So there was always something happening in South Hedland. It was an interesting town and we enjoyed our time there.

# As it Happened

You hear a lot of stories these days about the Stolen Generations. Most of them of course relate to how Aboriginal families were torn apart, and that's fair enough. It's tragic. But occasionally there were good things that came out of it too, and this is one of those instances.

Back in the early 1960s I was a police officer up at a small place called Coen, which is roughly halfway up Cape York Peninsula. There was this half-caste woman there. She'd married an Indigenous man and they'd had a big family. My wife and I knew them well. We'd had a lot to do with them, in a good way. In fact the woman, in particular, was a very good friend of ours.

Then many years later I came across a file in the police archives. It was a case surrounding an eighteen-year-old white boy who'd had sex with a young sixteen-year-old half-caste girl and she'd got pregnant. The incident happened back in 1937 when the Aboriginal Protection Act was still in existence and that act prohibited any form of sexual relations between Aboriginals — which included half-castes — and white people. For some reason the case fascinated me and I began to wonder what had ever happened to the sixteen-year-old half-caste girl. Where was she these days? How did things turn out?

I then started to do a bit of inquiring around. As you may appreciate, due to marriage and so forth, a young sixteen-year-old girl in 1937 would most probably have had a different surname by the early 1960s. Still, I began at the beginning and in this case I followed the girl through two different surnames.

When I got to the third, to my surprise, it turned out to be the half-caste woman that my wife and I were friends with.

As it happened, her true father was a white man. He was a miner, a prospector, around Cape York Peninsula. This white miner had had sex with a full-blood Aboriginal woman and the half-caste girl — our friend — was the result. After the white miner had moved on, the Aboriginal mother then took up with another full-blood Aboriginal. He was a half-wild nomadic Murri, which is what the Aboriginals are known as up that way, and he'd neglected this young girl fairly badly. With the mother being subject to her Murri husband, she had very little impact on the welfare of this little girl. And so that was the girl's circumstances.

When the young girl was about nine years of age a police patrol discovered her in a pretty bad state. They decided that she needed a better chance in life and so they brought her into Coen, where she was placed in protection with a white grazing family who headquartered — lived — in town. This family had then brought the girl up as one of their own. She lived in the house with the family. She ate with the family. In fact, she slept in the same room as the missus when the boss was away out in the mustering camp. She even took on their surname.

When this girl was sixteen, she met a young eighteen-year-old white fellow. Their two families had gardens down the back of their adjoining properties. The half-caste girl used to water her boss's garden and this young white fellow used to water his boss's garden. That's where they met. Then one day they said, 'Well, hang on here. I'd like to get to know you better. How about we meet behind the cow yard tonight at 7 o'clock?' Which they did and unfortunately the girl became pregnant.

As a result the police were notified. They investigated the matter and the girl admitted to having sex with the young white fellow from next door. The police then got an admission from the lad and he was charged under the Aboriginal Protection Act for having sex with an Aboriginal. He was convicted and fined,

I think it was something like five pounds at that time, and he moved on. This girl, on the other hand, remained with the grazing family and when she was old enough, she and her child went out on their own. By then they'd become quite well adapted to town life and so they stayed in Coen.

By the time my wife and I arrived in Coen, the woman was still living in the town and she'd married an Indigenous man. They were a good solid respectable family and, although I never talked to her about her getting pregnant to the young white fellow, I did talk to her many times about being brought into Coen as a young nine-year-old and being placed into protection. When I asked her what her feelings were on the matter, she told me she was forever grateful to the police that she wasn't left to suffer out in the wilds as part of a 'nomadic group', so to speak. In fact, she said that being brought in by the police patrol and being placed with the white grazing family was, and I quote, 'the best thing that had ever happened to me. They treated me well.'

And that's just one story that had a great effect on me. A more humorous event that occurred when we were in Coen was when we intercepted a stolen vehicle from Victoria. This was back in 1964. As it happened, this fellow was employed as a waiter in a restaurant down in Melbourne. He was so well trusted by his boss that he was allowed to drive the other staff members home in his boss's car after they'd finished their shifts of a night-time. And he did this very well — very reliably — until, one night, he didn't come back with the boss's car.

There was apparently some sort of investigation or other but no, the fellow and the car had disappeared. They couldn't be found anywhere. Initially of course, being near to the opposite end of Australia, we didn't hear anything about it up in Coen. Then one day one of the Aboriginals arrived in town. He come up to me and he said, 'Sarge, I just got a lift up from Musgrave.' Musgrave's about a hundred miles south of Coen and, mind you, the journey's over some of the most shocking roads you could possibly imagine.

I said, 'Yeah?'

He said, 'It was with a white bloke in a Hillman Minx, would you believe it?'

Now a Hillman Minx in that sort of remote country was a complete no-no. In those days you'd hardly even get a four-wheel-drive vehicle up the track. Anyway, the white fellow had apparently hit a rock and he'd holed the sump and he'd asked this Aborigine to walk into town and raise the alarm. 'Sarge, this bloke, he's out there all broken down to bits.'

We then got in touch with a local who was a bit of a mechanic and asked him to go out and find the fellow, fix his sump and bring him and his vehicle into town. Which he did, but then we thought, Gee this's a bit strange, driving around the wilds of Cape York in a tiny Hillman Minx.

So we decided to do a police check on the man and the Hillman Minx. Communications were never good at the best of times on the overland telegraph line, but we eventually got through to Cairns, who passed our request on to Brisbane, who passed our request on to Sydney, who passed our request on to Melbourne, who found out that the Hillman Minx was, in effect, the vehicle that had been stolen two weeks previously. So this fellow had driven from Melbourne, all the way through Victoria, then all the way through New South Wales, into Queensland and right up into the north of Cape York Peninsula and he'd ended up just short of Coen.

When we got the word about the Hillman Minx being a stolen vehicle we went over and interviewed the fellow and he came out with it straight away. 'Yes,' he said, 'I stole the car. I wanted to go to Thursday Island and see the sights but I came to grief down the track a bit.'

Anyhow, we arrested him and we took possession of the little Hillman Minx, then we had to arrange an escort to fly up from Cairns and take him back down there to attend the court case. Of course, living in a remote place like Coen, to arrange all that from our end took a fair while and then it took the Cairns police another fair while to organise a plane so that they could come up to get the fellow. In the meantime we had him with us for two weeks or so and, in fact, he actually turned out to be a decent sort of fellow. Yes, he'd done the wrong thing obviously, but he was an okay sort of chap.

But to have come unstuck in a little Hillman Minx, thousands of miles away from blooming Melbourne was the irony of the whole thing. And what's more, on your way to Thursday Island of all places, just to see the sights? You can't quite understand some people, can you?

Anyhow, back then, the Coen lockup was basically just a tiny little cell in the backyard of the police station. As it got as hot as Hades in there during the day, it would've been quite cruel to have had him locked up in there from dawn to dusk. So, after he'd had his breakfast, we'd let him out. Sometimes we'd get him to do a bit of work around the place. Either that or he was free to just wander around the police complex. On occasions, of an afternoon we'd even take him out to the swimming hole, about two miles out of town, where we'd have a barbecue and a bit of a splash around. Come night-time we'd lock him back up in the cell.

It all worked well. He got to understand the rules soon enough. He knew that if he wanted to shoot through we'd have the Aboriginal trackers onto him pretty quick. Anyway, he was one of them real city types and he realised that he'd have to cover a hell of a lot of rough terrain before he got to any sort of half reasonable civilisation. So I don't think he even entertained the idea of escaping and, of course, we did look after him pretty humanely. So much so that, by the time he was escorted onto the plane to go down to Cairns, I think he appreciated how well the Coen police had treated him. But like I said, he was a decent sort of fellow; different but decent. In fact, I'd like to meet up with him sometime to have a chat about those old days, because I'm sure he'd remember his time in Coen with some degree of affection.

# Batman

At the time this event occurred I was working for TAFE, at Mildura, in the far north-west of Victoria. Mildura was the major campus in the region, then we had a reasonably sized one at Swan Hill and two very small ones at Ouyen and Robinvale. Initially I was a teacher and through the years I'd sort of scrambled my way up the ladder. I think by this stage I was a senior manager. Anyhow, once a year we had a joint Christmas party for the four campuses. It was usually held on a Friday afternoon and, so that Swan Hill, Ouyen and Robinvale didn't always have to travel to Mildura, we'd rotate the venue between the four campuses. To add to the fun of the occasion we'd incorporate a theme of some sort.

As it turned out, this particular Christmas party was to be held at Ouyen. The main reason we'd chosen Ouyen was that one of the staff members at the campus there had been instrumental in applying for funding to restore their local picture theatre, the Roxy. The original Roxy had been built in the mid-1930s and had fallen into disrepair. It was a beautiful wooden single-storey theatre, built in tropical style, with high ceilings, and where all the windows could open right out like wings, so that the breeze could come through and keep everyone cool on hot summer nights. The staff member and her group had subsequently received the grant and the community had got together and restored the old theatre. So, in celebration, it was decided that our Christmas party would be held in the refurbished Ouyen Roxy picture theatre. The CWA was organised to cater and on this occasion the theme was movies.

There were about five or six women in the administration pool I ran at the Mildura TAFE and we decided that we'd take on one of the Disney films of the '60s, *One Hundred and One Dalmatians.* I got all dressed up as Cruella de Vil and the women dressed up as spotted Dalmatian dogs. Actually, we ended up winning the prize for the best group. Some of the others — the executive team, for example — went as the Flintstones: Fred and Wilma Flintstone and their daughter, Pebbles, along with their next-door neighbours, Barney and Betty Rubble or whoever. There were lots of sci-fi characters. Another group went as people from the movie *Cleopatra.* Oh, and one guy dressed up as Dennis the Menace and annoyed the hell out of everyone with whistles and buzzers and all sorts of irritating stuff.

In fact, we had about three busloads coming from Mildura, then there was a bus from Swan Hill and a car from Robinvale. In all there would've been a couple of hundred people. If you haven't been through Ouyen, it's a sleepy little place centred within a wheat farming area. And being at the junction of the Calder and Mallee highways it's on one of the main roads from Mildura to Melbourne, so there's a couple of roadhouses, then there's a pub, there's a police station and there's the bakery. In fact, the town used to hold the Great Australian Vanilla Slice competition.

The story goes that when Jeff Kennett, the former Premier of Victoria, was in power, he stopped at Ouyen Bakery one time and declared that they made the best vanilla slice ever. So from that they decided to have the Great Australian Vanilla Slice competition. I'm not sure how long that ran for, but I think the competition's now been taken over by Merbein.

Another of Ouyen's claims to fame happened back in the early 2000s when, at a secret location near the town, five hundred women danced naked in the hopes they'd put an end to a prolonged drought. So that's a bit of the background, if you'd call it that, and, no, I don't know if they helped break the drought or not.

So we all turned up in Ouyen. There was no one else in town. It was as dead as a doornail. Nothing happening, and one of the characters had come along as Batman. And he's a big chap. He's not fat, just big and solid. He's a tradie. I can't think of his name offhand, but he looked absolutely spectacular. You know, with the rippling chest and the cape and the mask and all that sort of stuff and, of course, I'm trying to keep him from stealing my puppies — the women dressed as Dalmatians. In fact I've got a picture of him holding one of them in his arms.

Anyway, the local police station just happened to be right next to the Roxy Theatre. As I said, Ouyen was very quiet. Nothing was happening so, as you might be able to picture, there's these two young police officers in the police station, probably bored witless, sitting at their desks, doing a crossword or playing internet games or imagining what might happen during the next drought, when all of a sudden the front door bursts open and in walks Batman, in his full regalia.

'Hi, guys,' he says, 'if you need any help in the next couple of hours I'll just be next door.'

And these two police blokes just couldn't believe it. Here in sleepy little Ouyen, standing right before them is Batman — the Caped Crusader — direct from Gotham City. Their mouths dropped and their eyes just about popped out of their sockets. Then, thinking that perhaps boredom had led to a momentary flash of insanity, they did a double take to each other: 'Did you see what I saw?' And when they looked back, Batman had gone. He'd disappeared. Vanished.

So that was that. Then a few weeks later the CEO of the TAFE was at an official function where he overheard a senior police officer saying how two young policemen from Ouyen had recently put in a report stating that Batman had visited the town.

## Beady Eyes

When I first got into the shearing game I was living at a place called Maryborough, which is in the Central Goldfields region of Victoria. The thing was, there wasn't too much going on locally so I decided to head off to Queensland where I'd heard there was plenty of work out in the sheds up there.

Now just before I leave my Maryborough days, this was during the times of the old 6 p.m. swill in Victoria. So to enforce the 6 o'clock closing laws, each afternoon at exactly 5.52 the local constabulary would get together and they'd draw straws as to which pair of coppers was going to be the law enforcers for that evening. Once that was done, the chosen pair would depart the police station and head off on a relaxed leafy walk to visit the five pubs down along the main strip. At 5.59 exactly they'd get to the first pub, which was at the top of the street, nearest the cop shop. There they'd settle in and have a couple of pots on the house before they'd remind the publican that it was closing time. 'Last drinks,' the publican would shout and the two coppers would exit the pub.

They'd then move on down to the next pub, where they'd have a couple of pots on the house before they reminded the publican it was closing time. So pub by pub they'd work, and drink, their way down to the bottom of the street. By the time they got to the last pub it'd be around 7 o'clock — an hour after the legal closing time.

Of course, the publicans of the top pubs started to argue, and quite rightfully, that, by being the first to be visited by the constabulary, their trading was being disadvantaged. So they got together with the coppers and they said, 'Come on, boys, give us a bit of a break', and they came to an agreement where the police would alternate their pub-closing pattern. From that day forth, one evening the coppers would start up at the top pub, next evening they'd start at the bottom pub, and everyone was happy.

So that's just one little side story. Oh, and just before I get to Queensland; same town — Maryborough, allegedly. There was a timber cutter. A huge man he was. A real arsehole, I might add. Anyway, this feller was always in trouble with the coppers. Always pissed. Never had a driver's licence. Car unregistered. Any rate, one night he leaves the pub in his usual inebriated state, slides into his unregistered car, goes down the street, turns right and he drives straight through a bloke's garage door and halfway out the back. And that's where he comes to a stop. The front end's caved in. Roo-bar ends up on his bonnet. Steam's hissing from the radiator. He's stuck. He's going nowhere. The cops are called. They arrive and pull the drunken timber cutter out of the car. They line him up. 'So when did you have your last drink?' asks one of the coppers.

'I fuckin' well haven't yet,' comes the reply, and that's the sort of bloke he was; like I said, a real arsehole.

Okay, so there's just a couple of yarns from my Maryborough days. If I told you any of the others I'd probably end up in trouble. So we'll leave it there. Any rate, so there I am, a young feller; I'm off shearing and I take the train up to Brisbane then out to the central west of Queensland, to Longreach. I went solo, and I can tell you it was a hell of a long old trip from Melbourne to Longreach. When I arrived in Longreach, I headed straight to the Palace Hotel. That's where a lot of the shearing blokes stay. It's early January, as hot as hell. Sometimes up into the mid-forties. When I get to the Palace I'm told that the sheds haven't started yet.

So there I am, hanging around Longreach in the heat, spending too much time in the pub and I'm going broke. Luck comes my way and I get a job with a bloke who's got the contract to dig the footings for the newly proposed fire station out at Longreach Airport. There's about half a dozen of us and it's all pick-and-shovel work. Too damn hot. No shade. Relentless heat. Blokes are cramping up and dehydrating.

As it turns out, the boss was a good bloke. I forget his name just now, but he says, 'Bugger this.' He says, 'I'm rooted in this heat.' There's no disagreement there. He says, 'I've got an idea. How about we start work at six in the mornings, then around midday we'll knock off and go into town for a counter meal. After lunch we'll head down to the local swimming pool for a while, then we'll come back out to work at four and we'll go through till six.'

That broke the day up. Of course everyone agrees, 'Yeah, we'll do it that way.'

So that's what we did. We started early, knocked off at around lunchtime, went into town for a feed and some beers, then over to the pool, have a bit of a splash around, then get back to work at around four. It worked well.

Any rate, one day we're down at the pool and, as young bucks do, we're mucking about having cockfights and so on in the water. If you don't know, a cockfight is where you grab someone and try to hold their head under the water for as long as possible. It's kind of like trying to drown one another ... but you don't. Anyhow, we're there, mucking around in the pool having these cockfights and whatever and about six young blokes around our age come up and ask if they can join in the fun.

'Too right,' we said, always up for a challenge, and so they joined in.

Of course from then on it was more or less us against them and boy, didn't we give them heaps. There was one bloke in particular — a beady-eyed sort of feller — well, we took an instant disliking to each other and we went at it, hammer and tongs. It got serious. At one stage I thought he was going to drown me. At another stage I thought I'd drowned him, and in the end we had to be pulled apart. No love lost there, I can tell you. Any rate, it got to time for us to go back to work and a few words were spoken, none too kindly I might add.

That must've been on the Friday because the next day, being a Saturday, was a day off. That morning I get up and go for a walk down the main street in an attempt to shake a few of the previous night's cobwebs out of the system. I just happen to see this young copper, he's out testing someone's parking ability. He looks familiar. I look at him. Beady eyes. He looks back at me and he says, 'I've got my eye on you.'

That's when the penny drops. At Longreach there's an academy for young cadet police officers. 'I've got my eye on you,' he said, and by gee he meant it too. After that, everywhere I went around Longreach, there he'd be with his beady eyes watching, waiting for me to make a false move so he could nab me. So I was pleased when I finally went out into the sheds, shearing. It got me out of Longreach. Away from him.

So that's the story of Longreach. Oh and just a quick last one; once again in Longreach, allegedly. Before I went out into the sheds, as I said I spent a fair bit of time in the pubs. From memory there were about four SP — starting-price — bookies in Longreach and they were working out of a couple of pubs each. Of course SP bookies were a highly illegal identity. Highly illegal. But of course where you've got a highly illegal activity going on, you'll always find ways and means around the law — the law in this particular case being one of the local coppers.

Anyhow, we were drinking away this Saturday and this particular copper shuffles into this pub. He has a bit of a sniff-around and he spies one of these SP bookies plying his trade over in the corner of the front bar. He goes over and says to the bookie, 'So what's going on here? I'm gonna arrest you for illegal gambling.'

The bookie, being the sharp sort of bloke he was, replies to the copper, 'Hey, mate, come on. Give us a break. Look, what's the price of turning a blind eye?'

'Simple,' says the copper. 'I'll have ten quid on the winner of the previous race.'

## Biggest Beat in the World

Laverton's out in the eastern Goldfields-Esperance region of Western Australia, about three hundred and sixty kilometres north-east of Kalgoorlie. I did two years there as sergeant in the late 1980s. Back then Laverton was a mining and administration town of around two or three thousand people. Western Mining had something like 1300 staff. The Windarra nickel mine was still working and the Lancefield Goldmine was operating as well, and it was expanding. With Windarra only being twenty-four kilometres from town and Lancefield only thirteen kilometres, the workers were bussed in and out for work.

The town had the basics. We had a footy club. Cricket was ad hoc, but there was indoor cricket. We had an outdoor bowling club but, due to the extreme lack of water, instead of playing on lawn, we played on a black rubber surface made out of shredded tyres. That was a real challenge at times. On a hot day you nearly melted and, because you're basically playing on rubber matting, your shoes would get stuck to the surface. When that happened you'd make a divot and so when your bowl hit a foot-divot it'd shoot off in all directions.

As far as policing went, Laverton was known to have been the biggest police beat in the world. From memory it covered something like near on 600,000 square kilometres. From Laverton we did back-to-back seven- and ten-day patrols out into the Great Victoria Desert. We had a specially converted troop carrier, with a prisoner carriage on the back, and we'd take out as much food as our car fridge could handle.

First we'd go up to Warburton. That was a six hundred and

eighty kilometre trip on an all-dirt road. It wasn't in a very good condition most of the time so that would take a full day. At Warburton we stayed at the hospital. They were very kind to us in those days because they'd put us up in the maternity wing. Mind you, they weren't delivering babies out there any more.

From Warburton we'd set off on a loop. First we'd head north-east, up the Great Central Road to the Aboriginal community at Warakurna. That'd be a trip of around two hundred and fifty kilometres. Then we'd go over to the nearby settlement of Giles. Giles was a full-blown meteorological station, away out in the remote, about ninety kilometres from the South Australian border. The people at the meteorological station used to accommodate us there in a tin shed. There were seven or eight in the 'met' crew. There was a cook, a powerhouse operator, the boss and four or five weather observers. Even though Giles was in Western Australia, they worked on South Australian time, which meant they were an hour and a half ahead of us. So there was always a bit of confusion with the time difference. When they'd say, 'Dinner's at seven,' that meant it was at 7 o'clock South Australian time and not 7 o'clock Western Australian time.

With Giles, all their food and supplies were freighted in. At one stage they had a cook there who was an ex-SAS soldier. He was a bit of a hard doer. One night when we were in Giles it just happened to be my birthday. The cook got wind of it and so he decided to make me a special birthday cake. With me being in the police, instead of cutting the cake with a knife, he decided he'd use a long police baton. Out came the cake and when he went to give it a hell of a whack with the baton we all ducked for cover, expecting it to explode. But no; it didn't. The baton just bounced off the cake. He said, 'You don't need to worry. The cake's as hard as a rock. I cooked it.'

Little things like that made for some fun and there was always someone there who could play some sort of music. They also had one of Len Beadell's old graders there. You may remember Len as being the surveyor, explorer and roadbuilder who opened up a lot of that isolated desert country out through central Australia. And remember back in the early '60s when the Blue Streak rocket they were testing out at Woomera disappeared in the desert? Well, they found that it had come down out near Giles and so they've also got some of the remains of the rocket there as a historical memento. They also had a swimming pool of sorts. I remember the old dog they had there; it was a black-and-white Border Collie cross. Being as old as it was, the dog had lost all his teeth and so they'd named him 'Jaws', and old Jaws also used to provide some entertainment, especially when he was splashing around in the swimming pool trying to catch a ball with no teeth.

Then sometimes we'd meet up with our counterparts from the Northern Territory and South Australia. Around that time there was a lot of grog being moved between the states so if there was some sort of a border incident, we'd meet at Giles and exchange information. The South Australians seemed a bit more reserved than us, but the Northern Territorians were easy enough to get on with. One policeman from the Territory who stood out was Big Dutchie. Big Dutchie was a good-humoured, good-natured fellow who looked about seven feet tall. Apparently he went on in the Territory to reach quite high up the police tree.

From Giles, every now and then we'd go and have a bit of a sticky-beak across the Northern Territory border to Docker River, which is on the western end of the Petermann Ranges. Then we'd come back into Western Australia and visit Wingellina Aboriginal Community. The people there lived pretty much in the traditional way. There wasn't much more than a school and a shop. I found it quite a depressing, desolate sort of place actually. It had an odd feel about it. It was like it'd fallen out of the sky and lobbed on the ground. There were no trees or anything — as bare as — and if anyone did try to plant anything, there was hardly any water and so it'd die off pretty quick. Blackstone was another community we sometimes visited. The people at Blackstone were quite friendly and they seemed to have a lot of pride in their community. It was a neat sort of place. It was quite an oasis really. There were lots of trees and lawns and stuff.

Anyhow, from Wingellina we'd occasionally go to Surveyor Generals Corner. Surveyors Corner was only ten kilometres north-east of Wingellina. That's where the three states of Western Australia, South Australia and the Northern Territory meet. There's a cairn there that marks the spot and if it takes your fancy you can step from one state to another state to another state, all within a metre or so.

Another little community we used to visit was Jameson. Jameson was only sixty kilometres from Blackstone. That was an interesting place. There were some fiery people at Jameson. If any of the family groups had a falling-out, they'd orchestrate spear-throwing competitions at each other. They'd stand just far enough apart that no one would get speared, but near enough to be able to put the wind up each other. But that's how they sorted things out. It was more of a show of force as opposed to, 'I'm gonna kill you.' The spears they used were made very well actually. They were about six to eight feet long, and they'd throw them with the *woomera*. On one end of the spear there was a flint and on the spear end they had sharpened stones or kangaroo bone and everything was tied on with sinew. Then sometimes the women would have a fight over family issues or whatever and they'd sort it out with a mulga stick. Like I said, very fiery people.

Then we'd finish the loop back to Warburton. But while we were out on the patrol we'd do things like firearm licensing, drivers licensing, issuing warrants or collecting people who'd committed crimes. Public relations was also a big part of it. We'd play a bit of footy or basketball with the kids. It also provided a degree of comfort and security for the white people working out there — such as the school teachers, office workers and the administrators of the various communities — when they knew that every few days or so the police would be coming around. I guess you could say we made them feel a little less isolated than what they were.

As far as law enforcement went, within each of the communities the administrators would keep an eye on things. If an offence was committed the administrators would write all the details down and we'd take it from there. Usually we'd just issue an on-the-spot warrant and tell them that they'd have to appear in court in Laverton or Warburton on a particular day. We'd then bail them and off they'd go and nine times out of ten they'd be waiting for us outside the court on whatever day it was. If things were more serious and we picked up a prisoner, they'd come along and complete the patrol with us. They'd camp with us and share our food and they never tried to escape. They were basically very honest people.

# Caring

I grew up in the northern suburbs of Perth, around Duncraig and Watermans Bay. You could say that I had quite a disjointed childhood. Dad left home when I was seven, so there was just Mum, me, my twin younger sisters and an older one. Then because Mum was out working so much to try to afford to get us all through school and things like that, us kids spent a lot of time on our own.

Being the only male in the family, I guess I took it upon myself to care for my sisters. I'd say that's when I got the bug in me to want to do something to help people. When I was in high school I remember looking around at what sort of jobs there were in relation to the community services area. That's when the thought of the police came up. I must've been quite taken with it because one day a lady gave me a package all about policing and what you needed to do to join. From there it just snowballed. After I left school I had to wait seven or eight months before I could get into the force as a cadet. During that time I took on a few part-time jobs such as working in a daycare centre. I enjoyed that. I wasn't trained or anything. I was just an extra set of hands, but again it was that caring sort of thing.

Then when I got into the police force I did two years as a cadet. The best way to describe it is that it was like doing an apprenticeship. Every three months you were moved to a different section to gain experience and to get some idea of what you really wanted to end up doing. So I was exposed to a variety of stuff. There were some good placements and some not so good. Three months of data entry was one of the least appealing. I just hated sitting there.

After I completed my two years I worked in and around the city for the next five years. I thought Perth was the be-all and end-all of policing, but after I got together with my wife we decided that we needed to branch out. That's when we went out into the various country areas of WA, and we've loved it.

I'm currently in Karratha, a coastal town in the Pilbara region of Western Australia and, just as I did last year, I'm overseeing our local Police Legacy Bike Ride. I say 'overseeing' because our customs service officer actually organises the event, and she and fellow supporters sell it. It's just if any bigger issues arise, then people come to me.

Just to put you in the picture: Police Legacy is basically an independent offshoot of the police union that was formed to help care for the immediate family of any of our serving members who get injured or pass away. To that end Police Legacy runs various fundraisers around the state. Anyway, about twenty years ago, a few of the police officers up here in Karratha decided to do their bit also. That's when they came upon the idea: 'How about we do a charity relay bicycle ride from Karratha to Broome?'

How it works is that you have two teams of twenty riders who cover the eight hundred and fifty kilometres from Karratha to Broome. In all, the ride takes about thirty-five or thirty-six hours; that's day and night, nonstop, so not everyone's out on the road at the one time. Our police officers don't necessarily have to get involved but I do try to encourage the younger guys in particular. That's just to impress upon them the importance of Police Legacy and the necessity for it to keep going. So we put it out to the police first, then it goes out to the local community, then on to anyone else who wants to ride. You don't have to be a great bike rider. We're more after people who can work together as a team.

Of course, with it being such a big event, a lot of support people also get involved. If you take in both the riders and volunteers, anywhere between sixty and seventy people partake in the overall proceedings. We have a bus and up to ten other vehicles. We have police escort. We have hire cars. The army volunteers their time as part of their service to the community. St John Ambulance come along with us. A couple of fireys — firemen and women — usually come on board. Apex brings their van and every time there's a major stop or changeover for the riders they're there with their food and ablutions and that sort of stuff.

Safety's also a big issue. The volunteers don't usually get much sleep because we're constantly keeping an eye out on all the riders. I mean, let's be honest, if you're riding a bicycle up the Great Northern Highway in the middle of the night and you've got triple road trains whizzing past you at supposedly a hundred kilometres per hour — probably more — things can get a little bit hairy. To that end the bus stops every five kilometres. That provides the riders the opportunity to have a break and have a sleep and grab something to eat. It also provides the chance for a changeover of riders. My wife's riding this year. It's the first time she's given it a go. Her aim's to just do her best and that's fine because, if need be, she can get off the bike, get on the bus and have a break, then get back on the bike again so she can still be a part of it.

As far as the main fundraising side of it goes, each year we sell raffle tickets for a camper trailer. You might've seen them today, set up down at Kmart. Then with the horse race meetings at places like Marble Bar, Port Hedland and Roebourne being such popular social gatherings, we also take the camper trailer out and around to those places and sell tickets there as well. It all culminates in Broome. We organise it so that the bike ride ends just a few days before the Broome Cup race meeting. With about twenty thousand people turning up for the Cup meeting it's not only an opportunity for the riders to have a great day out, but it's also the perfect place for us to sell quite a few more tickets.

Over the years, in all, just from Karratha alone we've raised hundreds of thousands of dollars. This year we're aiming to raise between thirty-five and fifty-five thousand. Though of course, when you organise an event like this, not everything's donated, so if we reach fifty thousand we'll be very happy. We then hold the money in a special Police Legacy account until it's needed. Everything's audited properly and so it's all above board. I think the last cheque we handed over was somewhere around a hundred and ten thousand dollars.

So the Police Legacy Bike Ride's something that started a long time before me. But I'm proud to be doing my little part in keeping it rolling. Yes, it's another caring thing, I guess you could say. Then, seeing that we get moved around quite a bit in the police, next year who knows where I'll be? Though wherever it is I'll most probably be involved in one way, shape or form. I might even come back to Karratha especially for it. Who knows? Actually we've got one volunteer who used to work up here. He did the first ten or so charity rides. He now lives down south and each year he sets himself up in his local shopping centre, along with a photo of the camper trailer, and he sells raffle tickets for our Police Legacy fundraiser. People like that you'll never replace.

# Collar and Tie

To protect the guilty, let's say this particular incident happened at an undisclosed town, somewhere in Tasmania. Actually, if the truth be known, it was over near the east coast.

Anyway, it was a reasonably common occurrence that, when the local hotel closed at night, those of us males who were left would often continue on in the butcher's shop. This was when it used to be 10 o'clock closing.

You may well ask, 'Why the butcher's shop?' Well there'd be two main reasons I guess: one being that the butcher's shop was right next door to the hotel and the second being that the butcher, Athol Campbell, was usually one of the last ones standing at the hotel.

On this particular occasion, a few of us had been to a collar-and-tie dinner at the hotel. I forget just now what the occasion was but, as was our habit, we all ended up in the butcher's shop. The party was continuing on when there came a knock on the door. It was two uniformed policemen. One was our local copper, Constable Bert Simpson. We knew Bert very well as he'd often pop by the butcher's shop after he'd finished night duty. The other feller was Constable Tom Brooks. Tom had recently arrived in the neighbouring town so he was new to the district and he was fresh out of the academy.

'So what's going on here?' they said.

'We're just kicking on after our collar-and-tie dinner,' we replied.

'Well, we're just on our way home from a collar-and-tie police do over in Swansea, can we kick on with you?' Bert asked.

'Of course,' we said, and so the party continued on continuing, with the addition of these two uniformed policemen.

Then at about twelve-thirty there's another knock on the door. Constable Tom, the new feller from the neighbouring town, opened the door and there stood Wally Ambrose, dressed in casual clothing.

'What do you want?' says Constable Tom.

Now, just a little bit of background on Wally Ambrose. He's the local real-estate agent and he'd done the dirty around town on a few occasions; like when he sold off Mrs McTavish's block of land to a particular fast-food concern, against most of our wishes. What's more, he somehow managed to pocket quite a profit from the deal. As you might imagine, he's not the most popular bloke in town, not by a long shot.

'I want to join the party,' says Wally.

Constable Tom turns around to us and says, 'Well, what about it?' From the grumbles and groans Tom surmises that Wally's not too welcome, so he says, 'No, sorry, you can't join the party. As you can see, it's a collar-and-tie affair.'

'Oh, okay,' says Wally and he turned around and he took off back into the night and we congratulated Constable Tom on his lightning-quick thinking.

Some time passed and the party continued on continuing on continuing. Then, when Frank Baldock, the local bank manager, stuck his head outside to get some fresh air he saw Wally coming back down the road.

'Wally's coming back,' he announced, 'and he's all done up in a collar and tie.'

'Shit, what're we going to do this time?' said Big Bill Langley, the publican.

'Don't worry,' said Constable Tom, 'I'll sort him out.'

Knock. Knock. Constable Tom opens the door and there's Wally all done up to the nines in his collar and tie.

'What do you want?' says Constable Tom.

'I've come to join the party,' says Wally.

'No you haven't,' says Constable Tom, and in a flash he's picked up the butcher's knife and he's chopped off Wally's tie an inch below the bow and he's tossed it in the sausage mince. 'You can't come in here,' Tom says. 'You haven't got a tie on.' And he closes the door on Wally.

Well, that took us all aback. So much so that Constable Bert said, 'Tom, you can't do that,' and, in a flash, he's picked up another butcher's knife and he's chopped Tom's tie off. So Tom then cuts Bert's tie off. Then once they'd cut each other's ties off they start chopping off the buttons from each other's shirts — button by button.

Somehow the whole thing came to an end after that. But next time I saw Bert, he said that his wife had managed to sew all the buttons back on his shirt. 'But,' he added, 'she didn't seem to show a lot of grace in doing so.'

As for his tie, he told me that before the police department would issue him with a new one, he had to show due cause as to why he wanted a replacement. Not being able to come up with a plausible excuse as to why his tie had been sliced in two with a butcher's knife during an after-hours drunken prank with the neighbouring police officer, he'd taken it back to his wife and asked if she'd be able to sew the tie back together as well.

'So what happened?' I asked.

'Well,' he said, 'let's put it this way. Things are a bit frosty on the home front.'

# Derby

Derby's up in the north-west Kimberley region of Western Australia. It's a couple of hundred k's north-east of Broome and about two and a half thousand k's north of Perth. It's just one of those towns you either like or you don't. I was there for four years and, based on the time I had, it's probably my favourite place in the Kimberley. I loved my footy and cricket and I loved the fishing, and of course the people were great. It's that way of life and we've still got friends up there.

In its heyday Derby was a port town where a lot of the livestock from along the Fitzroy River properties were boated out from the jetty. But since the road trains came in, that no longer happens. Goldmining was pretty big back in the mid-1880s when there was a gold strike. There was also a black granite mine at one stage. That got up and going, then it failed. The hospital used to do a lot of training years ago. Even though these days it's still known as a regional hospital, they don't do any training there any more; Broome's now taken over that side of things.

All that may sound a bit grim but there's still the old diamond mine up along the Gibb River Road. The Royal Flying Doctor Service still runs its base out of Derby. There's quite a few houses going up and a new prison's just been built: the West Kimberley Regional Prison. I don't know if you know or not but currently about forty per cent of prisoners in our state jails are of Indigenous origin. That's a huge percentage, and a lot of those are reoffenders. That's how the new prison came about. It's not like your normal prison where everyone's locked in together. The West Kimberley Regional covers a large area so they can walk about during the day, then at night they live together in self-contained houses according to family ties and security ratings. It's a different approach to Indigenous incarceration and it looks like it's working.

While I'm on about the policing side of things; just out of Derby there's the large Boab Prison Tree. They say that it's 1500 years old. A door's been cut out of it and it's hollow inside. Local folklore has it that the tree was used as a staging point by early police patrols when they'd bring the prisoners in in chains and put them in the hollow of the tree or just tie them up there. Now, whether it's myth, legend, fabrication, fact, fiction or otherwise, who knows, but the story sounds good and it's now a registered Aboriginal Site.

Back in my day, as far as the town itself went, Derby wasn't as picturesque as Broome, and it still isn't. It doesn't have the large volumes of tourists coming through. It hasn't got the palm trees and the sandy beaches like Broome's Cable Beach. It's mainly mangroves and mudflats with ten-metre tides, and if you go swimming you do so at your own peril. That's because of the crocodiles. But, like I said, I had a good time. What's more, a bit of my own family history was there as well because, back fifty years or so, I had a cousin who was the OIC — officer-in-charge — there. So there was a bit of a connection to start with.

There's quite a large population of Indigenous people in town these days; about half. After equal pay was brought in for Aboriginal station workers a lot of the Indigenous people started to drift into the towns and were put on the reserves. That didn't only happen in Derby, it happened everywhere and that probably saw a downturn on the Indigenous side. Then there's the white community, which includes some South Africans. There's quite a number of Asians in town as well. They're mainly Malays and Chinese and they all pitch in. A lot of the families first came to the area back in the mid-1880s when the gold rush was on. When that petered out they stayed and got on with business; you know, market gardens and stuff like that and they've done very well for themselves and have intermingled in well with the whites.

But there was always something happening in Derby, especially when it came to sport. Derby's the place where 'mud footy' was created and it still remains a very popular community event. I don't know exactly how it all came about, but I get the impression that it began with a few people talking over a few beers, which is common in Derby. Someone said, 'Let's try something a bit different like setting up and playing mud football.'

Initially it was a fundraising exercise for the Flying Doctor Service then, as it grew and grew, other charitable organisations were included. Anyway, with the first one, after all the bureaucratic red tape had been cleared up, they put out promotional flyers along the lines of 'Who wants to put in a team?'. You know: 'Come and beat the coppers' or whoever, and the challenge was on. When they had enough interest they graded out a large bird's-nest dam down on the marsh, put up the goal posts, then they filled it up with a foot or so of water.

Mud footy's played along the same lines as Aussie Rules and they started off with about four teams. I can remember the first one. It was a comedy. Because they were playing in mud, if someone's pants got pulled off you wouldn't have known the difference. Actually I don't even know why they wore any sort of uniform. After about the first five minutes you couldn't tell who was who and who was in which team anyway.

It was like, 'Kick it to me.'

'But who are you? Are you on my side or not?'

It was utter chaos, but it provided a lot of entertainment and heaps of fun and, because you're playing in mud, a hell of a lot of effort goes into a game where it's nearly impossible to score goals. But my God, the following day you knew exactly who'd played because their eyes were fire-engine red from all the mud and grit. There were the bung eyes, the ear, nose and throat infections and aches; the lot. But it was fantastic for the community. Everyone pitched in and some money was raised for the RFDS, and that's why I enjoyed my time in Derby so much. They were the type of people who looked after and cared for each other and their community.

# Dinky-di

We got an email the other day warning us about talking to you. I don't know why, because a lot of these stories need to be told and recorded. If not they'll disappear, and that's not right. So I've got a few tales to tell, some with a laugh or two in them, some not.

The police force runs in my family. I'm ex-Sergeant 4862. I did forty years and my father did near on forty years. His registered number was 2189. Dad joined not long after World War Two and he served in lots of towns over here in Western Australia; at places like Bunbury, Bridgetown, Big Bell, Cue, as well as a few city stations. Then my father's brother, Uncle George, was also in the police force. I forget his number.

I grew up in Big Bell. Big Bell's in the Murchison region of WA, near Cue. When I was a kid it was a big mining place, though these days it's pretty much a ghost town. The pub's just about the only building still standing because it was one of the rare ones that was made from bricks and concrete. We lived about a hundred yards or so directly across the railway line from the pub. The police station and our house adjoined each other. It was pretty basic in today's terms with just a sand floor that had linoleum laid on top.

There's a couple of stories I remember pretty well from back then; this one in particular. Dad used to like his drop of beer and even though, as I said, we lived just across the railway track from the hotel, Dad never walked over there. Each afternoon he'd get on his police pushbike and he'd ride from our house, down the road a bit, go over the railway crossing and back down the street to the pub. Then after he'd had a skinful he'd get back on his bike and set off back home again. The thing was, on the return trip, he'd sometimes fall off as he rode across the railway crossing. This was great entertainment for the pub's patrons. So much so that the hotelier would take bets on whether or not Dad would fall off his pushbike when he rode across the railway crossing. This's dinky-di.

But what most of the patrons didn't know was that Dad was in cohoots with the hotelier and before he left the pub he'd let the hotelier know if he was going to fall off at the crossing or not.

Then after Dad had got on his pushbike to go home, the hotelier would call out, 'Right-o, fellers, a couple of bob that Frank'll fall off his bike today,' and the patrons would say, 'No, no way. He'll stay up today,' and they'd bet against the hotelier. That's how Dad got to pay for his drinks; from the money he made on whether or not he'd fall off his pushbike as he rode across the railway crossing. And he made a fair few quid out of it too. That's until someone happened to overhear Dad and the hotelier sorting out whether he was going to fall off or not. They had to put a stop to it then. But it worked for a while, and that was the funny part of it.

Dad was a good shot back in those days. And just as well too because another time I was playing out in the yard with this bloody tiger snake. Of course, being a toddler I didn't know that the snake was dangerous. I just thought I'd found a new mate. Anyhow, when Mum stuck her head out the door and saw what was going on, she started screaming. As it happened Dad was doing his rounds over in the town so, when someone in the pub heard Mum, they called out to Dad, 'Frank, come here quick.'

Now when Dad did his rounds he'd always take his .303 rifle along with him.

And when he saw what was going on he grabbed his rifle and, *bang*, he pinged the snake from the back of the hotel — a hundred yards across the way. That would've been in the mid-'50s and that's another fair-dinkum story.

Then in the early '60s our mother shot through and Dad couldn't sort of look after us kids. Back in those days, the rules were, if a police officer wasn't with his wife any more and he had children, those children were virtually treated like orphans. So that's when us kids more or less went to live with our uncle and aunty down at Pingelly, which is south of Perth, in the Wheatbelt region of WA.

Uncle George was the sergeant-in-charge at Pingelly and one of his jobs was to keep an eye on the Aborigines down on the reserve. Back then there was a law about how many dogs the Aborigines were allowed to have for sleeping with to keep warm and to help them in hunting for food. From memory it was either two or three and if they had any more it was up to the police to destroy the extra dogs. Anyhow, sometimes Uncle George would take me with him on his rounds. I would've been in my early teens by this stage and on this particular day he was going down to the reserve, so I asked if I could go with him. 'Sure,' he said and he grabbed his .38 long-barrel six-shot revolver and we got in his car. I forget just what make the car was, but it was an old wooden spoked thing with leather seats. It wasn't a police car. In those days the police used to claim something like threepence a mile for the use of their own vehicle.

Anyway we went down to the reserve and there's dogs everywhere. On this occasion I also took along my dog, Tubby. Tubby was a real bugger. He just loved a fight. In fact, I reckon he preferred a fight than a feed. And so, when we got there, I stayed in the back of the car with Tubby. So there's Uncle George trying to sort out all these bloody dogs; you know, how many belong to whoever and in amongst all the yapping and the yabbering and going-on, one of the Aborigine's dogs attacked Uncle George.

Of course, once Tubby sees the dog having a go at Uncle George, he's out of the car in a flash and he's into it. He starts beating the shit out of this Aborigine's dog. Then when all the other dogs see a scrap's going on, they're into it as well. So now there's a whole pile of dogs all getting stuck into each other. Anyway, I jumped out of the car and I grabbed the nearest stick I could find and I started whacking into these dogs, trying to get them off Tubby. As I'm whacking away, one of them bites me. So Uncle George is out with his .38 six-shot revolver and he starts sorting these dogs out. Then when the Aborigines see what's going on, they start dragging them away. Oh, there were dogs everywhere. Anyhow, after things had settled down a bit Uncle George drove me and Tubby back to the police station where he reloaded his revolver, grabbed some extra bullets, then he drove back down to the reserve. But he wouldn't let me go with him this time.

But those days were very different times. The other thing I can clearly remember is being down at the reserve when an Aboriginal woman approached Uncle George and said, 'Sergeant George, you take my granddaughter please.'

He said, 'Why?'

She said, 'Because she's got half-caste in her, the tribe won't let me look after her. They don't want her.' And that's true. If they had half-caste children they used to ask the police to take them away for their own good. And that's my memory of the Stolen Generations. That's what they did and I saw that happen on other occasions as well. Now I'm not saying that a lot of them weren't taken, but by gee it never happened in any of the country towns I ever lived in and I lived in a lot of places and I was in the police force for forty years.

As for myself, I first went to join the police in 1972, but my old man wanted me to finish my automotive mechanic's diploma. Anyhow, the bloke who was in charge of the police academy in Perth was a friend of my father's and he said to me, 'Son, as soon as you finish your exams, just let us know and we'll get you in,' which I did, and that was in October 1973.

Then just to finish with: one of the sort of funny things that happened to me was when I wasn't long out of the academy. I was a constable back then and I'd just been stationed out in the Eastern Goldfields region at Coolgardie when we got a call from Norseman to say that a couple of people did a drive-off from the local service station. Anyway, the sergeant and I go out on the highway and we set up and wait for them to come by. The sergeant had a .22 rifle and I had an old .38 revolver. After a couple of hours we saw them coming along and so we stepped out onto the highway to wave them down. It was a green Torana. But before we could do anything they jumped out of the car and they fired a shot at us. So me and the sarge, we took cover behind a rock. After we were waiting there a while and nothing had happened, I said to the sarge, 'What do we do now?' And I remember looking over at the poor old sarge and he's as white as a ghost and he's shivering in his boots.

Next thing they take another ping at us. So I jumped up from behind the rock and fired a shot with the old .38. Now I don't know if you know anything about the old .38s or not, but they were shocking old things. If you got hit they'd hardly puncture your skin. But the one thing they did was, when they went off, they went off with one hell of a bang. And this couple must've thought we had a cannon or something because next thing we hear them calling out, 'All right, we give up. We give up.' So we took them in and after we'd got back to Coolgardie and we'd locked them up, the old sarge started to get a bit of his colour back.

# Dope

Have you ever heard of the reality Australian television police drama called *The Force*? It was on a while back, but they still replay some of the episodes every now and then. I've been on that several times.

One time a junior female partner and I went to a job along with the camera crew from *The Force* and I'd somehow got the house numbers all mixed up so we ended up at the wrong address. It was night and so we all rock up at this house; the one that turned out to be the wrong place. My partner and myself, we're in full uniform with all our gear and torches. Everything's been planned down to a tee. Every minute detail's been checked. All the camera crew's there, out in the street, filming. I go and knock on the door — *knock* — but no one seems to be home like they should be. I knock again. *Knock*. Nothing. The house had this big plate-glass front window. The light's on inside and so I go and look in the window. I'm standing there and I can just make out this bloke sitting at his table, doing something. I keep knocking but he's just ignoring us. I'm thinking that he's perhaps a bit deaf or something so I knock a bit louder. *KNOCK*. Still no response.

The camera crew's getting impatient: 'What's going on? We're on a tight budget, you know.'

'Okay, okay,' so I take a closer look in on this bloke and that's when I see what he's doing. He's got all his cannabis — ganja as it's sometimes called — stacked up on the table and he's packing it all into little plastic bags.

I said to my partner, 'Quick, get round the back. He's got cannabis on the table. Get around the back.'

The same instant she's turned to go around the back, the reflection of her torch has flickered in his eyes, through the window. It alerts him. When he looks out the window he sees me looking in at him.

'Don't move!' I shout.

Anyway, he's off like a shot. He's scooped up all his cannabis and he's bolted. My partner, myself and the camera crew, we start scrambling around to the back of the house. When we arrive, he's standing there as innocent as the day he was born.

'Hey,' he says, 'how ya all going?'

I said, 'Mate, you're under arrest.'

'What am I under arrest for?' he says.

'Mate,' I said, 'you're under arrest for the possession of cannabis.'

By now all the camera crew's gathered in tight around him. But I can't see the cannabis. It's gone. Disappeared.

'Where is it then?' he says. 'I'm calling a lawyer.'

Just then I happened to walk past a little bench. It's like a trestle seat and it had some clothes on it, from off the clothes line. It's dark, like I said, and I accidentally knocked it and when it topples over all this cannabis fell out. He'd hidden it in the clothes.

'Well,' I said, 'you're definitely under arrest now.'

'You can't prove that was mine.'

We then went into this big argument about proof of possession and all of that. While all this was going on they were filming it for the show, *The Force*. Anyway, by the time we got him back to the lockup he'd taken it on the chin. The camera was still rolling and I'm asking him some questions. 'So what's with the cannabis?'

'Yeah, it's mine,' he said. 'I buy an ounce every couple of weeks' — which is about a sandwich-bag full — 'and I put it in smaller bags so that I know how much I have a night.'

This must've been when the tennis was on at Wimbledon, because he added, 'And I was just getting some ready because

Maria Sharapova's playing tonight and I just love watching her. She looks real good and she wears real short dresses.'

So I'd really spoilt this guy's night. Now I'm just being a little bit cheeky here, I know, but I always tell people that I not only took away his cannabis but I also took away his opportunity to perve at Maria Sharapova. So yeah, that's the story of how I made an arrest when I went to the wrong house, and that's been shown on television about six or seven times now.

The other story I was going to tell you was about an accident I had and this time it was me who ended up in trouble. I was off work for about seven months after I broke my kneecap, and I've still got the scars to prove it.

Anyhow, when I came back from one of my country stints I spent a while at a city police station. This particular time I was involved in a pursuit with a bloke who'd stolen a car. Off I go after him and he ended up pranging the car. He then got out of the stolen vehicle and he took off, with me after him. First he went up a sand embankment, then he jumped over a couple of fences, then he ran down a concrete path, then he ran down a street, then he ran back down some more sand and out onto a major arterial road, into the middle of a dual carriageway.

By that stage we'd run about a kilometre and a half and so when I caught up to him I was pretty knackered and so my legs were like jelly. But then he turned around to try to fight me. And as I tackled him, with both his weight and my weight right on my leg, the first thing that hit the ground was my kneecap.

This was at about 9 p.m. on a Thursday — a late-shopping night — and we were about four hundred metres down from a large shopping centre. Anyhow, after I got him to the ground I couldn't get up. I was stuck. Then as I was holding him down, trying to get him handcuffed, the traffic lights changed outside the shopping centre. When I looked up there were all these cars heading towards us. So now I'm going, Hey I'm in big trouble here. We're in the middle of this dual carriageway and I can't move and there's all these cars coming right at me.

What made matters worse was that I didn't have my high-vis clothing on. That was because when I'd first tried to stop the stolen car, the bloke had taken off so fast that, when I jumped out of my police vehicle, I didn't have time to put it on. Anyhow it was just lucky for me that the first car that came down the road had two off-duty fireys — firemen — in it; one great big burly bloke and one not so burly. Their initial thought was that there'd been a car accident and two people had rolled out onto the road. So the fireys pulled their vehicle up in the middle of the road to stop all the oncoming traffic. When they came over, I said, 'There's been no accident. This bloke's under arrest for driving a stolen car. Can you give me a hand?'

By that time I'd got one cuff on and I was struggling with the other one. Anyhow, the big burly bloke said, 'No need for the cuffs, mate' and he pretty well just picked this guy up off the road and dumped him on the verge. 'Sit there and don't move!' the firey said, and the bloke was so scared that he didn't budge an inch.

The two fireys then helped me up and they got me across to the verge. By now my adrenaline had kicked in so much that, even though I'd a broken kneecap, I was still able to stagger around a bit. So I went to my car and I rang in and everyone came running and the bloke was locked up.

The thing was, I didn't even hear a crack when my kneecap was broken. I just think my head was so filled with what was going on around me; you know, Here I am, I'm stuck in the middle of the road trying to hold down a bloke who's stolen a car. There's traffic coming and I'm going to get run over.

Yes, so I spent a fair bit of time off work with this broken kneecap. Then, because my wife and I had been in the country and we'd really enjoyed it, after that incident we decided that the city just didn't seem to be doing it for us. That's when I started applying for another country post and in the end I was very lucky in getting a supervisor position. Even more lucky was that I ended up having a very good crew around me. Quite a few of them had come straight out of the academy and so I used to call them 'the kids' and, because I'd been around a lot longer than they had, they used to call me the 'old sergeant'. They were great. They'd be off-duty and you'd ring them and say, 'Look, a report's come in that there's an offender on the premises of a shopping centre or whatever. I'll meet you at the station and we'll go down there and sort it out.'

'Yeah, okay,' they'd say and by the time I walked into the police station to pick them up, they'd be calling in with, 'I've already got the person in custody, could you hurry down here please?' So they'd gone straight there.

Then there was this one really funny incident. It was just like you'd see in the *Keystone Cops*. One night we had a car chase. As was usual I was with a much younger officer — one of the 'kids' — fresh from the police academy. Anyhow, we were chasing this stolen vehicle when suddenly the driver stopped in the middle of the road.

I said to my younger feller, 'Go get him!'

So my young feller's out of the car. Just as he does, the bloke in the stolen vehicle has jumped out of his car and he's taken off, holding a large potted cannabis plant. As it turned out he'd stolen it from someone's backyard. So he's off down the street hanging on to this cannabis plant. By the look of him he'd also been drinking. He's a bit unsteady on his feet. Anyway, down the street he goes with my young feller after him. I'm sitting in the car with the police lights flashing, thinking how it'll be an easy arrest; the bloke's been drinking and he's also carrying something — a cannabis plant. Next thing, he gets down to the end of the street and he runs around a tree, with my young feller behind him. But instead of going right, left or straight ahead, he heads back up the street still hanging on to the potted cannabis plant, and still with the young feller in hot pursuit. But the young feller's gaining.

I can't believe it. I'm sitting in the car with the police lights flashing and there he is coming back down the street towards me. I'm thinking, Far out, I'm going to have to get out of the car here. Next thing, he runs straight down the driveway of this house. The driveway's only the width of a car. I knew we had him then. I also knew the house very well, so I was sure he couldn't go anywhere when he got to the end of the driveway because it had one of those big barbed-wire fences across it. There was no escaping.

So he's down this driveway, still hanging on to the potted cannabis plant, and by now my young feller's right on his heels. So I get out of the car and I start to wander over towards the driveway. Next thing, the bloke with the cannabis plant comes running back past me with my partner still in hot pursuit.

Eventually we got him and we took him down to the station and he was charged with driving a stolen vehicle, drunk driving, having a cannabis plant in his possession and he also didn't have a driver's licence. So we processed him and he was given a date for his hearing. He's still a bit drunk so we put him in the lockup for a couple of hours where he could sober up. But I said to the young officer who was with me, 'How the hell did he get out of that driveway without you catching him?'

'Well,' he said, 'there was a wheelie bin at the end of the driveway.'

'So?'

He said, 'I was just about to grab him when he ran around the wheelie bin and so I ran around the wheelie bin after him and he headed back up the driveway, past you.'

I tell you, it was just one of those *Keystone Cop* moments. But then the story gets even worse. Eventually this bloke had sobered up enough and, now that he's under the legal limit, we decide to let him go. It was probably only about a couple of hundred metres to where the stolen car was parked, so we give him the stern warning, 'Mate, you're in enough strife as it is so don't go anywhere near that car. Just walk home or something. Don't even think about driving.'

'Okay,' he says. 'See yers.'

It was a very busy night and not long after he'd wandered off, another call comes in. It's an assault and a stolen car. So we scream off to this other job. There'd been a fight or something and the offenders had jumped into someone else's car and the car had been spotted. It was a high-risk operation so when we pull this stolen car over we had one of our police vehicles parked nose to it and my vehicle was parked directly behind it so that the offending car was blocked in the middle. It couldn't go anywhere.

It was quite a scene with all three cars having their headlights on and both the police vehicles with their warning lights flashing. Everything was lit up like a Christmas tree. By now it's like 3 o'clock in the morning. Next thing we know, our old mate, the one we'd just charged with stealing a vehicle, drunk driving, not having a licence and being in possession of a cannabis plant, he comes driving past in the car that he'd previously stolen.

We're going, 'Did you see that?'

'Yep, it was him all right.'

Being as occupied as we were with this high-risk operation we didn't bother to go after him. We knew he'd be under the legal alcohol limit, so there was no problem there. And seeing how we'd taken down all his details when he'd been at the station, we knew we could easily follow up on him later. So we continued on with the job at hand.

Next thing we see, our old mate does a U-ie further down the street, he drives back to us and he parks right behind the police car. He then gets out and he comes over.

I've gone, 'What're you doing, mate?'

'Well, I saw yers all standing around with all your warning lights and that on and because I was driving a stolen car without a licence I thought you wanted to pull me over.'

I said, 'Did anyone try to stop you?'

'Well, no, not really.'

'Then why didn't you just keep driving?'

'Oh yeah, I guess I shoulda then, shouldn't I?'

So then he wore another set of charges. I tell you, you meet some strange characters in this game, and he was just one of them.

## Drunks' Assessment Form

# Emoluments

The township of Birdsville is in the far south-west of Queensland. The Diamantina River runs just to the east of the town. Well, in actual fact, the Diamantina hardly ever runs at all. It's usually dry. Then if you head west of town you'll run into the Simpson Desert. So it's a pretty remote sort of location. Even Charles Sturt, when he came through back in the mid-1840s, described it as being, and I quote, 'a desperate region having no parallel on earth'.

It wasn't until the 1880s, when the station people began moving cattle through the Channel Country, down the Birdsville Track to the railhead at Marree, that Birdsville came to life. Being so close to the South Australian border, the Queensland government set up a Customs House there and pretty soon Birdsville had something like three pubs, a couple of general stores, a doctor, a bank, a police station; just about everything a town of around three thousand people and a few billion flies could want for. But after Federation, in 1901, interstate customs collection was abolished, and just about everyone left town, either through lack of work and/or from the living conditions being too harsh.

My first contact with Birdsville was back in 1963. That's when I ran the administration for the Compagnie Générale de Géophysique (CGG) during the construction of the French Line. The French Line was a rough sort of track we built across the Simpson Desert, which was used for the seismic work we were doing. By then the population of Birdsville had shrunk to eight whites and sixty-three blacks. I know that because I counted them.

But of course, a pub remained. Back then it just had a small bar. There was only one narrow entrance. The room to the right, as you went in the front door, was what's called the 'drunks' tank', which was where the drunks were sent to sleep after they'd drunk all of their money. Out the back were six rooms for accommodation. The existing western verandah faced the airstrip and, from the comfort of a chair placed there for the purpose of, say, a twilight drink, you could see the combined post office and police station across the way.

Now because it's crucial to this story I'll give you a brief rundown of the police station. Birdsville lockup consisted of only two cells whose doors had been removed so that the occupants could come and go during their wait for the next visit of the circuit magistrate. That could be anything up to six weeks. You might think that that's a bit lax but, considering how Birdsville's situated at the apex of the Simpson Desert and the Birdsville Track, even the dumbest of criminals would've realised that they'd reached the end of the line in about every respect, and escape was out of the question.

So now may I introduce the leading character in this particular story: the legendary police sergeant Eric Sammon; also known as 'Lord of the Lockup', plus a few more colourfully descriptive titles, the vast majority of which would be unprintable. Eric Sammon ran the one-man police station at Birdsville. His word was law in this, the second largest police district in Queensland. Eric was into everything that moved. Anyone with business in Birdsville had to deal with Eric at some stage or other because, other than being the local copper, he also held all the state and federal government agencies in town. In my capacity as administration officer for the CGG party, every time I came into the airstrip to load or offload gear, grog, mail and personnel, I had to deal with Eric. And as he would so proudly boast, 'I've got nineteen emoluments and I earn more than Bischof.' Bischof being the then Queensland police commissioner.

Now for those who may not know, an emolument is a small government payment, or stipend, that's given out for doing certain things, like looking after the post office, which was a part of Eric's duties. Then he'd receive an emolument for being the jailer and probably one for airport fuel. He also ran the Trans-Australia Airlines agency. I don't know what all the others were. It'd be interesting to know. Oh, he probably looked after the cemetery as well. Though, I must add that, to his credit, Eric also took on many honorary community jobs such as being an office-bearer for both the Birdsville and Bedourie Race Clubs. Though who knows what went on there. Not me. So these emoluments were government payments and no one had as many as Eric, not even his boss, Police Commissioner Bischof, who, coincidentally, not only hired Eric Sammon but was also responsible for hiring that fellow, Terry Lewis, who later on was convicted and jailed as a result of the Fitzgerald Inquiry into police corruption in Queensland. Interesting, isn't it?

Anyhow, when I first came to Birdsville it was the advent of late-night closing in Queensland, which only allowed drinkers to stay on a licensed premises until 11 p.m. On this particular evening a bunch of us CGG fellows were enjoying a few quiet drinks in the bar. Other than us there was the publican, Norm Portch, and his wife, Elva, two other guests and Eric Sammon's wife, Joan. Then, out of the blue, in strides Eric and issues a warning to the two women, Elva and Joan. 'If you two aren't out of here by 11 o'clock closing I'll come back and arrest you.'

And he did. Come 11 o'clock, Eric returns and says to Elva and Joan, 'That's it. You two, you're off. You're nicked.'

Now he didn't arrest the publican, Norm Portch. He didn't arrest Norm's two guests and he didn't arrest us CGG fellows. I'm just thinking now that that may have been because whenever we were in town the local economy was given a huge boost. And somewhere along the line Eric would most certainly have gained from that as well. But, anyway, he only arrested the two women

— Norm's wife, Elva, and his own wife, Joan. Naturally I was horrified. So was everyone else, apart from Norm, that is, and the two women. The two women hardly seemed concerned at all. 'Okay,' they said and off they went with Eric.

I only found out later that this sort of thing happened on a regular basis, and it all had to do with Eric lining his pockets through emoluments. See, to all intents and purposes — to the letter of the law — Eric had arrested two people, which allowed him to receive an emolument for having to look after the prisoners until the circuit judge came around. Seeing they were women, he may have even got a bit more. Meanwhile, he'd also get a payment for having to buy food for the two prisoners. But without any doors on the cells, these women were free to come and go as they pleased. In this case, one went back to work at the pub while the other one went back to her normal home duties where she was also being paid to cook for two prisoners — herself and Elva — plus her husband, Police Sergeant Eric Sammon. Then six weeks later, along comes the circuit judge. Joan and Elva go up before him, they're let off with a warning or something, and Eric pockets all the dough.

So there you go, that's just one story I know about an outback copper and I'm yet to meet anyone who'd disagree with anything I said about Eric Sammon.

# Enterprising

I served two years in the police force up at Kowanyama. That was from 1976 to '78. Kowanyama's on the Gulf of Carpentaria, on the western side of Cape York Peninsula. At that time we not only covered Kowanyama Aboriginal Community, but a fair bit of area around there, right up the coast to include Edward River Mission. From memory a police station wasn't established at Edward River until about 1983.

In my day there were only just the two of us stationed at Kowanyama: myself and a constable. My position was that of sergeant second class. It was an early promotion. I'd been going up the ladder pretty quick because I'd been around the traps, working in a lot of remote places and Aboriginal communities and things like that. In fact, I think the department saw me as being someone who fitted into that type of policing very well and that I knew how to handle myself in the situations that arose in those types of areas.

Anyhow, it was in the 1960s that the grog really started to come in and, in doing so, disruptive behaviour had become quite common. One of the main problems we faced was trying to stop the sly grog from being shipped into these places by various enterprising people. Like many, the Aborigines were very much into playing cards and gambling, and at times big money was involved. So some of the more enterprising people soon worked out that there could be an easy quid made out of selling grog on the sly.

One particular instance I recall: the canteen at Kowanyama was run by the Kowanyama Aboriginal Council. Each morning an allocation of eighty-five cartons of beer was placed in the cool room. Then when the canteen opened at 5 o'clock it went on sale for a couple of dollars per can. Of course there were times when we, the police, had to be in attendance to keep an eye on the behaviour and quieten them down when the nights got on a bit. And if things got out of hand we'd arrest the unruly ones and put them away in the 'Bastille' for the night to cool off.

This allocation of eighty-five cartons per day was worked out as a sixpack of beer for every eligible drinker in the community, and once the grog was gone, that was it. That's all there was. No more was handed out. As I said, this was all run by the Kowanyama Aboriginal Council, and in this case we found one particular chairman of the council to be very enterprising indeed. At about 9 o'clock at night he'd call out, 'That's it. No more beer. All the beer's been sold.'

But then people would come and say to me, 'Look, we have not got our allocation. There must be some beers there still.'

So we'd go and check and yes, there was the correct allocation of eighty-five cartons per day going into the cool room. Then, next day, people would come back again and say that they hadn't got their correct allocation. Something was wrong and on further investigation we worked out that this particular chairman was putting aside a few cartons of beer for himself to sell, after hours, at ten dollars a can, making himself a huge profit.

Things like that needed constant police supervision, just to make sure that the canteen was being run honestly. Or sometimes it was enterprising bargain hunters like the councillors themselves who'd get together and sell grog after hours at greatly inflated prices.

That was one particular problem we had at Kowanyama. Then there was Edward River Mission. Even though they had Department of Aboriginal and Islander Affairs staff there, they were more administrative-type people rather than law-and-order enforcers. Unlike at some of the other places I worked, we did have a police vehicle at Kowanyama. So we'd try to get up to Edward River about once a month, even if it was just to demonstrate a police presence. But if things broke out that required the stern hand of the law, that's when there could be problems.

As in Kowanyama, Edward River had no direct telephone communication to our police station. If there was strife up at Edward River and they wanted to get in contact with us, they'd have to radio back to the Department of Aboriginal and Islander Affairs in Cairns, who'd then contact their counterpart in Kowanyama, who'd then come over and advise us, 'Oh, we've got a problem up at Edward River.'

Now, even in the dry season when the roads were passable, it'd still take us about three hours to drive up to Edward River Mission. During the wet season, when the road was impassable, if there was any trouble up at Edward River, we were pretty much stuck at home in Kowanyama. There wasn't much we could do other than hope that things would settle down by themselves.

I mean, we'd try to hitch a ride on a plane that was passing through. But it was very rare for a spare plane to be flying around Cape York Peninsula. Though, in saying that, the police air wing did commence in about 1977. They had two ex-army Cessna 182s, as they were. But because they were supposed to patrol the entire state of Queensland they hardly ever came up around our way.

Bush Pilots Airways had a DC3 that came through Kowanyama, then went on to Edward River and to Aurukun; but that was only on a weekly basis. If that coincided with problems up at Edward River we'd most certainly try to get a seat on that. But then once we got there, we had to somehow work out how we'd get back home again; whether to wait a week until the plane came through again or to try to hitch a ride on a boat that was coming down the coast and into the Mitchell River and to somehow get home to Kowanyama from there. Yes, so in that sort of country you had to be very enterprising, and that was on all sorts of levels.

# Evacuation

In the early days of remote policing, police officers also took on the role of 'protector of Aboriginals' for their area. It was in that capacity that my father, John Bright Chambers, was the police sergeant-in-charge of the 1948 operation to evacuate the remaining Bentinck Islanders over to the Presbyterian mission on Mornington Island and to oversee their resettlement. In doing so, he was assisted by Constable Bob Hegarty from Gregory Downs. Both Dad and Bob Hegarty were to work with the mission people led by the Reverend Mr John McCarthy.

Mornington Island is a relatively small island, situated in the lower part of the Gulf of Carpentaria, Queensland, a couple of hundred kilometres north-west of Burketown and about fifty kilometres west of Bentinck Island. We're talking about the mid-1940s now and by that stage Mr McCarthy had been in charge of the mission for some time. His wife and children lived with him and, from memory, there were also six or seven other white couples living on Mornington Island who were teachers and support people and so forth. Our family used to go over there on holidays quite often and I particularly remember Mr and Mrs Belcher and their young family. The Belchers were teachers and devout Christians.

Mornington Island was quite self-sufficient. The mission ran its own cattle station and abattoir. There was an abundance of fruit trees. They had vegetable gardens. They reared their own poultry. As kids, we loved to check out the incubators full of eggs and of course there was much excitement as we watched the eggs hatch. Bread was baked at the mission house. School was held in the church and the local Indigenous children were like weekly boarders. They'd arrive on Monday morning and sleep in dormitories during the week then go home to their families on the Friday afternoon. The children and the dormitories were looked after by some of the native Mornington Island women. Everyone seemed to be employed at some task or other. I distinctly remember when Mrs McCarthy and several of the Island women made a set of terraces that went from the front of the mission house and the church-school, all the way down to the beach, and they planted shrubs and other plants in each terrace. It was beautiful.

Bentinck Island was a different case altogether. Dad described the Islanders as being a fierce, warlike race who'd had little or no contact with Europeans. Basically they were still in the Stone Age. In fact, they didn't even use stone. They made their spears from wood. They had few utensils, except for sticks and large shells which they used for carrying water, and smaller shells that they used for sharpening their spears and opening oysters. They lived completely naked all year round and they didn't have shelters of any type: they just slept out in the open and covered themselves with grass or mud to keep the mosquitoes and sandflies away. They ate fish that they caught in basket-like traps, turtles that they speared, and wild berries, nut grass and roots. They cooked on open fires and ate with their hands and, even though they were surrounded by water, they'd never learnt how to build canoes; all they used were primitive raft affairs made from logs, tied together with rope fashioned from bark and vines.

Mr McCarthy and some of the missionaries tried to befriend the Bentinck Islanders, but to no avail. They were too aggressive. They even declined the food stuffs that the mission people had left out for them on the beach. On one occasion during winter, the missionaries dropped off some blankets, but the 'natives', as they were called back then, tossed them into the sea. But then, over time, the missionaries noticed that the Bentinck population was starting to decline and those that remained appeared to be distressed and suffering from starvation. From then on the missionaries started to visit the island more regularly. That's when they came to the conclusion that some major catastrophe was occurring. The birdlife was disappearing, the vegetation and animal life was vanishing and the people were suffering severe malnutrition and were dying from starvation.

The missionaries then began dropping off wallaby and other foods that the Bentinck Islanders would recognise and they'd sit offshore in their boat to see what would happen. They did that for some months until the Bentinck Islanders became more comfortable with their presence. Then Mr McCarthy and a few Mornington Islanders began staying ashore after they dropped off the food. Eventually they even stayed overnight and ate with the Bentinck Islanders. Mr McCarthy noted how the men ate first, followed by the women and lastly the children. Dad said that this was because the men were the hunters and the women were there for the reproduction of future children, when the good times returned.

As it turned out, the fresh water supply on Bentinck had been contaminated with sea water, which explained why the birdlife had left, the animals had died out and the flora had also been so badly affected. The mission reported the situation to the Queensland government. As I said, this was back in the mid- to late 1940s and at that time the government didn't look upon their situation as being too important, which is why they, more or less, left it up to Mr McCarthy to try to get the Bentinck Islanders onto the mission boats and move them to Mornington Island. And as I said, my dad, as protector of Aboriginals for his area, was to oversee the evacuation and their resettlement.

I'm just thinking now that perhaps that's why we happened to be holidaying on Mornington Island when the first of the Bentinck Islanders were moved over. I remember that we were forbidden to go near the waterfront during their landing. Still and all, Mildred, one of the missionary's daughters, and I snuck down to see them arrive. And what a horrifying, sad and distressing sight they were as they either scrambled ashore or were carried onto land from the dinghies. The women and the children in particular looked like stick people with large heads, sunken eyes and enormous distended abdomens, and I distinctly remember that there were no babies among them.

The few Bentinck Islander children who had survived were brought up closer to the mission house area, near to the cook-house. Also, small huts had been built a little bit away from the mission and from the Mornington Islanders' camp. That was done to prevent any conflict that could've arisen between the two different tribal people. But the Bentinck Islanders had no idea what the huts were for. In fact, they were afraid to go inside them. Instead, the adults sat and slept outside and some of the huts were broken up and used for firewood. A large four-poster structure with a shady roof was then erected for the children to stay under. Most of the men were just strong enough to look after themselves, but many of the women were unable to care for themselves, let alone their children, as most of the children were just hanging on to life.

It was then decided that every able-bodied person on Mornington was to be given a person or people to care for, around the clock. My mother took on a small boy that she called Richard. Richard appeared to be only about eight or nine, and, like everyone else did with the person they were caring for, Mum helped feed and give fluids to him. It struck me as being odd how the children would sit cross-legged and upright in the dirt, with their heads lolling over, and when they wanted to sleep they'd just lean forward onto the ground. The wearing of clothing was encouraged but not enforced so none of them wore clothes.

Anyhow, after a few days of this constant care, most of the children were able to stand and a good number of the women were able to get up and walk and care for their own children. In the end, not one of those children that had been brought over to the mission on Mornington Island died. Not one of them, such was the care that was given to them by the mission people and the Mornington Islanders. It was just amazing.

Much later I found out that forty-seven Bentinck Islanders were evacuated in that first attempt. Then disaster struck when the mission boat was wrecked in a storm and so all communication was cut between the two islands. I once overheard Dad saying how some of the remaining Bentinck Islanders had tried to get to Mornington Island on their primitive rafts. I know that one group made it but another group apparently drowned. Then not long after, some of the missionaries saw smoke signals coming from Bentinck and, when the weather improved, Dad and Mr McCarthy completed the evacuation in a borrowed fishing launch. In all there were something like sixty-six souls that were saved and, as Dad said, 'They were the remnants of a once proud tribe.'

So that all happened back in 1948 and unfortunately many of the Bentinck Islanders never really interacted with the Mornington Island people. They still longed for their home island and in recent years I've heard that quite a few of them have returned and Bentinck is quite a little town now. But out of such sadness and struggle there came many a good story. In fact my mother was later invited to fly back to Mornington Island to see how things were going, and there to meet her at the airstrip clearing was a moderately tall, healthy-looking young man. Mum could hardly believe her eyes. It was Richard.

# Exemplary: Yalgoo's Bush Copper

My name is Bernard Arrantash. As a state school teacher at Walliston, an outer Perth suburb, I used to take groups of my senior students on annual camping safaris into the Murchison Goldfields region of outback Western Australia. I named our group the 'Walliston Wanderers'. Our trips involved a week or more of school-holiday time away, travelling in a convoy of four-wheel drives driven by parents. Each night we camped in tents, in various remote bush locations throughout the Murchison.

The idea was to broaden the outlook of these city-based kids by giving them a taste of the environment that lay beyond their familiar urban lives. On our safaris we included as many new and challenging experiences as we could: camping, bush cooking, learning about the flora and fauna, seeing the towns and the pastoral and mining industries of the region and meeting local folk who'd talk about their lives; what they did and how they lived. We learnt about Aboriginal sites, art and culture. We learnt about bush survival, map navigation, two-way radio operation, vehicle care and, in doing all of those activities, the importance and need for teamwork, consideration of and respect for others and protection of the environment.

As I thought it important for the local constabulary to know that our sizeable group would be in their area, before each safari left Perth, it was a precaution of mine to mail ahead our planned itinerary to each of the Murchison police stations along our proposed route.

On the twenty-seventh Walliston Wanderers safari, back in September 1996, our nine-day adventure involved eight four-wheel drives, seventeen adults and twenty-eight twelve-year-old students. One night we were camped on a sheep station called Dalgaranga, which is eighty kilometres north-east of the little Murchison Goldfields town of Yalgoo. We'd set aside the next morning on Dalgaranga Station to give the students the opportunity to try their skills at target shooting, with our .22 rifles. As you may imagine, this was a pretty special treat for these kids from the smoke. For safety reasons, we'd set up a range in a back paddock, firing east at targets in front of a huge breakaway of rock. Naturally this was all done with the knowledge and approval of the station owner.

Just as we were about to start, I happened to look back across the bush, to the west, where a flash of reflected sunlight had caught my eye. A vehicle was on the move out there. As I watched, I could see that the vehicle was winding its way through the mulga scrub, heading towards our camp. It took some minutes before it was close enough for me to see that it was a police vehicle, with a ute cab in front and a lockup cage behind. My immediate thought was along the lines of why the police would make such a long journey out to this very remote place. What's more, what could be important enough to warrant such a trip? That led me on to the terrible thought that someone in our group was about to receive some unfortunate news.

With that in mind, and so I could be the first to talk with the police officer, I walked a distance out from our camp. The policeman pulled up alongside me. I noticed how he was immaculately turned out in his police officer's uniform.

'G'day,' I said. 'Are you looking for the Walliston Wanderers group?'

'Yes,' came the reply, 'I'm Constable Mark Johnson from the Yalgoo Police Station.'

'Is there someone in our group that you're looking for?' I asked.

'Well, no. Nobody in particular. It's just that I received your itinerary in the mail and it said that you were doing some target shooting this morning.'

'Is there a problem with that?' I replied.

'Well, no. No problem. I just wanted to know if I could join in.'

With a silent sigh of relief I welcomed the constable. 'Of course,' I said, and I invited him to come and meet us all.

Typically, kids these days don't often get to meet or interact with the constabulary and so many of them have preconceived ideas about the police. To that end, kids can feel a little uncertain, perhaps insecure or even threatened around them. Such doubts as these can result from perceptions suggested by the media and perhaps unhelpful family and peer influences.

Anyhow, with the introductions done, the morning's activity began. The first thing that impressed me was how Constable Johnson showed no inclination whatsoever to dominate or take over the situation. He was comfortable with us running the show and conducting our activity with the elaborate safety conditions we always had in place on these occasions. His comments were always supportive. He was keen to assist and to be fully involved and, in doing so, it was amazing to notice just how quickly the students came to see Mark as a friend. He was on their side. He was one of them and so they relaxed and became confident in his presence. This was one of those unexpected situations that I wanted my students to experience and learn from. Perfect. The morning's activity ended with Mark showing the students his police van and explaining the equipment. Then our convoy rolled out of there, the paddy wagon included, and Mark joined our vehicle communications network with his own Walliston Wanderers two-way radio call sign.

As it turned out, that was the first of three successive years in which Constable Mark Johnson made a point of joining the Walliston Wanderers on those parts of our safaris that took us through his Yalgoo area. I emphasised to Mark that his first appearance among us each year should have him presenting himself in uniform; something he wholeheartedly agreed to, and over those years Mark initiated many special experiences for our group. He once ran a competition to see how many kids could fit into the cab of his paddy wagon. I forget the exact number we'd managed to squash into the vehicle before the competition was forced to its noisy conclusion when one of the students became entangled against the steering wheel, which in turn started the vehicle's horn blaring uncontrollably.

On another occasion Mark came into camp with some bush tucker — a *bungarra*, or a goanna. Digging into our campfire coals, he cooked it, telling us that when the tail pulled off, the meat of the goanna was ready to eat. When he offered it around, it was only the braver of our members who were prepared to sample the bush-cooked *bungarra*. And as so often seems to happen with exotic white meats, the consensus was that it tasted 'something like chicken'.

On yet another occasion, after sunset one evening, in a remote bush camp at a giant, imposing rock outcrop called Woolgerong, Mark turned on the red, white and blue lights on the roof of his paddy wagon. This created a 'disco' atmosphere. With the lights flickering off the rock and to the echoing sound of the *Limbo Rock* CD, the kids took on the challenge of just how low they could go under the limbo stick of a long-handled shovel. The colourful lighting also became the backdrop for some spirited line dancing around the campfire. The scene was surreal. It was just magic. Then on our final safari of Mark's appointment, we included his twelve-year-old daughter as a full participant with our group. After all the effort her dad had made in sharing our adventures, it was our absolute pleasure to be able to have her with us. What's more, it was particularly gratifying to see just how much she enjoyed the occasion.

On the morning our convoy was driving out through the bush from Woolgerong Rock, Mark's paddy wagon was following immediately behind my Land Rover. Suddenly there came the ear-splitting howl of the paddy wagon's siren, accompanied, of course, by the flashing lights. I did what I knew I must do; I pulled over. Mark, looking very officious and wearing his cap and carrying a pad of 'tickets', approached my driver's door. He licked his pencil. 'Show me your licence,' he demanded.

I produced it and he asked if I was aware that one brake light on the back of my vehicle was not operating.

'No,' I replied. 'Sorry, I wasn't. But I'll get it fixed just as soon as I can.'

The response was a cynical grunt. Then as Mark scribbled on one of his 'tickets', he proceeded around to the other side of my Land Rover, where he slapped a yellow 'unroadworthy' sticker on the vehicle's windscreen. All this time, while Mark and I were struggling to keep a straight face, the students were shocked at this remarkable turn of events. Of course, soon afterwards the reality dawned and my students realised that police officers — well, this one anyway — could actually exhibit traits of humour. All the same, after Constable Johnson had left our group to attend to his other police duties on his patch, it was with some degree of trepidation, and out of sight of the kids, that I even dared to remove that yellow sticker.

In conclusion, over the three years that Constable Mark Johnson made a point of joining the Walliston Wanderers, I reckon his boss would've approved of his great initiative and positive interaction with our group. The public relations work that that bush copper did in the line of his duty was, to my mind, exemplary. We warmed to his presence and we welcomed the excellent rapport he developed with our students.

# Eye-opener

Coober Pedy was an absolute eye-opener. When I first arrived in town, I pulled into the police station and over the road were two people, sitting cross-legged, whacking each other and throwing dirt at each other. I just went, 'Oh my God, surely this doesn't happen every day?' But it does in Coober Pedy; it does.

Each place you go to has its own uniqueness and Coober's certainly unique. In many ways it's like a last frontier. For a remote area it's quite a big police station and, like everywhere I've worked, we've got a good group of girls, absolutely. At Coober there's about five of us females and a dozen males and look, apart from our normal duties, we predominantly deal with Indigenous people. We're their guardians while they're in Coober Pedy. They're quite transient. They come down from the APY — Anangu Pitjantjatjara Yankunytjatjara — Lands. They've usually got nowhere to live. When they get drunk — *gubijer* — they sleep in the dirt around town and we pick them up and take them to the sobering-up centre. By doing that, at least you know they'll be warm, get clean clothes and have a shower and some food. Then when they need to dry out they go back to the Lands for a while before they come back again and the cycle continues. I mean, they're the loveliest, kindest, warmest people you could ever possibly meet but, to be honest, a lot of them are slowly killing themselves.

But there's some great characters around the place. There's Susie. Susie's a tiny little thing, about the same age as my mum. I don't know how many times I've had to pick her up off the street and take her back up to aged care. So Susie's a great character. Then there's Padaway. He's from Indulkana. He's nearly as old as my dad. When I first arrived in town, I came across a beautiful cowboy hat that had been left in the house I moved into and I thought, I'll give it to Padaway. And because they tend to swap, trade and barter so much I wrote his name in it. I said, 'Padaway, don't give this hat to no one. It doesn't matter what they offer you, this is your special hat.' It's been a few months now and I saw him just the other week and he was still wearing it. I've got a picture of him so, so far so good.

Then sometimes I'll go out with the women. Right, it's 6 o'clock in the morning and I just want to sleep and they all arrive. We're off looking for witchetty grubs. There's Susie, Maureen and a heap of other traditional women. We all pile in the car; I had this little Suzuki Sierra back then. I don't know how I got them all in because there's also digging sticks, shovels, spades; you name it. Anyhow, I'm thinking that we'll just go somewhere a little way out of town. Well, a hundred and twenty kilometres later we've rocked up at Cagney Park. Out of the car we bundle and then we go bush. We're way out. There's wild camels; everything. And I'm right into it. I've got this special tool like a crowbar, but much shorter and thinner. It's used to jemmy up the roots and stuff, so I'm ripping up these bushes and I'm digging and finding all these witchetty grubs and I'm putting them in a big bowl.

But I couldn't work out why Susie's following me around with this margarine container. Then when I took a look in my bowl, it was, Hey, I thought I had more than that. I said, 'Susie, give me a look at your margarine container.' And when I opened it, she'd been sneaking the biggest, fattest ones out of my bowl.

Then after we got enough witchetty grubs we all sat down and they handed me one. It was raw, so I thought, Oh well, and when I put it in my mouth it basically exploded. I've gone, 'Oh, yuck,' and spat it out. Then I thought, Oh God, that's a terrible thing to do. How embarrassing. So I picked it up, brushed it off, put it back in my mouth, chewed it and swallowed it.

Oh, they were in fits of hysterics. Shaking their heads and giggling and going on. But I much prefer them cooked in the coals; witchetty grubs and kangaroo tails. Kangaroo tail is magnificent if it's fresh and properly cooked. You cook it in the skin then you pull the skin off and go for it. I was working one Christmas Day and they're all hanging around the main street. They've got no home, nothing to eat, so I went into the local shop and I bought a whole stack of kangaroo tails and gave them out as Christmas gifts. They loved it.

While we're on that, I'll tell you a funny story. One time we had what's called a crossover. A prisoner was being transported down from Marla and we had to meet them halfway, then bring the prisoner on down to Coober Pedy. I'm with a guy who was unfamiliar with the area so I said, 'Look, I'll follow you for a certain distance, then you keep on going, meet the patrol and come back.' Anyhow, on the way up to the crossover I hit a rabbit and so I made a mental note to pick it up on my way back. When I came back, a kangaroo had been bowled over a couple of hundred metres before I got to the dead rabbit. So I chucked the kangaroo in the back of the van and I drove down a little further and I chucked the rabbit in with the kangaroo and off I go.

When I got back I went straight up to where the women were camping. I said, 'Look what I've got for you.' And they came out and they're all excited and one of the *kungas* — *kunga* means 'sister' — she's got the kangaroo out and she's pulling out its entrails, preparing it for cooking in a fire.

'Come back when it's cooked,' they said.

'Okay,' so I come back later on, thinking that it'd be cooked. But it's not; well, not properly anyway. It's extremely rare and they're eating this kangaroo. Loving it.

And this rabbit; I'd given it to a lovely girl from Fregon called Rosie. I knew it was her favourite and when she held it up for me to take a bite it's still got its fur on.

'Ah, no thanks,' I said. 'It might need a little bit longer.'

So I come back an hour or so later and she holds up the rabbit and it's burnt to a cinder. And she thought it was just the bee's knees. She loved it. But not only that, she's saved the prime bit especially for me — the raw kidneys.

I said, 'Sorry, Rosie, you can have that.'

Another great character is Maggie. Maggie's a ripper; absolutely gorgeous. I adore her. I can be walking down the street on a patrol or whatever and she'll call out, 'Hey, *kunga*.' So she'll be fantastic one day and the next day she'll tell you to bugger off, and when Maggie goes off, she's like a little bulldog.

But something that amazes me is how the more traditional Aboriginal people form really, really strong partner attachments. It's almost like their total self-preservation relies on the need for one another. It's very difficult to explain because they can flog the crap out of each other, yet they just cannot be apart. And gee, they get involved in some fights. I mean, we've had stand-up rows with Maggie. One time her partner, Whiskey G, had hit her about and so we're around there trying to get Whiskey into the police van and Maggie's come up from behind and she's whacking us with a thong because she just does not want him to be taken away and locked up. It's such a clash of culture and it's all laid bare in Coober Pedy. As I said, it's a real eye-opener. And the thing is, I've lived all over the world. I am not racist at all. I absolutely love these people, but I have no answers as to what can be done to change things. Nothing.

Anyhow, after about six months in Coober I applied for a position as a regional operations service reliever. ROS relief is like when someone goes on leave or something and you come in and take their position till they return. And I really, really wanted the job, I did. When I put in my resume I hoped I'd at least get an interview. Which I did, and after about eight months they told me that I'd landed the position. Up till then I was a constable. Now I'm a senior constable first class and, believe it or not, my first placement as a ROS relief was at Coober Pedy so I didn't have to move anywhere; well, not straight away, that is.

And I've fallen in love with the place. Coober's absolute magic. I've done the whole kit and caboodle. I've even bought a dugout. I'm also now an opal miner. I've got my own claim. I've got a friend, Talus. He'd already had a claim and I got the one next door to his and now most of my days off are spent mining. I do all the spotting. Talus uses a Bobcat and we dig big underground caverns. They're huge; probably about six or seven metres wide. But with Talus, because he also works my claim, when he gets a good stone, I get first dibs. Talus cuts and polishes the opal and everything. It works out well. As they say, 'A girl can never have too many opals.'

# Forty-five Minutes

My name is Peter Joyce. My incident happened on 28th February 1999, then in the following year I was asked if I'd be prepared to receive the Australian Bravery Medal. Whoever organises these things had obviously read all the police and trial reports and the newspaper articles and things, and I was very happy to receive the award. Though, with all due respect, mine was simply the result of about forty-five minutes of keeping cool under pressure. It really hit when a lot of the media and so forth were asking me, 'How did you feel when it was going on? Were you scared of being shot?'

I said, 'No, not really, but it did make me realise that life is short and that I'd better get off my bum and get my act together and move on.' And I did. From that moment I did all I could to be the best tour guide possible. In fact, it was what gave me the stimulus to go for the job with APT — Australian Pacific Tours. That was what I really wanted to do. I really dug in with that and I eventually got the job and I went on to do the driving and the commentary and the guiding throughout the Top End for many years.

I guess it's a bit of a long story but, after selling my small orchard in the Adelaide Hills of South Australia, I decided I needed a new start in life. So, along with a female companion, we got into a caravan and we went nomading. First we went to Tasmania, then we went up the eastern seaboard and we kept going until we reached Darwin. By that time we needed work. My partner, she got a job in a private hospital and I got work digging ditches to bury the pay-TV cables they were running out. But every morning

I could hear the tour coaches going past on their way out to places like Kakadu and Litchfield and Katherine, and it just got me stirred up. I said, 'That's what I really want to do.'

Being from a farm, I already had my heavy articulated licence and I also had an H endorsement for paying passengers. My female companion and I were still in the caravan park at that stage and it just happened that a neighbour of ours had been a coach driver. So I asked him how I should go about it and he said, 'What you need is a good basic knowledge of World War Two history in the Top End and a good knowledge of settlement in the Northern Territory.'

I then bought all the appropriate books and I started reading and after I thought I'd taken in enough knowledge, I joined one of the tour group in-takes. There was about ten of us in the group and the manager-operator gave us the rundown of what tour guides and coach captains did and what was expected of them. That operator's main tour was a three-day trip of the Top End; out to Kakadu, then down to Katherine and back to Darwin via Litchfield National Park, and I was quite happy doing that. But it was very seasonal work. In the peak season — the dry — we could work up to eighty or a hundred hours a week. Of course, that wasn't all driving, because we'd also be conducting interpretive rock art tours plus boat cruises, sorting out their meals and so forth. Then when the wet season arrived there'd be pretty much nothing. So I started moving around the various operators, just doing part-time work; a bit here and a bit there.

During that period I got some off-season casual work with Britz, as a relief coach driver, and that's when it happened. I had a load of about thirty-eight German tourists on board, plus their interpreter-guide, Ralf, and we were on a day outing. Normally we'd go down to Mount Bundy Station and have a meal there. But this was during the wet season and the road was shut, so we went and visited Litchfield National Park in the morning instead.

We'd just passed through Batchelor, heading out to the Stuart Highway, on our way to a late lunch at Adelaide River. At that stage the road was quite undulating and as I was driving along I saw a light-coloured Datsun four-wheel-drive ute coming down the road towards me. There was only the one lane, so I slowed down and I pulled as far over to the left as I felt was safe. When he still kept coming at me I slowed down some more, but he still kept coming, kept coming straight at me.

I'm thinking, What do I do here? If he's fallen asleep I'd better not pull out onto the wrong side of the road or he might wake up and drive across and we'll have a head-on. So I just kept going slower and slower until eventually it was obvious that he wasn't going to shift. I couldn't move any further over my way because the coach had what's called tag axles and, with it being wet season, if I dropped a wheel right off the bitumen, the coach could easily roll. So I left it as long as I could and just when he was about to hit me I jabbed the front around and he smashed into the side of the coach.

Now I'm thinking, What next?

Anyway, this fellow jumped out of the ute with a sawn-off rifle and he comes over and he starts banging on the coach door, shouting, 'Let me in. Let me in.'

He was a scruffy, untidy-looking fellow, without shoes, who had a glazed look about him. Mind you, I wasn't there to judge him and to be fair, that description could well relate to any number of people in the Top End. But it certainly got me wondering as to what his motives might be. Not long before this I'd driven a private charter with the Minister for Roads from the Italian Parliament. This was at the time when the Mafia or whoever were shooting selected Italian justices and anyone else who got in their way. Anyhow, this Italian parliamentarian had come over to Australia without bodyguards, which I thought was pretty brave of him, and so now I'm starting to think, Is this guy after one of the German passengers on my coach?

I only found out later during the trial that earlier that day this fellow had shot a drug dealer mate in the foot. After doing that he'd gone home and given himself some un-prescribed medicine which, in turn, gave him an extreme anxiety attack, and now he wanted to be with people. He had the deep yearning for company and when he saw the coach coming along he thought, Here's some people. I'll get in with them and they'll help me hide from my demons.

Of course, at that stage I had no idea about any of that and so I thought, Well, I'm not going to wait around to find out what he wants. I'm going to get out of here. The trouble was that the coach was sort of jammed up against his ute, with its front wheels off the bitumen. So I backed up and then I pushed the little four-wheel drive aside with the front of the coach and I started driving off. In doing so I put a huge scratch right down the side of the coach. But not to worry; there were more immediate problems to contend with because, in the meantime, this character's come around the front of the coach; he's stepped up and he's got his legs around the bull bar and he's hanging on to the windscreen wipers and the side mirror and he's now banging on the window with his sawn-off rifle.

At that stage, Ralf, the interpreter-guide who was sitting behind me, suggested, 'Well you'd better ask him what he wants.'

So I did and the fellow started calling out, 'I want to come in. The people in the red and the green and the yellow cars, they're chasing me. They're after me.'

That's when I really started to have my doubts. What have I got here? It's all in his mind about people chasing him because there's no one else around; no one's coming out of the bushes to get him and there's not a car in sight. So I just kept moving and he just kept hanging on to the bull bar and side mirror. And that's how we kept going and after a while he managed to put the rifle down in the front of his trousers. So then I thought if I got the coach going in a jerky manner perhaps I could shake him off.

Problem being, he was hanging on too tight for that. All right then, what next? If I drove too slow he could easily get his rifle out and start banging it on the window again and if it went off, who knows what could happen? Then if I drove too fast he could easily get even more agitated and again anything could happen. That's when I thought, Time will sort this out to a degree. I'll just drive nice and easy down to Adelaide River. There's a police station there and I'll park out the front. So I found a speed of about forty to fifty kilometres an hour where he just hung on and everything was going fine.

By this stage, my German passengers were quite disturbed and I was worried that, if he did fire his rifle, one of them might get hit, so I asked Ralf to tell everybody to move down to the back of the coach, which he did. He ducked down behind me and he kept talking on the microphone, trying to keep everyone calm. Mind you, afterwards we joked about how we ended up having something like thirty-four people squashed into the far back six seats of the coach while the other four had locked themselves in the toilet.

All during this time we were trying to contact the police by phone and through the radio, but got nothing. There was no service in any of the communication systems we had on board so I just kept driving until we got to the Stuart Highway. That's when I turned south and headed towards Adelaide River.

By this stage I'd opened the window just enough that he wouldn't be able to get the rifle through, yet I could still keep talking and negotiating with him. And that had worked. He'd calmed down a bit by then, but I still felt it was important to maintain eye contact. Still, mind you, with him hanging on to the bull bar and me at the steering wheel of the coach we were less than a metre apart and my grave concern was that, at any moment, he might go into a panic and shoot me. But by looking into his eyes and continually talking to him, I felt I could keep his attention for at least ten or fifteen minutes longer until I could get him somewhere where I could get rid of him. Not out in the bush of course, but with some sort of other help. That was my aim and so it became almost like a mind game between him and me; hopefully one where I could stay in control.

So we're going south, down the Stuart Highway, and then a couple of cars passed us, heading north. One was a private hire vehicle. The driver and I were in the same sort of industry, so we knew each other. But he did nothing about it. I was told later that, when his passengers had seen what was going on, he'd made a joke that the gentleman hanging off the front of the coach was just checking the noise in the front wheel as we drove along. But the other car — the second car — was being driven by a psychologist lady who was on her way to visit some friends out at Batchelor, and the moment she saw us she knew something was very much amiss.

When she got to Batchelor she went straight to the police station. It was closed so she then rang Operation Headquarters in Darwin and alerted them to the problem out on the Stuart Highway. While all this is going on I'm still driving south with this fellow hanging off the front of the coach. Then a police vehicle comes hurtling up the road heading in my direction. But he drove straight past, going north. It was Sergeant Glen Huitson, a well-known and respected cop throughout the Top End. Glen wasn't dressed in uniform. He just had his official khaki overalls on. You often see the police dressed like that in the bush, in the Territory.

Anyway, when Glen went past, I was thinking, Mate, I need you. I need you. Then I looked in the rear-vision mirror and I could see that he'd smoked the wheels as he pulled up and he'd begun to turn his vehicle around. So I then started to look for a place to pull off the highway, keeping in mind that this was a Sunday and it was in the wet so it was important that I find a hard spot off the bitumen because a) I didn't want to sink the coach and b) I also had to leave the highway clear because Sunday was the day when most of the road trains came through, loaded with fresh produce for the week.

Anyhow, I found a firm spot and I pulled off the highway. By that stage, Glen had come back and he'd parked about a hundred yards behind me. He got out of his car and he walked out onto the highway and he started shouting, 'We are the police. We will look after you. Put your gun down and step away from the coach.'

I was very much doubting that the fellow would move away from the coach, but for some reason he did. When he did I took the handbrake off and I put the coach in second gear in readiness for a quick start and take-off. Being such a low-geared vehicle, the last thing I wanted to do was to stall the coach, so I had one foot on the clutch and one foot on the brake. Then, when the fellow had moved far enough away, I revved the engine as hard as I could and I took off. As soon as I did he came running after me. He actually got his hand to within a metre of the mirror. But then I changed into a higher gear and we started to gain some distance. I watched him through the rear-vision mirror, still running after us, until he eventually slowed down and was left behind.

Now unbeknown to me, at that time, just over the brow of the hill, there was a stationary paddy van and a police Falcon with a detective in it by the name of Cole Chapman. At seeing the situation, Cole took off in a cloud of blue smoke. He and Glen reach the fellow at the same time and they hit him hard and took him down in a rugby tackle. It all happened so fast that when the fellow came around he apparently asked Glen and Cole, 'Did you shoot me? Am I dead?'

When I saw that they'd arrested the fellow, I said to Ralf, 'I'll pull over now. Can you ask everybody to get out and see that the man's been taken away? It'll provide some sort of closure for them.'

Which he did; though, mind you, at first they were a bit reluctant. Then they slowly started to make their way outside where they could witness the police putting the fellow in the paddy wagon and being taken off. But it was odd to see how differently everyone reacted.

As for myself, I was surprised as to just how calm and in control I'd been throughout the whole incident. Very surprised. I guess I hadn't even had the time to think about it, but everyone else seemed pretty stunned. Some were sitting on the ground. Others were walking about. Some just stood there, looking back down the road. Then one lady, a little old German lady, as I was helping her down the steps of the coach she slipped a folded five-dollar note into the palm of my hand and she said in her faltering English, 'You are my hero,' and I just burst into tears.

# Good Friends

Even before I was transferred to Gawler, I did a lot of relief work out at various country police stations in South Australia. Gawler's just north of Adelaide. From memory I arrived there some time in '48 and I stayed there until — oh golly, do you remember when that was, Patty?

*Well, we got married in 1950. I was a Gawler girl. I worked in a kind of mixed grocery business there and Bruce used to come in quite often.*

Back then single policemen either had to cook for themselves or eat at the pub, so I used to go into the shop to get fruit and vegetables, and I saw this beautiful-looking girl there. So we met up and here we are.

*That was sixty-four years ago.*

Yes, so we got married, and in '55 I was transferred down the south-east of the state to Mount Gambier. Then not long after we got there, Superintendent Bonython called me and said, 'Would you like to go to Oodnadatta?'

I'd already worked up in the north of the state and I'd enjoyed it so I went home and said to Patty, 'How would you like to go to Oodnadatta?' And she said, 'Yes, okay.'

*I didn't really know where it was but, oh, it didn't worry me. No, not at all. My dad was a drover and he always told stories about those places up through the north there.*

Oodnadatta was a railway town back then. It had been the end of the line up north until the mid-1920s; that's before the track was extended up to Alice Springs. It was the main centre for the whole area. I was the only policeman there for quite some time and Inspector Noel Smith used to come up once a year and check the books.

*I took to it like a duck to water. Our house and the police station were all in one. It was a big weatherboard place. There was also a single men's quarters, but that was vacant, and there were three galvanised iron prison cells just at the back. So in the middle of summer you can just imagine how hot they got.*

The Overland Telegraph went through Oodnadatta so we had the telephone and for radio we were attached to the Alice Springs base of the Flying Doctor Service. Most times we'd only be able to talk in the winter time, because in summer you'd have a lot of trouble getting through because of the weather conditions.

*Oh, it was terrible.*

We always had the train, of course. The Ghan came through once a week with passengers. Then a goods train, with just the one passenger carriage, came through on a Thursday. The goods train used to stop off at all the little stations between Port Augusta and Alice Springs.

*Even though it was a fairly isolated place there was a small public school there. We only had the one daughter at that stage and she was five, so she started off there.*

In those days only the white kids were allowed to go to the public school. But there were also a lot of Aboriginal kids in Oodnadatta and so Patty and I thought, Well, this isn't right. So we made the various connections and eventually the Aboriginal kids were allowed to go to the school.

*There were about twenty Aboriginal children that were staying over at the United Aboriginal Mission; the UAM. And even though the people there used to try to educate them the best they could, we felt that they should be educated properly. And of course there were the camp kids — the ones that lived around town but weren't in the mission — and so it was made a condition that, if the kids were going to attend the school, they had to wash their hair and have clean clothes. But their mothers and so forth used to look after them pretty well anyway, so the Aboriginal kids were always quite presentable.*

We used to get bails of clothing come up from various religious groups down south and we'd distribute them around the community.

*The Aboriginal Department used to send up some too.*

Also the government had a scheme where I was like a welfare agent. I had a book where I could write a slip out for, say, Joe Blow and he could take it down to the shop and get food. That was instead of just giving them money. So I did that, then there were my patrols. They covered 130,000 square miles of country, stretching right over to the Western Australian border and they used to take about fourteen days to complete. That's when I left Patty in charge, to run the police station.

*Oh, I did not, Bruce. Don't tell fibs.*

Not long before I got to Oodnadatta the patrols were all done on camels. So thank Christ they'd sold them and they were replaced by an old Ford Freighter utility. I remember when it arrived. One day we saw this green ute over in the railway yard and I said to the stationmaster, 'Whose is that?'

He said, 'It's yours.'

It didn't have any police markings or anything on it, and it was just a two-wheel drive.

*I don't think there were any four-wheel-drive vehicles in those days, so Bruce used to get bogged a lot.*

Yes, so that's what we used for patrols. There'd just be me, then I'd have a black tracker sitting on the back with all the gear and that's all. Old Tiger was the first tracker we had. Gee he was a good old fella, Tiger.

*His whole family were. Lilly was his wife, wasn't she? Moana was the daughter. She was about fifteen.*

Anyway, I'd just load up the Ford ute and away we'd go, old Tiger and me. Hell, we covered some ground. We were just lucky that Lenny Beadell, the surveyor-roadbuilder, had been wandering around out there and he'd bulldozed out a few bits and pieces, so at least we had some sort of a track to go on.

There were just a few cattle stations to go to and we'd also visit the Aborigines. The small Aboriginal community of Ernabella was three hundred miles west of Oodnadatta. That was started by the Presbyterian people. But many of the Aborigines were still nomadic. They used to go from Ernabella, right over the border into Western Australia, to another little settlement called Warburton.

Back then there were no cattle stations west of Ernabella. It was all Aboriginal reserve, then there was some mining exploration in the north-west of the reserve. And because the Aborigines were always passing through that way, sometimes they'd steal food and so forth from the mining camps. But, I can tell you, when you arrested someone it was a hell of a long journey back to Oodnadatta. It took at least three days and, with having to keep an eye on the prisoners, you got very little sleep.

Anyhow, at night I'd pull up to camp and — to my eternal shame — we had these six-foot-long chains, with links about so big. So I'd find the biggest tree around the camp and, I hate to say this but, on each end of the chain was a set-up that would go around a person's neck and you'd put a padlock on it. So we'd have the prisoners in a circle around a tree. That's the way it was done those days.

They weren't usually violent. In fact, they were mostly very quiet; a nice lot really. Then once we got them back to Oodnadatta, the Justices of the Peace would come up from Port Augusta on the once-a-week Ghan to sit in court. If they were given a light sentence we'd generally keep them in Oodnadatta for a fortnight and we'd feed them up and look after them before we let them go. Anything more serious and they had to go down to Port Augusta. Really, it was a bad set-up. We didn't like it, did we, Patty? That's why we used to try to keep them in Oodnadatta for the fortnight because, with us looking after them, most of them got to trust us.

*A lot of them even used to stay on, living around Oodnadatta.*

Yes, and the weather out there was another challenge. It could go from a prolonged drought and extreme heat to a sudden downpour and flooding so, when we were out on patrol, sometimes we had to virtually dig our way through the country. And more often than not our vehicle was packed with extra fuel and camping gear and other supplies, and if you had any prisoners they'd be sitting in the back, up on the tucker box. Then in '59 we were issued with a four-wheel-drive, four-cylinder side-valve, long-wheelbase Land Rover, with a canvas canopy on the back. But even though it was more suited to the conditions, it didn't have the carrying capacity of the old Ford ute.

*And up around there it used to get red hot in the summer, which made it hell when you were bringing in prisoners.*

One time we broke down out near Everard Park cattle station. Oh, that was when we had the Ford ute. We were held up there for quite a while. Eventually the boys at Everard Park had to come out and help us drag the old ute back into the homestead before we could get it going again. It was just lucky we never broke down anywhere further west, because there was nobody to help us out there.

So they were the patrols and I was responsible for a lot of other things as well, like stock inspection. With Oodnadatta being a railway terminus, I'd oversee all the cattle that came into the place — check their numbers and check the brands, and make sure they were okay to be sent down south on the train.

*Don't forget the dingoes' scalps.*

That's right, and the dingo scalps. People used to be paid a couple of quid per head and, to show proof, they had to bring in the ears and the tails of any dingo they killed. So they'd come into town with these rotten bloody ears and tails and I'd have to count them and make out a form; you know, 'Bill Blogs brought in forty scalps'. Then I'd have to put all the ears and tails into bags and tie them up with red seals and take them down to the railway station. And I can tell you, the stationmaster was none too pleased about it all either. I used to spray them with anything and everything I could get my hands on to try to stop the horrible stink but the stationmaster reckoned he could still smell them a mile off. Then they'd go down to Adelaide in the goods train and the authorities would send cheques back to the people ... and I had to do all the dirty work.

*And what about the burials. You were responsible for those as well, weren't you? At one time we had a resident coffin there, in the single men's quarters. It was a lead-lined coffin and, just to play a joke on me, Bruce had it standing by the window so I could see it from the house.*

Oh God, yes. Somebody would get in touch and say, 'Look, so-and-so's died, can you get a coffin and come out and oversee the burial?' We didn't usually keep coffins in Oodnadatta. They were sent down from Alice Springs in knock-down form and we had to put them together, just like IKEA, and I'd take them out to the properties and perform the graveside burial service. It all had to be done properly signed off, but because I'd only be travelling out there every so often, some of these people would've been dead for quite a while before I got there.

*But the Aborigines used to take care of their own. Tell him about their graves and how they used to look after themselves.*

What they'd do was, if somebody a long way out died, they used to dig a hole and put the body in there all curled up — not straight out. They'd then just cover it over with brush and it'd stay that way for anything up to three or four months. By that stage the body would've been fairly decomposed and so they'd then go back and hold a ceremony and sing the bones. And that was it. The deceased was never mentioned again. Never spoken of. Once they were gone, they were gone.

*But we loved it up there, didn't we, Bruce? Particularly the Aboriginal people. Our kids were reared with them. Their kids were our kids, and likewise.*

Hell, we used to have them camped out the back of the police station.

*We most certainly did. Of course we had fettlers up and down the railway line and they were pretty rough at times, poor devils. Most of them were just out of either Yatala or Port Augusta prisons — shaved heads and all — and they'd be put straight on the railway gangs who were living in the little fettlers' camps all the way from Port Augusta up to Alice Springs. Sent way out in the middle of nowhere, where they couldn't get up to too much strife. That's why, when they'd come to town, they'd sometimes get up to a bit of mischief.*

*Anyhow, the police station was up on a rise, just at the back of the town. It was a little bit separate, a bit isolated, and when Bruce was away on patrol the Aboriginal ladies would come up to the police station and say, 'Missus, we're gonna look after you.' And I'd often look out at night and there they were, all camped around the house, just to keep an eye on me.*

Anyhow, we did two stints up at Oodnadatta — we came back again in the early 1960s — and I think it was the first time that police were regarded nicely among the Aboriginal people. Before I first went up there I don't think things were as good as they could've been. But Patty and I, we admired the Aborigines and we had great respect for their tribal society. It was always in our minds that they'd had a hell of an existence and that I, as a policeman, was — how can I put it — that I was there to help them the best I possibly could. And, okay, we had some bad ones, like in all communities, but I believe that our respect for each other was mutual because during my time I was invited to attend quite a few of their rituals. I was also privy to many ceremonial rites, which were considered sacred to their Dreaming. In fact, just before I'd completed my first stint up there I was asked to attend a corroboree about a hundred and fifty miles west, out at Granite Downs, and at the end of the corroboree they presented me with two *tujungas* — sacred objects — which had been used in the ceremony.

And Patty will back me up on this: when we left Oodnadatta we left a lot of very good friends up there, didn't we, Patty? And a lot of them were black. In fact, we're still in contact with many of those people today.

# Green

I grew up in the desert country, at Windorah, in outback Queensland. I say that I 'grew up' there because I was actually born at Scone, in New South Wales, at Glenrock Station. My mother was pregnant with me when she was down at Scone visiting her sister and I came along a bit earlier than she expected and so I was a week old by the time I got back to Windorah. As for my dad, he was a roadworks engineer, looking after the design and building of the road from Windorah to a place about a hundred and fifty miles further out west called Betoota. And that was a pretty slow process. They could only tar a mile and a half a day due to all the stone pitching that needed to be done because of the floods that sometimes came through there. Dad also worked on other jobs as well, like the Quilpie road and Jundah road.

The first policeman I remember was a really good man by the name of Fillingham. He was from the city so he was very green to the outback. It must've been a real eye-opener for him and his family to come out to Windorah, because it wasn't as if we had a Myer Centre or a Coles or anything like that. We didn't even have a local store where you could buy bottled milk. You had to go up to Mrs Guyver's goat yard. That's where everyone got their milk. You just took an old tin or a jug and it was only goat's milk.

I'll never forget this Mrs Fillingham, the policeman's wife. She was a real city type. Mum used to tell us how she'd once asked Mrs Guyver if her milk was full cream or not. But there was never no full cream about it. You just got what you got and that was it. I doubt if the old girl Guyver even strained it. It came straight out of the teat and into the tin. When we were kids we used to make money out of it because a lot of the old drovers that came through used to drink wine in the flagon. So when they were empty we'd go and wash the flagons out and sell them to all the ladies who'd use them as milk bottles, because the milk kept better in glass. What's more, we used to get fifty cents a flagon, which was a lot of money back in them days.

From memory I think there was just the three or four in the Fillingham family. There was the girl we went to school with and I think she had a younger brother who wasn't old enough to go to school yet. But the father — the policeman — coming from the city, out to a little place in the desert, I think he thought he'd have a pretty easy life of it. He didn't realise all the extra jobs a copper had to take on in the bush. He couldn't get over how he'd also have to be the undertaker, the marriage celebrant, the local magistrate, the welfare officer as well as doing all the other little jobs that he had to do around town. He even had to tow the tourists that had broken down back into town. Not that we'd get too many tourists.

On top of all that he also had a big area to police. He not only had to look after Windorah, but his district went right out to Betoota. Then there used to be another pub in between called the JC. It was a beautiful big old pise hut. A pise hut's made out of spinifex and ant bed and sand, and they mix it all in together with water. Then the gel that the ants use in the ant bed and the sap out of the spinifex grass sticks the whole lot together.

That old pub was still standing when I was a kid, then one afternoon a big dust storm came along and flattened it. After that, nobody bothered to look after it and so the sand built up and it eventually covered it all. And that was a shame, because there were so many of the old names carved into the walls. There were also about fifty or sixty sandstone graves out behind the pub. They're also covered in sand now, but I know exactly where they are. I can still remember them. I'd love to go back there and have that sand taken away because there were some sad stories on those graves. I remember reading some of them; about how mothers had lost four or five kids in the one hit through a bad flu that went around back in them days. Then there were the graves of young fourteen-year-olds that had died on droving trips. At fourteen they should've been home with their mums. But in those days they had to get out and earn their own money because things were so tough.

But that policeman Fillingham and his family, they were only there for a few years, then they went back to the city. I don't think they could handle it. To my thinking they send a lot of green police out there just to toughen them up a bit. And I can tell you, out at Windorah, there was no carnival of flowers to greet them.

That reminds me of another story. One night a mob of young fellers had pinched a motor car and the police were chasing them across the salt pan. Anyway, these police were having trouble getting across this salt pan in the vehicle they had so the young fellers got away into the bush. The police then went and got in a four-wheel-drive troop carrier — a troopy — to go and catch them. Their plan was to cut the young fellers off at a place the other end of the bush. But just as they got there a mob of horses ran out and one of them hit the side of the troopy. No joke, it not only broke the windscreen but it put the biggest dint right up one side of the vehicle.

Of course, they then had to go and explain it all to the sergeant. But see, they were real worried how he mightn't believe them when they said how a horse had run into the side of the police vehicle. At that time the sergeant was down at the pub. So they drove the damaged troopy down there and they went inside to see the sergeant.

I was there at the pub too and my mate Ray Hassler asked me to move his car. Which I did — but I didn't know the police troopy was parked right behind Ray's car and so, when I backed out, I dinted the other side of the police vehicle. That's the other side from where the horse ran into it.

So when the young police fellers brought the sergeant outside to show him where the horse had run into the troopy, he just happened to look around the other side of the vehicle and said, 'And so did the horse also run into this side of the vehicle as well?'

That gave them something to think about. I was standing right there, but I never said nothing. But fancy parking their troopy right behind me like that. Like I said, the coppers they sent out to Windorah back in those days, they were so green some of those fellers.

Talking about green; this one happened up at Cloncurry — the Curry — which is a bit over a hundred mile east of Mount Isa. My sister and a girlfriend of hers were speeding down the main street one day and the local policeman pulled them over. He was a young constable, a feller by the name of Frank. Frank was also green to the outback. My sister's friend was driving the car at the time. She'd already had a couple of speeding marks against her name and so they had to somehow pull a swiftie over Constable Frank, otherwise she would've done her licence. Now if you'd ever met my sister's friend, she's a very, very big woman — huge — and so when Constable Frank pulled her over, she said to him, 'Can you deliver a baby?'

'No,' he said. 'Why?'

She said, 'Well, if you hold us up any longer you're going to have to deliver one right in the front seat here.'

After Frank took a closer look at the size of my sister's friend, he rang the sergeant to see what he should do. Of course, the moment he explained that he'd pulled over a woman who was just about to have a baby, the sergeant said, 'Get her up to the hospital immediately.'

Which he did. He escorted them up to the hospital with all the sirens and everything going. When they got up there, they asked him to leave them in the emergency car park. 'We'll be all right from here, Constable,' they said, and then they waited in the hospital foyer until he went away. And you wouldn't believe it; that afternoon my sister and her friend were back driving downtown and Constable Frank saw them, so he pulled them over and he said to my sister's friend, 'Well, what did you have, a boy or a girl?'

She said, 'A little boy, thank you, Constable. He's at home with the father.'

And the poor bugger believed them. 'Well, congratulations then,' he said.

But baby or not, that's what used to happen out there. If a woman had a baby before 8 o'clock in the morning she was allowed to go home at lunchtime if she wanted to. That's true. My sister had a set of twins out there at 9 o'clock in the morning and she was back home by half-past twelve. Yeah, brought them home. I was there at the time, sitting with her husband, and I still remember it. She walked into the house and the first thing her husband said to her was, 'So what's for lunch then?'

And boy, didn't she give him a dirty look.

He said, 'What's that bloody dirty look for?'

I didn't say nothing. I just sat there. But nothing like that happens these days. Not even the police are like they used to be.

# Guilty?

My name is Allan Peters. Though I've never served in the force I've been the official police historian here at the Thebarton Barracks, in South Australia, for the past nineteen years. My interest in Elizabeth Woolcock began when I was a very small child, visiting family over on Yorke Peninsula, at a town called Moonta. I remember — it must've been around 1940 — sitting out the front of my grandmother's place and being told, 'Don't go down that end of the street. Poison Flat's down there. That's where that woman poisoned her husband.'

As a young kid, the thought of a woman poisoning her husband very much intrigued me, but when I questioned further I was told, 'Oh, you don't need to know anything about that,' and so I let it go. Then in about 1982 I started researching my family history. I was going through some old newspapers from around the Moonta region when I came across the story of Elizabeth Woolcock and how she was the only woman to be hanged in South Australia. Again it grabbed my attention. So much so this time that the family history was thrown in the bottom drawer and I've gone on to write two books on Elizabeth Woolcock: *No Monument of Stone: Elizabeth Woolcock's struggle through life* and *Dead Woman Walking: Was an innocent woman hanged?*.

Elizabeth Woolcock was born Elizabeth Lillian Oliver, in 1848, in the mining town of Burra, South Australia, where she and her family lived in a dugout — rooms — cut into the bank of the local creek. That was not unusual for poor mining families in those days, and evidence of the dugouts can still be seen to this day.

Then, as a very young child, a flood washed away the dugout and Elizabeth moved from Burra with her family, which included a younger sister, to the goldfields around the Ballarat region of Victoria. There they lived in a tent, as so many did. This was quite a turbulent time, not only in Australia's history but also in Elizabeth's life. Not long after the family arrived in the goldfields her sister died from dysentery and her mother took off with another man and returned to South Australia, leaving Elizabeth with her father.

Close on the heels of that upsetting event, at the age of five or six, Elizabeth witnessed the murder of one of her father's friends. This happened during the Eureka Stockade uprising of 1854 when a number of policemen shot the friend after he'd been slashed across the head by one of their compatriots. Following that, they trampled his body with their horses. If all that wasn't traumatic enough, a year later Elizabeth was raped and beaten and virtually left for dead by an Indian traveller who was passing through the area. Her father died from consumption two years later.

So, at the age of nine, Elizabeth went into service with the family of a Melbourne pharmacist, learning the principles of housekeeping. After completing her traineeship she got work in a guesthouse. By this stage she had become addicted to opium. Then when she was fifteen she heard that her mother was living in Moonta and so she decided to contact her with the view of moving back to South Australia. This she did, and she moved into the house with her mother and her stepfather and their family. To support herself she worked as a housekeeper and taught Sunday school on weekends.

Elizabeth was around seventeen when she applied for the position of housekeeper to Thomas Woolcock. Woolcock was a miner-cum-amateur veterinarian who was in his mid-twenties. His wife and eldest son had died of fever, leaving him with a young son who, from memory, would've been about seven years of age.

Oddly enough, Elizabeth's stepfather was far from pleased when rumours surrounding this live-in arrangement started. I say 'oddly enough' as it's rather ironic that the stepfather was upset by his stepdaughter being so closely associated with a single man, when he himself had returned from the goldfields with Elizabeth's mother and had had two children out of wedlock before they married. Anyhow, to avoid the gossip Woolcock agreed to marry Elizabeth, who would've been around eighteen years of age by that stage.

But, as it happened, Thomas Woolcock turned out to be a heavy drinker and a bully and he gave Elizabeth very little money to housekeep on. After reading my books a lot of people have misinterpreted what I said and believed that he also beat Elizabeth. I didn't intend it that way. All that's recorded was that, at one time, he slapped her across the face after she'd said something that upset him. Whatever the case, Elizabeth was unhappy in the relationship. On several occasions she attempted to leave Woolcock and even attempted suicide by hanging herself. It was during this time that she became addicted again. Her addiction became common knowledge within the community and, after the local chemist refused to prescribe any more drugs, she began sending her stepson to various local pharmacies in an attempt to procure them.

After they'd been married for about six years, Thomas Woolcock took ill. In Moonta at that time they didn't have a hospital, so patients were treated in their own home. The first doctor that was brought in was a Dr Bull, who himself had a reputation for mistreating people and was known to have been a heavy drinker and a drug addict of long standing. Dr Bull diagnosed Woolcock as having nothing more than a sore throat. To that end he treated him with rhubarb pills, which contain the poison oxalic acid. Dr Bull also administered a second medication, which contained traces of mercury — another poison when overdosed.

When Woolcock didn't improve under Dr Bull they brought in a second doctor, a Dr Dickie. Dr Dickie's diagnosis was that Woolcock was suffering from some sort of gastric fever. But then, when Woolcock's health began to deteriorate even further, a third doctor was brought in, a Dr Herbert. It was noted that, under Herbert's treatment, which included his diagnosis of mercury poisoning, Woolcock's health did improve. But unfortunately, Herbert's fees were so high that Woolcock was soon reverted back to Dr Dickie who, for the next six weeks, continued treating him for gastric fever, after which time Woolcock died. That was in September 1873.

After Woolcock died, rumours began to spread about how Elizabeth had been trying to buy various drugs from the three different chemists in town. Now it's my belief that, with Woolcock having also set himself up as an amateur veterinarian, many of those drugs could well have been for use in the treatment of sick animals. Anyhow, the rumours persisted to such an extent they prompted the authorities to call an inquest into Thomas Woolcock's death.

On the first day of the inquest, an autopsy was called for. The findings suggested that Woolcock may well have died of mercury poisoning. To that end, Dr Dickie insisted that nothing he did in his treatment would have harmed Woolcock. And Bull, when he was able to testify, stated that his treatment contained such a minute amount of mercury that it wouldn't have had any effect. So then suspicion fell on Elizabeth. She was arrested and transported by stage coach to Adelaide where she was housed at the Adelaide Jail in readiness to go on trial for the murder of her husband, Thomas Woolcock.

The court case was held at the Supreme Court in Adelaide. With Elizabeth being unable to afford a decent lawyer, she ended up with a man who had never practised in South Australia and who — mind you — never participated in a major case in the state again after her conviction. While much of the prosecution's evidence focused on Elizabeth's purchase of different chemicals and drugs from the various chemists in town, her lawyer offered no evidence whatsoever on Elizabeth's behalf; not even the knowledge that Thomas Woolcock had been well cared for by Elizabeth throughout his illness.

During the trial there was no mention of mercury but, after the organs from the deceased had been sent to Adelaide and analysed, an amount of mercury was found to be in the body. It was also discovered that Thomas Woolcock was suffering from consumption and other illnesses and that he most likely would've only lived another two years, possibly less.

So whether all that played a part in Thomas Woolcock's death we'll never know. But the important thing was that the coroner's report never actually stated just how much mercury was in the body nor whether there was enough to cause the death.

One of the world's leading toxicologists of that time had previously written about the various legal aspects that can or cannot be presented within a court trial. Now if Elizabeth's lawyer had used some of that information, he could've argued how the essentials of any poisoning case are that, firstly, there has to be proof of a fatal quantity of toxic substance in the body and, secondly, that quantity has to be clearly stated which, as I've said, in Woolcock's case it wasn't.

Another aspect of murder by poisoning is that the person has to have no awareness that the poison was being administered to them. And if he, Woolcock, was aware that it was being administered to him, in that case, his death would have to be classified as a suicide. So there's yet another complication.

To make Elizabeth's case worse, as was the ruling of the day, it was not permitted for an accused person to give evidence on their own behalf. But if Elizabeth's lawyer had done his homework he'd have found out that there was one person who he could've presented on her behalf. His name was William Ey, an assayer and chemist who'd given evidence in similar cases.

Ey would've been an ideal person to have countered the medical evidence that had been presented by the prosecution.

Anyhow, that didn't happen. It was only after Elizabeth had been sentenced that Ey wrote to the Attorney-General stating how the medical evidence presented in the case against Elizabeth was wrong on at least twenty points. But it was all too late and his letter was ignored.

In those days, the date of a hanging was set at three weeks from the date of conviction. But as that three weeks terminated on Christmas Day it was thought unseemly to hang someone on such a day. So they delayed the hanging until the 30th December 1873 and to this day her body remains buried between the inner and outer walls of the old Adelaide Jail. In an added twist, after the trial, Dr Bull was committed to a psychiatric hospital and committed suicide several months later.

In stating all I have researched, it is my belief that Elizabeth may well have been wrongly convicted of the murder of her husband, Thomas Woolcock, and, to date, I've petitioned the Governor of South Australia twice, seeking a posthumous pardon, but have been rejected in both cases.

# Gutted

Now here's one for you. This is going back before I was born, around the late 1800s, early 1900s — around my grandfather's time — and we're looking up into the central highlands of Tasmania. As it transpires, there's a little town up in that highlands area called Bothwell. It's a beautiful little village, just beautiful. A very 'frontier' type of place with a lot of sandstone buildings. Bothwell was settled by the Scots, going right back. And now here's a point of interest: having been settled by the Scots, Bothwell was known to have had the first golf club in the southern hemisphere. True, so there's a little side yarn for you.

Anyhow, several miles out from Bothwell was a family by the name of Lawson. I remember the name because I'm a great fan of Henry Lawson, the Australian writer. But this mob of Lawsons lived away out in the real wild country, out on an area known as Misery Plains. And it was a pretty miserable existence. They didn't have any form of transport, not even a horse. They had to walk everywhere. And they were a huge family. Maybe twenty or more. All inbred, so no one knew who belonged to who. All in together. And unlike the few poor farming souls that also lived out in that area, the Lawson mob didn't own any property or anything. They were more a family who lived off their wits and so they survived by fishing and hunting and there was a lot of poaching going on too, I might add, both in and out of season.

Now I don't know if you've ever had anything to do with snaring or not, but snaring's a very primitive way of catching animals. There's basically two types of snares for land-dwelling animals:

'neckers' and 'treadles'. The Lawsons would've used neckers. It's where you get some rope or wire and tie it like a noose and you attach it to a 'sprunger', which is a supple young sapling. Then you might lay some bait out next to the snare-trap to entice the animals in and when one has a go at the bait — *snap* — it gets strung up in the noose and you've got it. Real primitive, like I said. Anyhow, this Lawson family used to snare a lot of their food; things like small kangaroos or wallabies, wombats and quolls and whatever. But of course, say if you've snared a good number of large animals all at once, there'd be quite a heavy load to carry home, wouldn't there? Too heavy. So what they used to do was, after they snared an animal, they'd gut it on the spot, which would lighten their load for the walk back home. So they'd carry these gutted animals home, cook them up and that's what they'd eat; the whole family. It was their tucker, and that might give you an idea as to just how these people lived. They'd even eat snakes and lizards and frogs.

Anyhow, as I heard it, one time back at the turn of the century the local policeman from Bothwell was riding his horse through that wild country. Apparently a farmer had reported that some of his stock had gone missing and the copper had come out to investigate. So this copper's riding around the wilderness and he stumbles across the Lawson mob living in this huge old barn sort of thing. As rough as guts it was. If you can imagine a large open dirt floor, with a few sheets of holey tin propped up with saplings as a roof. It had a big old Metters oven up one end and at night they'd all bed down together within the rusted corrugated iron walls of this barn.

So right out of the blue the policeman arrives at the Lawsons' and there's all this family gathered around the old Metters oven, grinning up at him in an odd manner and going on. Anyhow, the copper took old man Lawson aside and he said to him, 'This's just not right.' He said, 'Look at all these people you've got. You just can't live like this. You've got to divide off the bloody house.

Turn it into bedrooms and that, to keep everyone separate, you know, from getting into each other's beds and so forth.'

'Yeah, okay,' says old man Lawson.

Then the copper tells old man Lawson that he'll be back in a couple of weeks just to make sure that the job's all done. 'You just can't live like this,' said the copper. 'It's just not human.'

'Yeah, okay,' says old man Lawson, and the copper heads off, leaving all these people huddled around the Metters oven, grinning and going on at each other and so forth.

A couple of weeks later the copper comes back to check on the situation; you know, to make sure they'd divided off the barn into separate spaces and so forth. Of course, he expects to see all these walls and doors and that. But no; what old man Lawson and his tribe had done, they'd gone out and nicked a stack of farm posts, fencing rails and hinged gates and they'd put those up inside the barn. So all they had to do was jump the fence at night and they'd be back into it.

Anyhow, that was just part of the story because the real one I wanted to tell you was that, while the copper's there checking on the building project, he's poking around outside and he comes across all these little mounds with markers on them. So he asked the old feller Lawson, 'What's the go here?' and old man Lawson tells him that they're the grave mounds of the stillborn children that various members of the family had had along the way.

The cop said, 'Look,' he said, 'you can't do that sort of thing. It's illegal. If you don't declare a death, you could go to jail.' He said, 'The law states quite clearly that, if there's a birth in the family or if anyone dies, you've got to let the proper authorities know so that it can be legally recorded. And in that case the proper authority around this area is me.'

'Yeah, okay,' says old man Lawson, so that's that.

Anyway, as it transpires, old man Lawson's missus dies, so he thinks, Well, I don't want to get into any bloody trouble over this.

If I bury her out here, the copper's sure to find out and I could end up in jail. So what he does, he puts her in an old chaff bag, tosses her over his shoulder and off he heads to Bothwell to show her to the policeman. As I said it's a hell of a trip under the best of circumstances but, when it's stinking hot and you've got the dead weight of quite a large body to lug along over your shoulder, you can just imagine what a walk like that would be like.

Anyhow, old man Lawson sticks with it and a few days later he eventually makes it to the outskirts of Bothwell. He walks into town. It's another stinking hot day and he gets as far as the Bothwell pub. By crikey, he thinks, I'm pulling in here for a drink before I take her to the police station. So he stumbles into the pub with the chaff bag over his shoulder and he dumps it down on the floor. When it lands with a thud, the publican says with a start, 'My word, it'd be bloody hot out there carrying a load like that, wouldn't it?'

'My oath,' says old man Lawson.

'So what's in the chaff bag then?' the publican asks as he hands over a beer.

'It's the missus,' he says. 'She carked it and the copper said that, under the law, I had to bring her into town and show her to him.'

'Where did you walk from?' asks the publican.

'Out Misery Plains way.'

'Christ,' says the publican, 'she'd be a fair weight to carry all that distance.'

'My oath,' says old man Lawson. 'She was a pretty hefty woman to start with so, to lighten the load, I stopped along the way and I gutted her.'

# Indicators

In the '70s I was in the Northern Territory, working out on Bathurst Island, at a place called Nguiu. Being such a small, isolated community there was no permanent police presence in those days and, what's more, visits from the mainland constabulary were very infrequent, and that's to say the least. Because of this, the enforcement of the laws, particularly in respect to motor vehicle registrations, driver's licences and so forth, were pretty lax. Well, more than pretty lax, really. To give you a clearer idea, the general rule of thumb was more akin to the use of vehicles on a private property, in as much as hardly anyone even bothered to follow the law. That's the way it was.

Then out of the blue some bright bureaucratic spark decided that 'in the interests of public relations and to improve interaction between police and remote communities, a programme of regular visits was to commence'.

We were rostered for one such visit per fortnight so, on the due date, a constable arrived from the mainland. Now, back then, our community was a fairly peaceful one. Apart from the odd donnybrook, not much else happened that would be of interest to the Territory's finest. Consequently the visiting police officer didn't have a very big case load to attend to during this, his first visit. But he did happen to notice how very few of the local motor vehicles and motorbikes were registered and, being the smart cove he was, he also rightly assumed that there wouldn't have been too many current driver's licences around the place either.

This then, he decided, was to be the thrust of his particular law-and-order initiatives in our community. To that end, the approach he decided to take was to firstly educate the populace as to their responsibilities and, once that was done, he'd then begin to enforce the law more vigorously. So to set the example for the rest of the community it was agreed that all work supervisors — like myself — plus our community leaders were to rectify their discrepancies. This was to begin at his next fortnightly visit.

The allotted date came and rather inconveniently I found that the constable had been offered my office as his temporary police station for the day. This was a little tricky because my usual mode of transport was my trail bike and, as it turned out, I had quite a few discrepancies to rectify; far too many in my mind. Not only was my motorbike unregistered, but it had a lack of any form of reasonable brakes, and the indicators, well, they went west during my first bush bash out to Moantu, on the western side of the island, after cyclones Tracy and Wilma had reorganised the vegetation out that way. On top of that, my not having a bike licence may have also been an issue so, being the responsible citizen I am, I decided that the trail bike should stay at home, just for the day. What's more, in fairness to the constable, I also thought it not opportune to drive the work truck to the office as I didn't have a truck licence for that either. So today's trip to work would have to be on shanks's pony.

Oh, that's right — though I didn't have a car over on the community, I did have a car licence; the only problem being, it was still my old one from down south and it'd long needed to be changed to a Territory licence. This, the good constable seemed more than happy to do. 'Yep,' he said, 'I'll sort that out,' and he took my details and scribbled himself a reminder on a piece of paper.

Gee, I thought, that was easy. I'm on a bit of a winner here, so I then asked what I'd need to do to register my motorbike.

'What have you been doing up till now?' he asked.

'Well,' I said and, while I was aimlessly fishing around in the hopes of finding some sort of half-decent excuse, he said, 'Well we'd better fuckin' well get you sorted out with one of those also, hadn't we? What sort of bike is it?' he asked.

'Yamaha,' I said.

'Done,' he replied, as he scribbled himself another reminder on the same piece of paper.

This was all going far better than I had expected it to, so I then asked if I could possibly upgrade my car licence to a truck one.

'What do you want to drive?' he said.

'Well, everything, I guess; you know, just in case,' I said.

'Oh,' he said.

I could see by this stage that I'd perhaps pushed our newly formed friendship a little too far so, to waylay any of his concerns, I quickly replied, 'It's okay, I'm willing to show you that I can drive the work truck,' to which he gave me a steely look and said, 'Sounds like you've obviously been doing it.'

Anyhow, as he started to scribble himself a reminder for the upgrade of licence, down under the reminder for the change of state licence and the reminder about the motorbike registration, I marvelled at the power of this policeman. Here he was, sitting at an old rickety desk, in a galvanised tin shed painted pink, miles from anywhere, exercising powers that would pretty much require the approval of a cabinet minister down south.

'Thank you very much,' I said with great admiration and appreciation. Then, feeling proud of my achievements, I walked home for lunch secure in the knowledge that I'd be able to ride my trusty old trail bike back to work and even legally drive the work truck out to the airstrip to meet the afternoon's Connair flight.

After having had a bite to eat and a bit of a snooze I jumped on my motorbike and was heading back to work, taking particular care to keep to the left-hand side of the dirt road as was required.

All was going well until I saw my new-found policeman mate flagging me down on the road ahead. Though I was fairly sure he'd spotted the missing indicators and maybe even the worn tyres, I was hoping like heck he wouldn't test the brakes. Anyhow, as I coasted to a stop alongside him, his first comment was, 'This isn't the bike that I registered earlier today, is it?' to which I mumbled, 'Well, it sort of is, maybe, perhaps. Yes, kind of.'

'Well, get the fuckin' thing fixed before I see it again.'

'Yes, sir,' I replied, and that was it. The following week my new Northern Territory state licence to drive anything short of an aircraft carrier landed on my desk, along with the registration papers for my motorbike. And I did attend to the bike. I still have it in fact, and the brakes are still fine, the tyres are borderline okay and, well, as for the new indicators, they're still in the box they came in, ready for the next inspection. I mean, they were quite expensive so I'd hate to lose them out on another bush bash, wouldn't I?

# Kip and Me

Kip's a ripper. He's an Australian Kelpie and he's just about the most laidback dog you could ever imagine. I got him a while back now, from this guy called Goatie who had a goat station on the Danggali Track. You know the Danggali Track? It's basically a sand track that goes up the South Australian–Victorian border fence line, then into New South Wales.

Goatie had a litter of about ten little Kelpie pups. They were just absolutely gorgeous; all different colours. I took one look and I said, 'I'll take that one.' He would've only been six weeks old; the size of my two hands. Anyway, I took him home and that was it. That's Kip. We've never been apart since. Everywhere I go, Kip goes with me. He doesn't get much choice. The only place he doesn't come with me is when I'm at work, then he stays at home and rules the roost.

So far, Kip and me, I reckon we've been to just about every place in the far north of South Australia. When Oodnadatta was vacant we went there. If you take out the APY — Anangu Pitjantjatjara Yankunytjatjara — Lands, Oodna's probably the remotest police posting you can get. Basically the whole community's Indigenous, bar the people at the Pink Roadhouse, a couple of nurses down at the clinic and a few teachers. But you know what, Kip and me, we just had the best fun in Oodnadatta, absolutely.

When we first arrived in town I parked at the roadhouse just to get my bearings. I was dressed in my police uniform and the moment I got out of the car, this big Aboriginal man came storming up to me. I'm thinking, Oh my God, this could really go pear-shaped.

But no, he wraps me in this big bear hug and he goes, '*Kunga, walka walgen.*'

I'm going, Oh my God, he's saying 'young woman police officer'. And that was my greeting to Oodnadatta. His name was Jeremy. He had FASD — foetal alcohol spectrum disorder. But Jeremy was a real gentleman. Without fail, each night, he'd visit me at the police station. He'd have a glass of orange juice and we'd watch a bit of telly and we'd have a chat and he'd pat Kip. Kip loved him.

I was the only police officer in Oodnadatta; one female — me. The Indigenous CC — community constable — was there for the first few days after I arrived and then he went off on leave, so I was sort of on my own for a while. At first I was a bit worried because, even though I'd already worked as a solo patrol member, I'd never been to Oodnadatta so I had no knowledge of what to expect. I mean, just for starters, there I was, a single female officer, with very few creature comforts, in this remote little town, with the nearest police station being two hours away.

But just about every night I got called to the pub. They'd see me coming and when I walked in I'd line everyone up and I'd tell them in no uncertain terms to pull their heads in and go home. And that'd be it. It was never aggressive. I never felt threatened. But you know what? I never had any issues because it's all about how you speak to people; particularly Aborigines. I always say that if you can build a rapport by being able to speak to them in a bit of their own dialect, they'll listen. And the thing about Pitjantjatjara is that it's only a spoken language, it's not a written language.

Before I got to Oodna I already knew a few words of Pitjantjatjara. I could basically get across what I needed to. But I wanted to learn more, so one of the first things I asked was, 'Do you know someone who can teach me some of the language?'

'Audrey Stewart,' they said. 'She's a North Melbourne supporter.'

Audrey was one of the traditional women. She'd been a long-time jillaroo out on Macumba Station before she moved to Oodnadatta. She was getting on a bit so she didn't really work any more. When I tracked her down we came to an agreement that each time we got together she'd teach me three words of Pitjantjatjara. Three words. So when I was off duty, Kip and me, we'd go up and see her.

We all got on really well — terrifically, in fact. We'd go off for long walks, looking for meteorites. She'd also teach me some of the culture. You quite often see the old ladies chewing this big wad of stuff. Well, that comes from the bark off a special tree. The traditional ladies take the bark and they smoulder it in a fire till it turns to ash, then they mix the ash up with a native herb and they chew it. It's meant to be a hallucinogenic sort of thing but look, I don't think it is. But you know what? The old women would just about sell their souls to have a tin of it. They just love it.

So little by little I learnt some of the language, and I was always asking about their culture and things like that. And because they could see I was interested in them, I was made more welcome into the community. And it wasn't only people like Audrey that I became close to. I was very fortunate at Oodna to have a fantastic Indigenous community constable called Bobby Bales. Bobby was one of the loveliest, most beautiful gentlemen you could ever meet. He taught me a lot. We'd go out hunting and Bobby would cook the food up the traditional way. Things like that.

Yeah, so Oodnadatta was a great experience. Kip absolutely loved it too. He was great company. If we weren't out with Audrey or Bobby Bales or any of the others we'd go off for long walks, just the two of us together. He hates the car though. Can you imagine that? A Kelpie who hates cars, and he can't jump for shit either. So he's a Kelpie who also can't jump. I have to lift him into the car. I think I might've spoilt him a bit too much.

# Lame Dick

I was born and bred in Portland, Victoria, a fishing and meatworks town over near the South Australian border. When I finished my schooling I joined the Victorian Police as a police cadet, but after about eighteen months I decided to have a bit of a break and I had a year off.

Then when I was about twenty-one, I saw a piece in the *Herald Sun* newspaper where they were advertising for police to come up to the Northern Territory. In the advertisement they showed a big burly policeman standing next to a Ford F100 and I thought, Gee, that looks exciting. So I went into it a bit more and I saw that the Top End of the Territory had all these amazing river systems that were stacked with barramundi. I liked my fishing, and I was still single, with no ties, so I applied and I got interviewed and I got the job.

Originally we were supposed to start training in Darwin in early January 1975, but because Cyclone Tracy had hit Darwin on Christmas Day '74, we ended up driving to Darwin later on, in the March of '75. It was my first time in the Territory and my immediate impression was of a vast wilderness. Nothing for miles and miles. But being young I looked upon it as an adventure and anyway, whatever happened, I was only aiming to stay for just the two or three years and that'd be it. Though, mind you, it didn't turn out that way.

Arriving in Darwin was a shock. Being so soon after Cyclone Tracy there wasn't a leaf on a tree anywhere and there was still a huge mess to be cleaned up. But it worked out really well. A whole bunch of us single fellows ended up living in the old police barracks. There was no hot water or anything like that, but we did have a room each, just a little room, and we all got on well. In fact, many of us have ended up mates for life.

For me, it was exciting being in a new place and getting out and about as a policeman on the street. I was a constable, nothing overly exciting; just a lad on the beat. Though not that long after I'd arrived in Darwin I was sent out to do a relief stint at a place called Hooker Creek. Hooker Creek's now known as Lajamanu Aboriginal Community and it's about five hundred and sixty kilometres south-west of Katherine. In other words it's way out in the middle of nowhere. Actually, I think they used to send us young single fellows out to some of these wild and woolly Aboriginal settlements just for the experience; maybe to toughen us up a bit.

Whatever it was, it turned out to be a long two months for a single fellow like myself. There was just me and my officer-in-charge. That was all. I stayed in the house of the constable I was relieving. He'd gone on holidays, and I guess you could say that it was a good experience ... sort of. Because, having grown up in country Victoria and then basically only recently having arrived in Darwin, to be then sent to an Aboriginal settlement out in the middle of the sticks was a bit of a shock. There was no special sort of training or anything. You just had to go out there and do your best. And that wasn't easy, especially when you ran into someone like Lame Dick.

Lame Dick was an Aboriginal fella from out at Hooker Creek. He's dead now and he wasn't named Lame Dick for any reason other than he had a real old limp about him when he walked. He was probably only about six stone in weight — as light as a feather — and he was a wiry little bugger. He could just about twist himself inside out. And he was the biggest troublemaker I've ever come across, especially when he got on the grog. People in the community would be forever knocking on our door and saying, 'That Lame Dick, he's down the back causin' trouble again.'

So you'd get down there and you'd be struggling to get him in the van and he'd be doing everything he could to cause you injury. He'd be biting. He'd be kicking. He'd be scratching. He'd be mouthing off left, right and centre and, while you're also trying to protect yourself from his onslaught, the people in the community would all be crowding around going, 'Ay, you can't treat 'im like that. He's one of us.'

And I'm thinking, Yeah, it's all right for you but he's just about bitten my frigging fingers off.

So that was Hooker Creek. I hated it actually, and so I was very pleased when my eight weeks was over and I could get back to civilisation. And that was the end of Lame Dick ... or so I thought.

It must've been a couple of years later; he must've come up to Darwin for some reason or other and a fellow constable had a run-in with him. Of course Lame Dick was up to his old tricks — kicking, scratching, biting and mouthing off — and so the constable bundled him into the van and he took him down to the police station where he locked him up and charged him with assaulting a police officer.

By that stage I was a court orderly and on the day of Lame Dick's hearing I can still picture the magistrate. It'd been a long day and when they called the next case, in hobbles Lame Dick — still as thin and weedy as ever; real pitiful-looking he was — and the magistrate took one look at him and said, 'I'm not hearing this case. Out the door, closed, finished. This poor man would not be capable of assaulting an ant let alone a police officer.'

And I'm sitting there thinking, Yes, he could, your Honour. No doubt about it. No doubt at all.

Oh, he was a nasty little bastard. In the twelve years I was in the police force up in the Territory I can tell you I had to make some pretty rugged arrests and Lame Dick would've been amongst the very worst of them.

# Malachi Martin

In my early teens I was in the Scouts, in South Australia, and I remember when we went on a camping trip down to a place near the southern end of the Coorong, called Salt Creek. Our Scoutmaster was a nice bloke but, every now and then, he'd try to put the wind up us. Anyhow, one chilly winter's night, while we were around the campfire at Salt Creek, he told us the story of Malachi Martin.

The story was set in the mid-1800s and back then each fifteen miles or so the Cobb and Co. coach service had a stopover place where they'd feed, water and change their horses. That's how Salt Creek came into being. It was on the main route between Melbourne and Adelaide and there was an inn there called the Traveller's Rest. Other than being a pub and providing a few beds for the weary traveller, the Traveller's Rest also acted as a general store for the locals; a place where they could buy the basics like flour, sugar, tea and so forth.

Now Malachi Martin grew up on a farm just south of Adelaide. Our Scoutmaster said that Malachi wasn't particularly well liked as a child; always getting himself into some trouble or other and then, when he was a teenager, he was arrested and charged with stealing from the local post office. He was tried and found not guilty. But the odd thing was, just a few days after the trial, Malachi's pregnant mother disappeared under mysterious circumstances and, after a search of the family farm, the police found her body in a dam. An inquest was held into her drowning and it was deemed that she'd committed suicide — many say due to the shame she felt for her son, Malachi.

So that was that — or so it seemed, because a few years later Malachi moved to Salt Creek, where he got work as a Cobb and Co. mail coach driver. In doing so, Malachi befriended the couple who ran the Traveller's Rest, William and Nellie Robinson. Malachi and Nellie started having an affair and not long after the affair had started, Nellie's husband, William, disappeared under mysterious circumstances. So the police were called in. The nearest police station to Salt Creek was about sixty miles away at a place called Wellington, which is on the Murray River, just south of Tailem Bend. They came down the highway on horseback from Wellington and, after a search of the area around Salt Creek, they discovered William's body not far from the Traveller's Rest. He'd suffered horrific injuries and his throat had been cut from ear to ear.

All the locals knew that Malachi and Nellie were having an affair, so the police questioned Malachi, but he wasn't charged. As the Scoutmaster told it, immediately after the murder had been committed, Malachi had jumped on his horse and he rode, flat out, all the way down along the ocean beach to the mouth of the Murray River. He then swam the Murray mouth to Goolwa where he created merry hell in one of the pubs and he was arrested for being drunk and disorderly and locked up in the slammer. The next day, after he'd sobered up, the police kicked him out of jail and told him to head home and stay out of trouble. And that was his alibi. When the Wellington police questioned Malachi about the murder, Malachi replied, 'Well, I couldn't have been in two places at once, could I?'

Anyhow, not long after he'd returned to Salt Creek, Malachi took off to Sydney for a couple of years. But here's the odd thing: when the heat had died down after those two years, he came back to Salt Creek and he married Nellie Robinson.

So that was that — or so it seemed, because, during Malachi's time in Sydney, Nellie had employed a servant by the name of Jane Macmanamin to help with things around the Traveller's Rest and after Malachi's return, Jane disappeared under mysterious circumstances. When the police came down from Wellington and questioned Malachi about Jane's disappearance, he told them that Jane had recently gone to live in Mount Gambier — Mount Gambier being down near the Victorian border.

Now Jane had always kept in contact with her sister and so when the sister hadn't heard from Jane for a while, she wrote to the police telling them how she was worried that something had gone terribly wrong. The police in Wellington then asked some of the local Aborigines to do another search of the area, which they did, and they came across Jane's body half-concealed in a wombat's hole, not far from the Traveller's Rest. Jane had suffered horrific injuries, she'd been raped and had her throat slit from ear to ear. Then in a crude attempt to hide the body she'd been partly stuffed down a wombat's hole. That's how our Scoutmaster described it — 'partly stuffed down a wombat's hole'.

After hearing back from the Aborigines about their gruesome find, the Wellington police were convinced that Malachi was the murderer. There was no doubt. But the last thing they wanted was to spook Malachi by letting him know they were onto him. So, instead of coming down the highway, this time they went across the Murray River at Wellington where they jumped into boats and rowed overnight down the Coorong to a spot just six miles west of Salt Creek. That's where they camped for the night, and that spot's now called Policeman's Point. That's how it got its name. Next day, the police were up before daylight. They'd previously borrowed some horses from one of the locals and so they rode into Salt Creek, where they caught an unsuspecting Malachi in bed with Nellie, and charged him for the murder of Jane Macmanamin. Malachi was then taken back to Adelaide where he was found guilty of first-degree murder and sentenced to death by hanging. As the records show, Malachi was hanged on Christmas Eve 1862 and he was buried within the walls of the Adelaide Jail.

So that was that — or so it seemed, because, while Malachi had been living at Salt Creek, there'd also been a few other mysterious disappearances. One was a jeweller who'd disappeared without a trace and his damaged jewellery box was later found near Salt Creek. The second missing man was also never found, but a torn piece of handkerchief was later discovered, which had his initials embroidered in one corner. As it turned out, both men had been staying at the Traveller's Rest.

The local Aborigines also believed that Malachi had murdered one of their teenage boys. They said that, just before his mysterious disappearance, the young man had been seen having an argument with Malachi. It wasn't until much later that a group of Aborigines came across the teenager's badly decomposing body while they were swimming in a waterhole near Salt Creek. The boy had suffered horrific injuries, his throat had been slit from ear to ear, then his body had been stuffed in a bag and weighed down by a large stone. There were also rumours that some of the local Aborigines had died from arsenic poisoning after eating flour and sugar they'd stolen from the Traveller's Rest.

So that was that and that was the story of Malachi Martin, pretty much as our Scoutmaster told it, and, as I said, he was always out to put the wind up us. And it definitely worked on this occasion, because after we went to bed that night we were so terrified that Malachi Martin might somehow extricate himself from the walls of the Adelaide Jail, find his way to Goolwa, swim across the Murray mouth, jump on a horse and ride, flat out, all the way down along the ocean beach before making his way to Salt Creek, where he'd inflict horrific injuries upon us before slitting our throats from ear to ear and stuffing us down wombat holes, that not a single one of us dared to venture outside our tents that particular chilly winter's night — much to our own physical discomfort.

Anyhow, the following night the Scoutmaster gathered us together to go on a treasure hunt. Of course, we were pretty apprehensive about it all but, buoyed by scouthood courage, we nervously gathered together to go out on this treasure hunt. With our torches in hand we grouped in single file and ventured out into the dark chill of the night. Now, unbeknown to us, during the day our Scoutmaster had got a dead horse's leg bone and he'd tied a boot to the top of it and then jammed it down a nearby wombat hole. So there we were — there would've been about ten or twelve of us — tentatively making our way through the scrub when the leading boy's torchlight hit the leg bone with the boot attached to it. And that was it. All hell broke loose. The kid let out a blood-curdling scream, he shot up in the air about six feet, spun around and he took off back to camp, with the rest of us in hot pursuit.

# Memories of Maffra

My name is Roman Kulkewycz and I'm sitting here in my recliner chair, reminiscing on how the police force has changed over the years. In small country towns like Maffra, which is in the central Gippsland region of Victoria, when I was young, the police were highly respected, admired and trusted members of the community. Everyone wanted to be the local copper's friend, though underneath this thin veneer of mateship, there lay a crippling fear of the constabulary. In those early days the local bush policeman had a lot of clout in the community. He was sort of like a judge and jury all rolled into one, as well as being the dispenser of punishment whenever us young blokes strayed off the mark.

Of course, if your father just happened to be a friend of the copper, us young blokes hoped like hell that, if we ever got caught doing something wrong, a simple apology would be enough to keep us from fronting the visiting magistrate and getting a mention in the local paper. But more often than not, our punishment would have been meted out well before it came to that. If we were caught doing something wrong, the copper usually gave us a stern verbal warning and a twist of an ear, followed by a kick up the bum. He'd then take us home and tell our fathers, who would inflict Part Two of the punishment. Back then, the parents always backed up the coppers. There was no discussion as to whether you were right or wrong. So we got a double whammy if we got caught. No wonder the court house in Maffra was so small. There was so little need for a judge.

These days, of course, the tables have turned and the aggressors have all the rights in their favour. There's no respect for authority these days. It's now the police who are on the back foot. If they swear at a kid or twist an ear or, woe betide, kick one in the arse, the parents of that young person would soon have a bunch of lawyers onto them. Today, police run a fine line and, in doing so, they do a fantastic job under such conditions. Perhaps it's because of those many restrictions having been placed on the police that we have so many bashings and robberies. I don't know.

At eighteen, when I bought my first car, I made it my business to be well informed about who the policemen were at Maffra, where they lived, and who to fear. In those days, the Maffra Police used their own vehicles so you could always tell who was on duty by which car was parked out the front of the police station. I also remember how some of the young blokes had cars that went much faster than the cops' cars, which usually meant the police would not even bother in a chase. But still we didn't ever really get away with it. Word travels fast in a small community and so these perpetrators were soon rounded up and were meted out their just deserts.

Of course, back in those days, 6 o'clock closing of pubs was the law. Though in Maffra, closing time much depended on which particular policeman was on duty. It was not uncommon for one of the coppers to come into the bar and walk away with a carton of longnecks under his arm or a bottle of scotch, without any money changing hands. This smooth operation allowed the publican a discreet extension of closing time. There was no need for a direct command from the policeman because 'no one saw anything, no one heard anything and no one said anything'.

Then one time a relief policeman arrived in town, determined to make his mark, in the hopes of a promotion. To prove his point, he decided to book the few patrons who'd stayed behind well after closing time. Anyway, amid much complaint, he lined these crestfallen drinkers up against the wall and started taking down their names. As he worked his way down the line of Smiths, Joneses, Johnsons and Thompsons and so forth, he came to this dishevelled-looking inebriated bloke.

'What's yer name?' asked the policeman.

'Mein name is't Siegfried von Dittler,' came the slurred German-accented reply.

Being new to town, the copper thought that the drunk had made the name up and put on a foreign accent just to avoid conviction. 'Come on, mate, I didn't come down in the last shower. Don't give me that bullshit. What's yer proper name?'

'Siegfried von Dittler.'

'No it isn't.'

'Yes it is.'

'No it isn't.'

It was then that the remaining drinkers decided to step in and try to help clear the matter up. 'Yes it is,' they called out to the policeman.

'No it isn't,' shouted the policeman in reply.

'Yes it is!' came a louder chorus.

By now the policeman was thinking they'd all made up their names and, if the higher authorities found out that he'd been taken for a fool by a mob of drunks, any hopes of a promotion would be dashed. So he gave up the ghost.

'Oh, bugger off, the lot'a yers,' he said, and he put away his notebook and walked out of the pub.

Yet most of these police were very kindly, caring men with a good sense of humour and a good understanding of what was 'fair'. If we ever got into mechanical trouble or we needed to be pulled out of a ditch while we were out in the sticks, the local policeman was usually the first on hand to help.

A couple more stories: people always tell of how they obtained their licences back in the early days. I remember when a mate of mine drove to the police station to get his licence. The policeman saw him coming down the road and when my friend arrived he was told to get back into his car and drive around the block. By the time he got back to the police station, the policeman had written out his licence.

Another mate went for his licence in a similar fashion. When he walked into the police station and said that he'd come for a driving test to get his licence, the policeman replied, 'I've seen you driving around town. I thought you already had one.'

'I was just practising,' my mate said.

'Oh, okay,' replied the policeman and, without batting an eyelid, he wrote out a licence.

But the classic story of obtaining a licence was my own father's. My parents had come to Australia as displaced refugees, after World War Two, and because Dad worked such long and hard hours at the local milk factory, he never had the time to learn to read or write in English. Of course, without English he was unable to get a driving licence and so he always rode a pushbike. As it happened, the road to work went past the local Ford dealership. Time and time again, the car salesman would stop Dad and try to convince him to buy the latest model Ford Falcon. But Dad's reply was always the same: 'I can neither read nor write English so I would never pass the licence test.'

Then one day the salesman said, 'Well, Pete, how about you buy the car and I'll look after the licence.'

This was in 1967 and, pretty soon after, a brand-new blue Falcon arrived in the driveway. When Dad opened up the glove box, there was his driving licence. And Dad had never been near the police station.

Finally, I must tell you this last story. By this stage we had proper police cars in Maffra. They were blue in colour and had a blue flashing light in the middle of the roof. Each year the local police sergeant would play the role of Santa at the local aged-care hostel where I was working. To make Santa's entry as exciting as possible for the residents, this sergeant would arrive in the police car with the siren blaring and the blue light flashing.

This particular year I had my four-year-old son, Mathew, at the residents' Christmas Party with me and I'd purchased a gift for him to go into Santa's sack. Anyhow, after Santa finished distributing the gifts, he bent down and asked young Mathew if he'd ever ridden in a 'real' police car.

Well, Mathew's eyes widened and his mouth fell open. 'No, sir, I haven't,' he replied.

'Well, how about we go for a bit of a spin then?' said the police sergeant.

With that, Mathew was taken for a wild ride around the sleepy streets of Maffra with the blue lights flashing and siren blaring which, just between you and me, caused great concern amongst the locals as to what tragedy had happened. Of course that was many years ago now but, as Mathew would tell you, even to this day, that was the most exciting Christmas present he has ever received.

# My Grandfather, Tracker Williams

*Are you recording? Right, okay; my name is Paul Roe and back when I first got involved in the local history of Bourke, I looked at it and I thought, These are really great stories. And so I got some of them together and, with the help of the local radio station 2WEB, we broadcast them and for the first time, Bourke got a real opportunity to hear its own voice; to hear its own story. In the process I learnt the power of storytelling. It's an age-old thing, I know. The Aboriginal people used to say that the storyteller was the richest man in the tribe because he could articulate the songlines of who they were, where they came from, where they were going to and I felt a bit like that. So I then started telling these stories to the travellers who were passing through town and we've been using the quote of Henry Lawson's, 'If you know Bourke, you know Australia' and if you use that ...*

Sorry, I don't mean to interrupt but I couldn't help it. I'm Tracker Frank Williams' granddaughter. If you knew the history of Bourke, then you'd know Tracker Williams and how he was awarded the Imperial Service Medal in appreciation for all the years he spent working for the New South Wales Police. They even took him down to Government House in Sydney to give it to him and he would've been the only Aboriginal person to have received that award. Though, just the other day, someone said that an Aboriginal man called Riley had also got one. But I'm not sure about that.

Anyway, all our family's history is being written up by my first cousin on my mother's side. He's the oldest member left on our Aboriginal side. He lives in Sydney now and he's putting a book out in November, at Tranby Aboriginal College. He'll be having a big book launch and everything and I'm hoping to get down there for that. But he's the one who knows all the stories. You should talk to him because see, originally our side evolved down through two full-blood Ngemba women. Ngemba's spelt about fourteen different ways but that's the one I use. The Ngemba totem was the *goo-gaa* — the big goanna — and those two girls survived the massacre out there around the Warrego. That was in the middle of the 1800s, back when the soldiers used to go out and shoot and kill all the children so there'd be no more breeding. That was the reason they did it and they'd leave the elderly people because they were too old to breed.

My old great-granny was one of those elderly people who survived through the massacre. She was from the time when the women used to wear a big bone through their noses and she'd use that bone as her needle when she'd sew up the possum skins for clothing for the winter. Then when she saw the soldiers coming, she took her two little grandgirls and she raced them up the top of the mountain and she hid them in a cave and she told them that they weren't to come down till they saw smoke, which was to signal that the soldiers had gone.

I'm sorry to disturb you in this way but, when the two girls came down from the mountain, because their mother had got killed, my old great-granny took them to a close-by squatter's property where a family of white people lived. She knew them somehow, and my old great-granny just left those two girls there, then she went and she stood back away from the house. So the girls' last memory of their grandmother would have been seeing her standing way back, watching and waiting, and then the white lady came outside and she looked over to old great-granny and she took the girls inside. That was because she knew about what was happening, about the massacres and the shootings of the Ngemba Aboriginal children. Then the two girls were given jobs there in the squatter's house as domestics and that's where they stayed, working there so they'd survive.

Then when the girls got older, two men came to Australia on a ship and both of them got jobs out on the property as horse-breakers. One of the men was named Ted Williams and he was from Worcestershire, England, and the other man was named Wilson and he was a Scotsman.

That's how we came down the line. One girl, who the white people had named Fanny, she married the man Williams and the other girl, who'd been named Rosie, she married the man Wilson. Fanny and Rosie had proper Aboriginal names too, but we don't know what they were. Then I came down from the Ted and Fanny Williams' side. I didn't even know they were officially married till twelve months ago. I always thought, No, not back then did a white man marry an Aboriginal woman. But there was a marriage certificate. When I got a copy of it sent over from Brewarrina it was just so wonderful; it was very special.

Ted and Fanny Williams, they had three children, Frank, Peter and Maude, and Frank was my grandfather, and he became the tracker. That's his photo on the table there. It's very old so it's not really clear, but that's his photo. On the back it is written how Tracker Frank Williams was born in 1881 out on a station property on the Warrego River. He was nineteen years old when he first started working as a tracker and the police only paid him in rations. That would've been like sugar and tea and flour. Basic rations, that's all. That was when he was at a little place north of Cobar; I think it was called Drysdale or something like that. And when he'd go out on a patrol with the white policemen, if they stopped at a station property, he wasn't allowed into the big house. He'd be left outside to sit on the porch in his police uniform and he'd have to eat his meals out in the cookhouse with the other Aboriginal workers. So that's where he started and then he also worked for the police at other places as well. In the end he was twenty-five years at Byrock and for his last twelve years he was at Bourke.

Some of my mum's memories are that, when they allowed him to join the New South Wales Police in Byrock, part of the government conditions were that he could live in town but he was no longer to associate with his own people. And he agreed to that because he wanted his children to go to the white school and be educated in that way so that they'd have a better life and more opportunities than he'd had. But my mother said that, when she went to the little Byrock School, all the other children were white and so Mum and her brothers and sisters had to sit up the back of the classroom on a bench, on their own, and they had to drink out of a separate water bubbler and they had a separate wash bowl and a different toilet and they couldn't play with the white kids; they could only play amongst themselves.

Mum also said that, when they lived in the town, they had to live at one end while their own Aboriginal people lived at the other end, on the outskirts, in a special reserve. And so they were separated and the white kids didn't want to play with them, and Mum and her brothers and sisters weren't allowed to go down and play with the black kids. That's how Aboriginal people were treated in those days and, because they lived in the town like they did, there was a lot of jealousy and so they were even disliked by a lot of the Aboriginal families from down the reserve.

Then after my grandfather started working with the Bourke police, that's when I was born. That was in 1951 and when I was young, Mum had to go out and work and, because she held down two or three different jobs all at once, she couldn't stay at home with us kids like she wanted to. So it was my granny and my grandfather who reared us and my granny was like a mother figure to me. But Mum would come up and see us, just to make sure everything was all right, and she'd give Granny money for looking after us. Then she'd leave us to go back to work again and that was very hard because us kids, we didn't understand why we hardly ever saw her and why she didn't spend much time with us. She never sat us down and explained things.

But with my grandfather having to agree that he'd no longer associate with his own Aboriginal family, when we were in Bourke, I know that he sometimes did. But that was without the government knowing. When I was very young, every once in a while, all these full-blood Aborigines from down on the river at Brewarrina, they'd arrive at our house on the back of a big old Ford truck. And oh, they were as dark as dark, and they'd all clamber out and come inside, and Granny would hunt me out of the house and tell me to go off and play and not to come back till they'd gone again.

But sometimes I didn't. Sometimes I'd sneak up and I'd hide around the side of the house. There were holes in the tin — the old corrugated iron — and I'd look in through the holes and I'd see these people in the lounge room and when my grandfather put his hands up like that, they'd all sit down in a circle on the floor. And because the sounds they made were in their own language, I couldn't understand it. To me it was unreal. It used to scare me. Then when my grandfather would raise his arms like that, they'd all go quiet and they'd listen to him; listen to what he said back to them in their own Aboriginal language. Then after they'd all spoken, he'd raise his arms again and they'd get up and they'd go back outside and they'd all get in the back of the big old Ford truck again and they'd drive off back home to Brewarrina.

I remember one time when they came, I was still inside and because I had fairish hair and bluish eyes that'd come down to me from Ted Williams, from Worcestershire, England, these people tried to touch my hair and I got so frightened of them that I ran down to our friend who owned the drycleaners. He was a white man and he asked me what was wrong — why I was so upset — and I told him that there were all these black people at our house and that they scared me. And I still remember him saying, 'Don't worry, darlin'. They are your people, just like you, and they'll look after you till the day you die.' Yes, I still remember that, I do.

Another memory I have of my grandfather is that every now and then a white man used to come up to the house on horseback. I forget his name just now but he had the old butcher's shop here in Bourke. He was well known and well respected. That's right, it was Old Percy Robinson; that was his name. And then my grandfather would get on his horse and they'd go off together. I don't know where they went, but sometimes they'd be gone for days. So maybe that's when he went out tracking, I don't know. My granny never said.

Then when I was about four, he took sick. He'd retired by then and I just have these pictures of memories about him. He was a big man, I thought, and I used to sit up on his bed and I'd give him soup out of a teapot. And he always kept a gold watch that the white police officers had given to him on his retirement and he had the photo of when they gave him the award — the Imperial Service Medal. Then after he died he was buried with a proper police funeral, which was a very rare thing to happen to an Aboriginal person.

Anyway, I'm very sorry for disturbing you but I just heard you talking about the history of Bourke and I thought I'd tell you a bit about my grandfather, Tracker Frank Williams. But I can't wait to go down to Sydney in November and get this book my cousin's putting out because he's the one that knows all the stories; you know, about the girls up in the mountain and the massacres and everything and I bet the story's in there of when a full-blood Aboriginal man murdered a young boy in Brewarrina and then the murderer took off bush. So the police got my grandfather and my grandfather tracked the murderer for miles and miles, right up to near the Queensland border. And because the man was a full-blood Aborigine he purposely went through creeks and over rocks so that no one could ever track him. But my grandfather tracked him down, all right. He eventually found him asleep and he had him arrested. So it should be a very interesting read, that book by my cousin, don't you think?

# No Power

My name's Sandra Cole and my husband is Malcolm. Mal was stationed in the Kimberley for the best part of his police career. In fact, the author Peter Conole wrote a book called *Protect and Serve: a history of policing in Western Australia* and there's a number of stories in there where Malcolm was involved.

Mal and I first met in 1966 when I was up in Port Hedland working as a waitress. Back then, Port Hedland was a big iron ore place where you could earn good money, and your accommodation and all that sort of thing came with the job. So that's where I first met Mal, then I came back down to Perth. A couple of years later I was waiting on Perth Railway Station for a friend who was coming in on the Kalgoorlie Express and Mal just happened to be there to pick up some police stuff. He remembered me and eight years later we married.

Our first posting as a married couple was on Cockatoo Island, which is about a hundred miles out of Derby. Malcolm was also the policeman for nearby Koolan Island. Back then both islands were owned by BHP, so once a week Mal used to catch the barge across to Koolan. Those were usually day trips. If there were any big problems they'd send a boat over to pick him up and he might've then had to stay over in Koolan for three or four days, depending. But that was pretty rare and I didn't worry about spending a few days by myself because it was safe as houses on Cockatoo Island.

For our supplies, there was a little store on Cockatoo Island. BHP owned the store too and you could buy most things; you know, like your meat and fresh vegetables. BHP were very good really. They were the kings of the iron ore industry back in those days. Then sometimes we'd get on the plane and fly to Derby to do some shopping. Other than that you could place an order down in Perth and the state shipping line would bring it up within two or three weeks, depending.

But living on Cockatoo Island was wonderful. We loved it. It was like having a two-year holiday on a tropical island. It was very social. We were taken out fishing on weekends, on people's boats, and it was a very quiet life because no one was allowed in unless they were invited by BHP.

Really, Koolan Island was where BHP had most of their administration and that, but the police station had been on Cockatoo Island for so many years that they just kept it there. Then after we left, they closed Cockatoo Island down and moved everything over to Koolan and I think Bondy — Alan Bond — bought it and made it into a resort. Funnily enough, some time later I saw photos of the development and it actually looked quite good. I don't know what happened after that because it sort of didn't go ahead. But we had some fun while we were there and it was a great experience. Anyway, do you want to speak to Mal now? He's waiting right here next to the telephone.

*G'day, Mal. How's things going?*

Oh, all right. I'm eighty now. I've got a few problems but I'm battling on all right.

Now, you wanted to ask about my time in the police force. Well, I was originally a city slicker. When I was a little walloper I grew up around Perth, then I joined the force right back in 1961. I almost missed out because I was twenty-seven at that stage and, by the rules, I was too old. Anyhow, I'd already put my forms in so they accepted me.

After my training I did six months in Perth, then I saw where they had a vacancy way up north in Broome, so I put in for that and I got it. Broome was all right; it was very good actually. It was a nice town. Oh, there were problems at times, just like you get in every other joint, but I enjoyed it. Broome was a regional office for a lot of the north. Our district went inland, right over to Halls Creek, near the Northern Territory border. Then it went right down around Port Hedland way.

I was only in Broome for a few months before I went up to Wyndham. Wyndham's right up the top of the Kimberley. It had a big meatworks. They used to ship meat all over the place, so there was the big wharf in town and there was the police station and a hospital. Out of town you had the Six Mile pub and the airport. The old school in town had shut down by then and they'd moved it out to Three Mile. The powerhouse was also out at Three Mile and they'd only got the power put on to certain places in Wyndham.

When I first went there I had nowhere to live, so they put me up in a little room out the back of the police station. There was no power, so the sergeant let me run a lead from his house over to where I was bloody camped. Then a few months later, the chappie who was living up at the old schoolhouse residence, he moved out and I asked if I could move in there.

'Yes,' they said and so I did.

The old schoolhouse was only a hundred yards from the police station, which was good for me. It had a gas stove so I could do a bit of cooking, but it didn't have any electric power; it was torches and lanterns and things like that. And there wasn't any hot water so it was cold showers and washing all year round. Anyhow, I scrounged around town and I borrowed this and borrowed that and I set up camp there for a while. Then a chap who was doing different jobs around the place, he moved in as well. It was pretty good really, other than not having any bloody power, that is. So in the end I went to the house next door, to where some public works boys were living, and I said, 'Can I run an electric extension lead over to my place?' and they said, 'No, it's not allowed.' I said, 'Okay then. I'll sort something out.'

Anyway, I got onto a few contacts and in the end it all got approved and I ran a lead from next door over to where I was camped. I stayed there until I moved into another quarters that had both gas and electricity. I think I was about two years at Wyndham and after that I went off and worked in a lot of places around the Kimberley.

But it's all changed now. The police have air conditioning and everything these days. They've got it good. They wouldn't go near a place that didn't have the power on. But I enjoyed it. Actually, I enjoyed most of my thirty-three years in the police force.

# Not a Wink

As a matter of fact I do have a couple of police yarns from Tasmania for you. Both are true. One's set just after World War Two and is quite humorous. It's about a much liked and greatly respected country cop from around this area by the name of Tom Cornelius, now sadly deceased. The second is a more recent anecdote concerning my aging self and one very young, very small policewoman.

Okay, to the first one; the one about the much liked and greatly respected Tom Cornelius. Now, how familiar are you with Tasmania? Well, just to fill you in, this concerns our Central Highlands, which have a lot of lakes. It's quite often referred to as 'the land of a thousand lakes'; the Great Lake being the largest. And just after the war years, if you were living around, say, Deloraine way and you wanted to go to Hobart there was a short cut up over the lakes. That's what we'd say — 'up over the lakes'. It's up over the mountain country into the head of the lakes and you cut right through to Hobart.

Back in that older era, the constabulary down here were equipped with Harley Davidson motorbikes with sidecars. I don't know what it was like over on the mainland, but down here just about every cop had one — ex-army of course. Well, there was this local policeman by the name of Tom Cornelius. I don't recall his rank just now, but Tom would do just about anything for anyone. He was one of them real old-time gentleman coppers. If anyone was in strife, you'd guarantee Tom would be the first on the scene, ready and willing to help. Anyhow, this time Tom had been called to Hobart for some reason or other. I don't know, it could've been for an inquiry or to give evidence in a court case or whatever. Now from Deloraine to Hobart, gee, you'd be looking at around a hundred and twenty-five or a hundred and fifty miles, up over the lakes.

So Tom jumps on his Harley and he goes to Hobart and he does whatever he's supposed to do and he's returning home up through the lakes. That's what you say when you're coming back from Hobart to, say, Deloraine; you describe it as coming 'up through the lakes'. Anyhow, it's just on dark and Tom's riding along on his Harley with the sidecar and he sees this bloke thumbing a lift — hitchhiking. Tom being Tom, he stops and asks, 'Where are you off to?'

The bloke says, 'Deloraine way.'

'Oh,' says Tom, 'that's where I'm heading too. Jump in, mate. I'll give you a lift.'

'Thanks very much,' says the bloke and he hops in the sidecar and off they go.

Okay, so Tom gives this bloke a lift back to Deloraine. When they pull up outside the police station Tom says, 'Well, this's as far as I'm going.'

'Thanks, mate,' says the bloke. 'Greatly appreciated.'

'That's okay,' says Tom. 'Any time I can be of help, you know where you can find me.'

'Yeah. Cheers,' says the bloke and off he strides into the night.

What a nice bloke, thinks Tom. Good manners. Hope he's all right. And Tom puts the bike away and he goes home.

A couple of days later, Tom's sitting in his office. The newspaper arrives and when he opens it up, there, blazoned across the front page, is a picture of the hitchhiker bloke he'd picked up on his way back from Hobart. The headlines read: 'Axe murderer escapes Hobart Jail.'

So that's the first little yarn. The next involves my aging self and a very young and very small policewoman.

Now to predicate this story; when I left school I applied to go

a) into the police force and b) into the fire brigade. In both cases I never ever got past the initial stage because you couldn't get a job with either of those noble establishments if you were under five foot seven, and I was five foot six and a half. They were very strict about your height back in those days, so I was knocked back. That half inch put me out. I'm sixty-eight these days, I've got children in their forties, I've got grandchildren in their twenties, and it's still something that niggles at me.

Anyhow, just a while back a mob of young blokes moved into the place diagonally across the road from where the wife and I live. I'd say they would've been around the eighteen to twenty-two mark. That sort of age. So they move in and right from day one they're playing this bloody boom-boom-doof-doof music and it's going night and day, day and night. Boom-boom-doof-doof. Drove us bloody crazy it did. It was near lifting our roof off, let alone theirs, and so me and the wife, we just couldn't get a wink of sleep. Not a wink.

Of course I soon get pretty sick of all this business and so I go over and knock on the door. A couple of blokes answer. They're not looking too good. Both of them look like they've been bowled over by a train. They've got grey, pallid, pasty skin. They're dishevelled. They've got bloodshot eyes.

Anyhow, I shout out above the racket, 'Can yer turn that bloody crap down!'

They stare back at me as if I'm some sort of aging alien that's just landed on their doorstep. 'Yeah, okay, dude,' they say and they shut the door in my face and stumble off and turn it down.

No sooner do I arrive back home than it starts up again. Boom-boom-doof-doof. And this goes on and on and on and on. The wife and I, we're at our wit's end. Not a wink of sleep. And no matter how many times I go over there and ask them to turn the bloody racket down, they just look at me with that strange distant stare of theirs and mumble, 'Yeah, okay, dude.'

But they never did.

Now, in my younger day, I was a bit of a pug. I could go a round or two with the best of them. And in my younger day, I would've sorted this mob out myself. But being in my late sixties and with them being in their late teens, early twenties, no matter what condition they were in, I felt they'd be a bit too much for this old feller to take on. I wouldn't have liked my chances. So we start ringing the police and the police would come around. Boom-boom-doof-doof. They'd go to the door, have a word to these young blokes. They'd turn the music down. Then no sooner had the coppers got to the end of the street than it'd start up again. Boom-boom-doof-doof.

So one day I got sick of it. 'Bugger this,' I said to the wife and I went down to the local police station. I explain the situation to the copper on the desk and I say, 'I'd like to see someone in authority. I want this mob'a yahoos sorted out.'

'I'll get someone for you, sir,' says the copper. He disappears and out comes this tiny little policewoman. I'm five foot six and a half and she only comes up to my chin. She's about five foot nothing, and she's extremely young. Of course my first reaction is, 'Dear oh dear,' I said, 'I'll need someone a lot bigger and taller than you are, my young girl. I'm looking for someone about seven foot.'

Well, she immediately jumps on the defensive, doesn't she? 'Okay,' she says, 'please yourself. Just forget it,' and she starts to walk away.

Anyhow, I took stock of the situation and I calmed down a little bit. 'All right. Okay,' I said and we sit down and we discuss the problem. I tell her how I've been over to the house on numerous occasions to tell these young yahoos to turn their bloody music down but they don't take any notice, and how I've also complained to the police and they've come around but, as soon as they drive off, the bloody racket starts up again and the wife and I haven't had a decent night's sleep since this mob have moved in and we're both sick to bloody death of it all.

By now I'm all worked up again and, I know it's a generational thing but, in my best grandfatherly manner I'm now wagging my index finger at the young policewoman like I do when I'm going crook on the grandkids. Of course that only compounds the problem, doesn't it? And boy, didn't she go off the deep end. 'Don't you dare point your finger at me like that,' she says.

Well, it was obvious to me at this point that we'd reached an impasse, so I said, 'Well I'm not getting anywhere here.' And I get up and I walk out of the police station, leaving her sitting there.

I get home. I'm still in a huff. Boom-boom-doof-doof. That afternoon, a police car arrives. The wife and I, we're looking out from behind the lounge room curtains. But when I see the tiny little figure of the female copper get out of the car, my hopes fade. She walks up to the front door. *Knock knock*. One of the young blokes answers. She goes inside. The music's turned down. All's quiet on the western front. About half an hour later she comes out of the house, jumps into the cop car and she heads off.

The wife and I, we sit in the lounge room waiting for the boom-boom-doof-doof to start up again. But no. Nothing. Comes evening, we have our dinner in silence; dead silence. We go to bed. Still nothing. Not a sound from across the road. We just lay there, waiting. Expectant. Listening. We try to get to sleep. But no. Not even a whisper. We toss and turn. Not a wink. Not a wink. Not a wink. Not a wink. Not a wink. Not a wink.

# Nowhere to Hide

Between May 1965 and December '66 I was party leader of a geophysical survey crew that operated out in the Simpson Desert. We were working for a mob called Austral Geo Prospectors, who'd been contracted to carry out seismic surveys for an American oil company called Amerada. As we were operating in the south-eastern corner of the Northern Territory, you might be able to imagine just how isolated we were. The nearest town was Finke, which was about eighty miles out along a rough sandy track from our nearest habitation of Andado Homestead, which was out along an even rougher sand track. At that stage, Andado held pastoral leases of about five thousand square miles.

In our operation there were two geophysical crews operating: Party Two and Party Three. The camps were pretty rough and ready sorts of affairs; just a caravan or two as a mess and accommodation, plus a couple of vehicles, and not much else. I was in charge of Party Two.

How it all worked was that, initially a surveyor would lay out straight survey lines, then a bulldozer would run along those lines to make it trafficable for vehicles. That would be followed up by a drilling party, who'd come along and drill shot holes at quarter-mile intervals. From memory, each of the shot holes were loaded with about thirty pounds of dynamite. Then the recording group came through, the shot holes were detonated, the ground movement was taken and in this case the results were shipped to America for processing.

To cover both camps we had just the one bulldozing contractor operating, a man called Arty Hearne, and, because the two crews could be a hundred or so miles apart, he had a bulldozer stationed at each base. To move between the two bases, and, say, if he needed to get spare parts in a hurry and that sort of thing, Arty operated a small aeroplane. Arty's idea of an airstrip was one that was just a little wider than the wingspan of his plane and roughly three hundred feet long. Obviously at that width, after he'd landed, he couldn't turn around, so he'd hook a vehicle on the back of the plane and tow it down the other end of the strip before he could take off again. Of course, there were no trees out there to get caught on and, being all sand, he had to keep the tyres on the plane at a fairly low pressure.

So that's the background, and now to the story. At this stage we were camped at a place on Andado, called North Bore. Anyhow, one of the men from Party Three — a bloke called Tom — had driven into Finke to get some supplies. It was getting well on in the day and he should've been back, but he wasn't. So the leader of Party Three asked Arty if he could fly out and see if Tom was on his way. You know, in case he'd broken down or had an accident or something along the track. Like I said, these tracks were pretty rough.

So Arty set off in his plane and about thirty miles away he spotted Tom's Toyota Land Cruiser heading towards the camp, with another Land Cruiser in front of it. Arty didn't recognise the leading vehicle so, to get a closer look, he circled around and he came in right over the top and he gunned the plane engines about four feet over the cab of the vehicle, then he landed a bit further up the track. He'd just shut the plane engines down and was somewhat taken aback when the two vehicles pulled up and written in large letters across the door of the leading Toyota was 'NT POLICE'.

It turned out that the policeman was out there in his role as deputy census enumerator. He'd been told by his boss, 'Look, we know there's two seismic crews out there somewhere. Go and find them and get them all to fill in their census forms.'

Anyhow, they proceeded to the camp of Party Three and sorted out the census forms there. Then, when the policeman found out that Party Two was about a hundred and twenty miles, or seventy sand dunes, away, he more than gratefully accepted the offer of a lift in Arty's plane.

The policeman then arrived in our camp and, of course, the first thing you do when you arrive in a camp, especially in such a remote place like that, is that you head to the kitchen-caravan for a cold beer, because that's the only place that's got a fridge. So the policeman enters the kitchen-caravan and as soon as he does he sees the young cook trying to shrink as far as he can into the corner of the caravan. The policeman recognised him immediately. 'Ah,' he said, 'gotcha. I told you that I'd track yer down, didn't I?'

It appeared this young man — the cook — had previously been working with a mobile railway gang well out along the track from Finke. One Saturday night, half the crew jumped onto one of the rail-trolleys and they went into Finke on an expedition with the boss to visit the pub, leaving the rest of them back at the camp. The blokes that had been left behind were a bit pissed off about being left out and so somewhere around midnight, after they'd knocked off the remaining beer stocks, they hit upon the bright idea of joining their mates at the Finke pub. So they jemmied open the trolley shed, stuck a rail-trolley on the track and off they headed.

Now you have to realise that, although these trolleys were motorised, they didn't have lights. Still and all, they thought the chances of them running into anyone else on the track at that time of night was next to Buckley's. Of course, the inevitable happened and they ended up having a head-on with the other rail-trolley as it was making its way back to camp.

Luckily no one was killed, though among the scattered bodies, there were a few serious injuries. But the long and the short of it was that the ringleader of the trolley shed break-in ended up in the lockup in Finke. The next morning, one of his mates —

a young cook — was handing stubbies through the bars of the back window of the cells when a voice thundered out behind him, 'So you want'a join him in there, do yer?'

Anyway, the young bloke dodged the policeman and he bolted. Off he ran, in a cloud of dust, with the policeman calling out to him, 'I'll track yer down, yer little bastard.'

As it turned out the young cook had then got a job out on our seismic crew and, as per chance, the policeman did track him down. But as the copper said, 'Oh well, you'd probably get into less strife being stuck out here in the middle of nowhere, as being stuck in the lockup with me having to feed and look after you,' and he left it at that.

# Nullarbor Highway Patrol

I'm currently on fifteen months' long-service leave and when that's done I'll retire from the police force. No, I'm not going back. It's been thirty-nine years, with most of it being remote, and while, yes, it's been a great experience, I reckon it's time to do something else, like a bit of fishing and opal mining.

I grew up over here on the Eyre Peninsula. My father was a timekeeper in the railways so we moved around a fair bit; places like Minnipa, Port Lincoln, Kadina then Adelaide for a short time. I started school when we were at Minnipa. There would've been about sixty kids, maybe more. I still remember most of the people. One of the teachers, Mr Reynolds, he was a bit of a surfer. He drove an EH Holden, which we thought was pretty good. I still remember him and also getting into strife over certain things. Oh, like the time when a few of us kids grabbed one of the teacher's cars and we put it out of gear and pushed it down behind the oval. I mean, it wouldn't have been hard to know who done it, especially with me in the mix. So we were all lined up and given the cuts. But it was worth it just to have seen the look on the teacher's face when he walked out and he saw that his car had disappeared.

Football was big at Minnipa. We were in the Le Hunte League along with towns like Wudinna, Kyancutta and Poochera. We had a mini-league, then there was the colts — the under-eighteens. Then you had the seniors, both A- and B-grade, and on Saturdays everyone would pack up and they might drive a hundred bloody mile or so just to go to a footy game. But someone you might remember: I played with a bloke by the name of Greg Phillips.

Greg went on to play for the Port Adelaide Magpies in the South Australian Football League then he went off and played for Collingwood in the old VFL — Victorian Football League.

Back then, the west coast was mainly all farming. Though whereas you had, say, thirty farms with thirty families on them, now you've got thirty farms owned by just five families. So the population's dwindled. In fact, nowadays Minnipa's just about buggered. They can't even support a footy club so they've joined in with Poochera and they've called themselves Central Areas.

Anyhow, I initially wanted to be a shearer so I put my name down with several contractors. When nothing come back I thought, Bugger it, I'll put in for the police force. This was back in the mid-1970s when there was probably about two hundred and fifty cadets going through the academy at any one time. Every three months they'd take in thirty to forty new recruits. There were thirty-six in our course, but then they started backing off and cutting it down. We were the last of the three-year course, then the next one was two years and nine months, the next one was two years and six months till they got down to the twelve-month intakes.

We lived at the academy and we had one night out — Wednesday night. That was from 5 o'clock till midnight and before you went out you'd have an inspection parade. They'd check that you were dressed properly and you had a tie on, and that it was tied right, and your shoes had to be nice and shiny and all that sort of stuff. Mind you, the tie only lasted till you got out the gate. Then it was off.

With the midnight curfew, when you got back from your night out, there was an old bloke on the gate who'd put you through another inspection and make sure you were sober. Half the bloody time you'd be half pissed and you'd stand there trying to look like you were sober. But they put you through hell, it was that regimented. They just pushed you to the limit to try to break you. If you did something wrong, it was, 'All right, everyone's doing a twelve-mile run through the sand hills.' And you did it. No question. If you were out on the parade ground and you were walking out of step they'd make you get down on the ground and do fifty push-ups or you'd have to run around the parade ground with a typewriter.

Anyhow I'd only been there a few weeks when I get this letter from Cartwright, the shearing contractors in Port Augusta. It said, 'Start on Monday.' But I thought, Nah, I've got through all this crap so far. I'm not stopping now.

Of course, these days they'd call it bastardisation and when you were actually going through it, granted, it was pretty tough. But I don't reckon it hurt anyone. I reckon the discipline was good. You look back on it now and it was the best thing ever. It certainly prepared you for a career with the police. To my mind, it was all about mateship and comradeship. Everyone was real tight. Nowadays that doesn't happen. Today you're trained to sort of beat each other — be better than the next feller — whereas in my day we were tight in together.

We graduated in January 1978 as probationary constables. After that you worked with a senior man for nine months where you attended tasking just like anyone else and, if everything went well, you went up to constable. That's what I did and I spent eighteen months in the northern suburbs of Adelaide, at Para Hills. In those days, Para Hills looked after Elizabeth, Salisbury and Gawler and at night we'd do Two Wells as well. It was certainly a good learning area. If you didn't get three or four domestic disputes in a shift there was something wrong. So you either drowned or you learnt to swim and I learnt to swim, and bloody quick.

But I always wanted to go back to the bush. I kept putting in for Ceduna and Coober Pedy, but I wasn't having much luck. Then they said, 'There's a spot at Port Lincoln.' So I went there and two years later I got Ceduna.

Ceduna was interesting in those days. It was a big farming town where they sent out a lot of grain. That created a fair bit of local industry and, because of the number of Aboriginals, there was a lot of government agencies to support them. And again I worked with some fantastic blokes. Back then there was only nine of us and we worked hard and we played hard and everyone was tight; like real tight. Our housing was provided. But police housing in those days was pretty substandard — just transportables mainly — and they'd generally put you in the poorer areas, like next to a troubled Aboriginal family or whatever, which created problems.

I remember the house next to me had this mob in it and, mate, they were just nothing but trouble — parties every bloody night, night after night after night. I hardly got a wink of sleep. Anyway, I'd had enough so I went over and said, 'Look, any more parties and I get woken up, someone's bloody well gonna get locked up.'

They're thinking I'm full of bullshit, so they go, 'Oh yeah, yeah, yeah.'

Then about two nights later they're having a party and I hear all this shouting, 'Get fucked,' and all this carry-on, so I rang my mate and said, 'Let's sort these bastards out.' So we did. We arrested a couple of them and we chucked them in the cells and locked them up, and that slowed them down.

In those days we were doing three highway patrols a fortnight across the Nullarbor to Eucla and back. Eucla's four hundred and ninety k's from Ceduna, just over the Western Australian border. We'd leave at 9 o'clock in the morning and we'd basically stop everyone and go right through them. This was just after they'd bituminised the Nullarbor Highway so, because people no longer had to drive on the shit dirt road it used to be, everyone just went on holiday. Problem being, it also opened up the gateway to a lot of movement by crooks. It was just unbelievable. So we'd get some pretty good detections with stolen cars and drugs and that. Then if you arrested someone, you'd have to turn around and take them back to Penong to drop them off at the police station there before you went back out and continued on your patrol. Sometimes you wouldn't get to Eucla till late at night.

Now while we're talking about highway patrols across the Nullarbor; one time a mate and I got called to a fatal accident forty k's east of the Western Australian border. Just at that time they'd sent us over a relief police car. It was one of those Toyota coffin-shape things. A complete load of crap. Anyhow, a lot of road trains were crossing the Nullarbor. They were only supposed to travel at a hundred k's an hour but they never did; a lot of them went in excess of a hundred and forty. So we're heading out to this accident in this old Toyota. We were going flat out and there's all these bloody road trains overtaking us. And we're going, 'Hold on, something's not right here,' and they're going that fast, we could hardly even get a registration number off them.

Anyhow, this old Toyota didn't even have a radio fitted into it so they'd sent us out with a little box with a Codan high-frequency portable thing in it. So me and my mate, we get to the accident scene. It was a head-on; road train against road train. From point of contact, the crash scene was about eight hundred metres long. It was an absolute mess. They must've both been doing about a hundred and forty k's when they hit and they just exploded. There was one deceased and so forth and we've got to call back to Ceduna because we need tow trucks and ambulances and all that. So I open up this box with the Codan radio in it and inside there's also this roll of wire and there's the instructions. They read, 'Tie wire to a rock and throw rock up into a tree as an aerial.' And me and my mate, we're out there in the middle of this bloody dead-flat nowhere, with not a tree in sight, and we're going, 'What the hell do we do now?'

It was a bloody joke really. But luckily one of the truckies was able to talk to his boss in Sydney so we got him to send a message through and they then rang back to Ceduna. But with that particular prang, after the ambulances came out, we then had to clear things up and wait for a crane from Melbourne to lift the trucks clear, so we were out there for three days straight.

But hot; it got bloody hot out there. One day, me and a mate were on highway patrol and, when we pulled into Yalata Roadhouse, it was 55 degrees Celsius in the shade. We were wearing police-issue boots — pretty much like the ones I've got on now but with the clear rubber soles — and it was so hot that, when we went to get out of the vehicle, our boots had stuck to the floor. That's true. There was no insulation between the floor matting and the actual floor itself. That was in the old Ford F100 351 V8, and when it got stinking hot it'd only do eighty k's an hour because the fuel would keep vaporising.

Then there's another one: it was another stinking hot day and this Japanese bloke was pushing a cart from one side of Australia to the other, and he was very determined to do it too. But by the time we pulled him up he was struggling; mate, he was really struggling. He was dehydrated and any exposed skin was covered in massive burns. What made matters worse was that he couldn't speak a word of English and we couldn't speak a word of Japanese and we're trying to communicate with him. We're going, 'Ah, mate, have you got anything for the sunburn?'

So we finally get that across to him and he's nodding, 'Yes. Yes. Sunscreen all okay.' Then he pulls a spray can out of his cart and its bloody Mortein fly spray. 'Yes, yes,' he goes and, to shows us how he uses it, he goes *shhhhhhh* and sprays it all about.

I mean, no wonder he was so burnt, and we thought, Nah, we're going to be picking this feller up off the road and carting him off to the mortuary if he keeps on going. And there he was, he thought Mortein fly spray was a bloody sun lotion. It only made it worse. It would've fried him. But he was that determined to push this cart of his right across the Nullarbor that we had to fight him to get him in the back of the van. Anyhow, we finally got him in and we took him to Ceduna hospital and, oh, he was as wild as hell about it too.

# Once Was Lost

I suppose one of the more interesting and controversial events I was involved in as a police officer was back in 1999 with the Bogucki search. If you might remember, Robert Bogucki was that thirty-three-year-old Alaskan who went off into the Great Sandy Desert and got lost. My understanding of it was that he was quite a religious feller who'd read something in the Bible about proving his faith in God and he'd interpreted it as, if he could get across the Great Sandy Desert, he'd gain some kind of spiritual enlightenment.

Whatever it was, the first we heard about it was when we got a call from a couple of blokes who'd been driving down the Pegasus Track, about thirty k's inland from Sandfire Roadhouse. They said, 'We've found this pushbike bogged in sand and there's a note attached to it saying that he's walking to Christmas Creek.' Christmas Creek's on the other side of the Great Sandy Desert, out between Fitzroy Crossing and Halls Creek.

After we got the call, we went out and did a reccy — reconnaissance — of about a kilometre around the spot where the bike had been left. After seeing where his tracks were leading, it was obvious that we weren't going to easily find him. That's when we decided to extend the search. We got some four-wheel-drive vehicles and we loaded up with a few SES — State Emergency Services — volunteers. Then as the search got protracted we also took along a couple of Aboriginal trackers from the nearby Bidyadanga Aboriginal Community — Bidyadanga being the old La Grange Catholic Mission set-up

— along with an Aboriginal police aide, a fella by the name of Johnny Birch. In fact, Birchy's just retired. Police aide no. 8 he was.

We then started tracking Bogucki into the Great Sandy Desert, camping out as we went. But it was funny to see how these trackers operated. What would happen was, they'd sit up on the front of our vehicle while we slowly drove along and they'd just lead us with hand signals; like they'd give a wave to go forward, so we'd go forward. Then they'd put their hand up to stop. We'd stop. They'd get off and they'd scratch around in the dirt a bit.

But, the thing was, they then wouldn't come around and say, 'We've found something.' They'd just go and perch themselves back on the front of the vehicle, get back into position and wave us on again. And this continued day after day; on, stop, off, have a bit of a scratch around, back on again and wave us forward. It was a painfully slow process and by then we'd also mounted an aerial search, again without any initial results.

Anyhow, after we'd covered about a hundred and fifty kilometres, Birchy came and saw me. He said, 'Hey, Sarge, these boys, I think they've had enough of this tracking business.'

I said, 'Why's that, mate?'

He said, 'They're a bit worried 'cause we're getting closer to some other tribes' lands.'

It was purely for cultural reasons. And it just wouldn't have been right to make them continue, so we cut them loose. Birchy also went back with the trackers. That left me; Ben Martin, who was a reporter with the *West Australian* newspaper; Rob Duncan, the photographer; and there was Ted Thompson, another sergeant, and we still had the SES fellers with us too. We then did the tracking ourselves for about another hundred kilometres and that was relatively easy because Bogucki had never deviated off the track.

Anyhow, we got to a point about two hundred and fifty kilometres into the desert and that's where Bogucki's tracks seemed to stop. When we took a closer look we could see where he'd walked around. He must've been thinking about things; you know, what to do, which way to go. Then all of a sudden he went straight over the first sand dune, heading due north. To my mind he'd obviously decided that he couldn't get to where he wanted to get, which was east, out to Christmas Creek. So he thought he'd better try to head to the Great Northern Highway, and I reckon he must've had a compass because his tracks headed dead straight north.

We then followed him over about five sand dunes. But a lot of that country had recently been burnt out and, with all the little trees having been broken off during the burning, they were like nails and we ended up staking a few tyres. It was obvious that we couldn't go any further by vehicle, so then we decided to focus on the wider aerial search. There were three main tracks out through that desert country. There was the Pegasus Track. There's another track about seventy kilometres north called the McLarty Track. Then further north again there was the Looma Aboriginal Community access road. So we saturated the area by air between McLarty Track and Pegasus Track. But still no sign.

Bogucki later said that he'd seen the planes, but he just thought they were tourists so he didn't try to attract their attention. That's what he said, though, mind you, there are also those who have suggested that, because of his single-minded determination to prove himself to God, he might not have wanted anyone to find him at that stage, a suggestion that he has denied. Whatever the reason, it further complicated the search and after something like twelve days with no sign of him, I guess the correct way of putting it was that we decided to downsize the search.

On several occasions I was asked by the media if I thought Bogucki had perished out there and I always said, 'No, I don't think he has.' There's a few reasons for that. First of all, he'd been a volunteer fireman back in Canada and he'd had a fair bit of bush trekking experience, so he knew how to survive.

Secondly, there was heaps of water out there, especially if you knew where to find it. Thirdly, this was in July; it was cool during the day and yes, it would've been cold at night, but he came from Alaska so I didn't think the cold would have bothered him. If it did, all he had to do was dig a hole in the sand and bury himself overnight and he would've been okay. I mean, if he'd been out there in the heat of November or December, it would've been a very different matter. He would've only lasted a couple of days at the most.

So that was that. Then out of the blue I get a call from my OIC — officer-in-charge. He said, 'I've got this email here from an American Miami-based mob calling themselves the 1st Special Response Group.'

I said, 'Who's that?'

'I don't know,' he said, 'but their motto is "Anytime, anywhere".'

This 1st Special Response Group turned out to be a privately funded search-and-rescue mob led by an ex-army feller called Garrison St Clair. Apparently Bogucki's old man was a high-profile person in the United States. He believed, like I did, that his son was still alive and he'd managed to organise for this team of search-and-rescue specialists, plus their dogs, to come out to Australia and continue the search. So the boss — the OIC — called me into the office and said, 'Look, it's a private search but we need you to go out with them as an advisor.'

Initially I wasn't that keen on going out again. Anyway, after thinking it over, I said, 'Yeah, okay,' and I went. I flew out in a helicopter with two of the 1st Special Response Group trackers. They wanted me to show them where we'd last seen Bogucki's tracks. They were a couple of white American guys who, mind you, actually turned out to be pretty good at what they did. The helicopter pilot was a feller by the name of Davin O'Brien. Davin's since passed away, but back then he owned the King Sound Resort Hotel and so he'd offered up his chopper in the hopes of getting some free advertising. He said to me, 'Ray, if those guys pay for the fuel I'm happy to do it. But only on the condition that, when we land, they pan the cameras down both sides of the chopper.' That's because one side had 'King Sound Resort Hotel' written on it and the other had 'Royal Mail Hotel, Meekatharra' written on it; the Royal Mail Hotel being another of his business concerns.

Anyhow, first we flew down to Dampier Downs station. Dampier Downs is a couple of hundred k's south-east of Broome and we were going to use it as a staging point to fly out to where we'd last tracked Bogucki. By that stage, Garrison St Clair had employed a local by the name of George Morris, who'd done a lot of seismic work out through that desert country so he knew the area like the back of his hand. So along with Garrison's 'convoy', as I'll call it, they'd all loaded up and they were heading out about a hundred and forty k's further north of us, along the Looma access road.

After staying overnight at Dampier Downs, the next morning we flew down to see Bogucki's tracks. No sooner had we got there than Ben Martin, the reporter from the *West Australian*, called in from Garrison St Clair's convoy and said that they'd come across some tracks up on the Looma access road. After we measured and compared the tracks, we were confident that they were Bogucki's and that he was trekking due north, into the Edgar Ranges.

We then flew up to the Looma access road to help in the search up there. By then Garrison St Clair's convoy had come across a Bible, an empty water bottle, a notebook, a tent and tarpaulin. Now, there's one thing that sticks out in my mind that I'll never forget: this Garrison St Clair was a short, stout, ex-army fellow. Anyhow, after we arrived, we were out in the desert, near the Edgar Ranges, and I said to this Garrison St Clair, I said, 'Garrison, be careful. This's death adder country.' I said, 'If any of your crew or your dogs go sniffing around and they get bitten, it'll be the end of them.'

Garrison used to smoke these big fat cigars and he was standing there dressed in his green fatigues and he looked up and he replied in his American drawl, 'Ray, I started my military career in Vietnam and I ended my military career during Desert Storm and in all that time I never lost a man in combat. Not one, and, Ray, I'm not about to lose one out here in the goddamn Australian Great Sandy Desert.'

Ben Martin, the reporter, was with me at the time and, after Garrison had said that, I looked at Ben and Ben looked at me and we wondered, Is this feller taking the piss or is he serious? I tell you, I'm sure both Ben and I were waiting for the American flag to unfurl behind us and a band to burst into 'The Star-Spangled Banner'. It was unreal.

Now the one thing I do regret out of this whole saga is that it was mid-afternoon when we were at the Edgar Ranges and I said to Ben Martin, 'Maybe we should go down and have a look where those tracks of Bogucki's go into the Edgar Ranges?'

Then we decided, 'No, it's too late in the day. We'll set up camp here for the night and head off into the ranges tomorrow.' And I still reckon, if we would've followed those tracks that afternoon we'd have found him. Anyhow, we didn't and the rest is history. By that stage, a Perth-based Channel Nine news team helicopter had joined in the search and they found Bogucki a day or two later. By then he'd been out there for forty-three days and when they came across him in a place called Geegully Creek, he was okay but he was in a pretty worn state. I think he'd lost something like twenty kilos and he'd been surviving on plants and flowers and he'd been digging into the sand in the dry creek beds and drinking the water that had seeped into the dig-holes.

So he was found.

But the story doesn't stop there. There's actually some very interesting stuff in the media about it. Richard Ackland, who back then was the host of ABC Television's *Media Watch*, got hold of the film footage of the retrieval and he gave Channel Nine's *A Current Affair* a huge serve for what they did. What happened was, when they'd landed the helicopter, they interviewed Bogucki for about ten minutes before they even offered him any clean water. What's more, they didn't bother to call in for any medical assistance. *Media Watch* suggested that they just wanted to pick him up and bring him straight back to Broome, presumably so that he could be exclusively theirs. Problem was, the Channel Nine helicopter only had four seats and all four seats were already occupied. So what they did was, they kicked the photographer, Rob Duncan, out and they left him there with some water and a handheld EPIRB and they put Bogucki in the chopper. And then it was only while they were on their way back to Broome that they started to make arrangements for another helicopter to go out and pick Rob up.

Also, interestingly, if you look at the *Media Watch* report, you'll see the original footage of Channel Nine talking to Bogucki in the gully, dressed in a dirty old T-shirt and holding a bottle of muddied water. But what they showed on Australia-wide television that night as being the moment they found him, was a shot of Bogucki on the ground with a clean white T-shirt on. What really happened there was, after they found Bogucki, he changed into a clean white T-shirt he'd been holding on to for when he got to the highway and needed to hitchhike. His thinking there was, and quite rightly so, that no one would pick him up if he looked filthy dirty.

But then with hardly having eaten for the past week or so, when they were taking off to bring Bogucki back to Broome, they offered him a banana. Once he ate the banana, he felt that he was going to be sick. So they landed the helicopter, let him out, and, not to miss a sensational filming opportunity, they lifted the chopper off again and took a shot of him from above and that was the footage they presented to the television audience as being the moment they first located him.

So in reality, he was found in a dirty shirt, filmed in a clean white T-shirt and by the time he arrived in Broome he was wearing a Channel Nine T-shirt. I think it was a shoddy piece of journalism all round and when Richard Ackland of *Media Watch* got hold of all the footage, he served it up to them in spades. And it wasn't only him. There were a lot of other people who were disgusted by Channel Nine's behaviour, a) for not calling for immediate medical aid for Bogucki and b) for leaving Rob Duncan behind and c) for concocting the footage of the moment they rescued him. I guess it runs along the line of that old saying: 'Never let the truth get in the way of a good story.'

Anyhow, that probably would've been one of the highlights of my time in Broome and even though it was of significant cost to the police, we didn't ask for compensation; though, from memory, I think Bogucki's father did later contribute somewhat toward police search costs. Then of course, to top that, he had to pay Garrison St Clair's costs and I'd suggest they would've been somewhere in the order of eighty to a hundred thousand dollars. So it was a costly exercise all round. But we never charged Bogucki with any offence.

So that's the story of the Bogucki search and funnily enough his bicycle is still out the back of the police station. You can come and have a look if you like. It's nothing special.

But in a local twist of humour, the whole Bogucki affair has sparked a Broome group of Lycra-clad bike riders to name themselves the 'Bogucki Riders'. You might even run into them while you're up here. You can't miss them; their motto is 'Getting lost to find ourselves'.

# Over the Moon

Both my parents were Aboriginal. They were from the Wirangu people and also from the Mirning people. I was born at a town called Penong, which is out on the Nullarbor Plain, an hour west from Ceduna. Penong's known for its windmills. You can't miss them. When you come into Penong, you go down a big hill, then down on the flat, and just on the edge of town, you'll see them all. When the Europeans came they built all the windmills to get to the artesian water.

In our family there's six girls, including me, and two boys. Dad worked as a shearer and a station hand on sheep stations out on the Nullarbor. Then we moved back to near Bookabie, which is about a twenty-minute drive on the western side of Penong. I started school at Bookabie School. Then, when Dad leased the property at Colona Station, us kids, we went to Coorabie School. It would've been close to an hour on a bus each way. There was just the one teacher at Coorabie School and about twenty kids, and me and my brothers and sisters and the Cox kids were the only Aboriginals at the school. A lot of kids I went to school with back then, I still see them now.

Then in 1974 I went to Concordia College, which is a girls' boarding school in Adelaide. That was all done through the Lutheran minister from Yalata Aboriginal Community. Yalata was just up the road from where we were living at Colona Station. But I only stayed at Concordia a year. To tell you the truth, I got a bit lonely and so I came back to our family homeland. I preferred it there. I felt better.

I'm now fifty-five and I've got three children: my eldest son is thirty-five, then I've got a thirty-one-year-old daughter and a twenty-nine-year-old son. He's got his own band. They're called Desert Sea and they play everywhere. One time they were going on tour and so me and my sister, we went with them all the way right up to Broome, in Western Australia, then right over into the Northern Territory and across to Darwin. My son, he first started off with his dad in the Coloured Stone and he's followed in his dad's footsteps. They've got their separate bands now, but his dad might say, 'Jason, I need you to come and help me with this concert thing,' and so Jason will go with him.

Then how I got into the police was that one of my cousins, Wayne Miller — Wayne's deceased now, but he said to me, 'Jenny,' he said, 'I think you should join the police force and become a community constable.' A community constable is the more up-to-date term for what used to be an Aboriginal police aide.

I was only in my early thirties back then, and I said, 'Oh, I don't know.'

'Well, think about it,' he said.

So I did. I thought about it and I applied for it. There were three positions going in Ceduna and my brother also went for a job. But I can tell you, the night before my interview, I was that nervous about it all that I just did not sleep. Then when I went for my interview down at the police station, we'd only just started and the senior sergeant who'd come up from Adelaide to help with the interviews, he goes, 'I think we've heard enough from you now, Jenny. Thanks.'

I thought, Oh, is that it? And I didn't have too good of a feeling as to how it all went.

My mum was still alive back then. We were living in Ceduna at that time and when I got a letter back, I opened it and I said, 'Mum, I got the job,' and we both sat down and we cried. Yeah, I was just so over the moon; over the moon, I was.

But I think that what was behind me wanting to go for the police was that I'd lived in a domestic violence situation. We wasn't together at that time, but he was always coming back and forth. So I thought, Well, if I join the police force, perhaps he'll stay away from me. Which he did. It really helped, you know, because I could never go back to that sort of situation again. Not now. Not ever.

But through it all I was never out of a job. I've worked all my life. I used to work for Aboriginal hostels. That's helping with accommodation for people who have got nowhere to live. That's just down on Mackenzie Street. It can be anyone, black or white. Then the last job I had before I joined the police was at the fresh seafood shop over there, just near the hotel.

As a community constable I do just about all the same duties as a fully fledged copper does. When I first started, because I had to learn, I had a partner and he showed me everything from doing arrests and interviewing people and how to do witness statements and all of that. I worked with him for twelve months, then I went out with other coppers, just doing whatever jobs they did.

That was a way back. Then over the years, I've slowed down a bit. Now I do more things, like going to community meetings and helping with domestic violence issues. It's more of a liaison thing. I can understand their language so I deal a lot with the local Aboriginal people and the people from out at Yalata Community. My job's never-ending for twenty-four hours. I live just around the corner over there and sometimes people will be waiting on my doorstep or they'll be ringing my door bell, night and day, or they'll just talk to me when I'm walking down the street.

I help out wherever I can. Perhaps they might want a bit of food or I'll help them out with clothing and blankets. The Red Cross give me a lot of stuff, and so do the people from around town. And my workmates, they'll always help out. So I just put it all in my shed and it's there when anyone wants it. Then if I haven't got what some of the women want, I'll go through my wardrobe and grab something out of there for them, and that's okay.

Being a community copper's a real eye-opener. It was all sort of scary at first because when you see the police shows on the TV, you think, Is that for real? Then when you're out there and you're doing it, you realise, Yes, it is. It is for real; like when you go to domestics and jobs like that and you think, Oh, he's gonna come out and bash me up. But over the years you toughen up a bit and you learn how to deal with it. So I'll go out on patrols and I'll make sure I'm there to assist when they do the arrests and all of that.

But talking about it being like it's on telly: one time me and this other police officer, we were on night shift and an alarm went off at one of the clubs. So we jumped into our police vehicle and we go racing down there and as we do we passed a car that's got two kids in it. 'That's them,' so we spun around and we chased them and as they turned a corner, their car door flies open and this boy comes rolling out.

I said, 'Stop the car,' and I jumped out and I grabbed the boy and the other lad just drove off. We didn't catch up with him till a couple of days after. But, oh, my heart was really pumping, I was that worked up about it. And the boy that'd fallen out, he was in a pretty bad way, so we took him to the hospital. He was okay in the end. But when I think back about that time, I go, Did I really do that? That's just like it is on the telly.

Then in early May I went to a job — a domestic — with this other copper, while a third copper stayed in the police station to look after the prisoners we had in there. So we went to this job, but it was a very threatening situation so I said to the copper I was with, 'Let's go back and talk to the copper back at the station.'

So we went back and told him the situation and then, after he'd sorted things out, he came back with us to help make the arrest. I was assisting at the time and I'd put my leg on the offender's leg, where he was laying. The second copper had the other leg and the third copper was trying to get his hand out from underneath to put the handcuffs on. So I had my leg over there, just like that, and I'd just grabbed his hand when I saw all this blood everywhere. I just thought it must've been the offender's. So when he was under control, I went and washed my hands with the antiseptic we had in the car. But my knee just didn't feel right. To start with, I thought I'd just strained it. It wasn't until after we'd got back to the station and done all the paperwork that I went to get up to go to another job and I said, 'Gee, my knee's really aching.'

But that was all right and I started walking okay — you know, not real good but just okay — and I went to this other job and at the end of the night I went home. Next morning I go to jump out of bed and I couldn't walk properly. It turned out that I'd torn something in my knee and so I've been on light duties ever since. I've just got to stay in the office. I can't even go out on patrol.

So now, tomorrow I'm flying down to Adelaide to have keyhole surgery on my knee. Apparently I've also got a couple of cysts in there and so they're going to give it all a good clean-up and that should fix it. I don't know how long I'm going to be off work. Probably a couple of weeks, then I'll take my holidays and when I come back I'll be back on the road again.

# People of the Outback

Marla's in the far north of South Australia, on the Stuart Highway about a hundred miles south of the Northern Territory border. It's a lovely little spot. I'm not exactly sure what the population was when I was there, but the roadhouse was the biggest employer in town, and still is. Then there was just a few Mines and Energy people, a couple of nurses from the medical clinic and a few private citizens.

There were eight of us stationed at Marla: four constables, two senior constables, a sergeant and a senior sergeant. Our primary role was to police the APY Lands — the Anangu Pitjantjatjara Yankunytjatjara lands — up to the Territory, and we'd also do eight-day patrols right over to the Western Australian border, to Pipalyatjara. How that worked was that two of us would head off on a four-day patrol out to Pipalyatjara, then they'd fly the police Cessna out to pick us up and they'd drop off two other officers and they'd drive back for four days.

As in any normal society, the APY Lands had its issues. There was the usual petty crimes such as assaults, driving without a licence, unregistered vehicles, with just the occasional serious crime. But there was quite a big problem with petrol sniffing and alcohol consumption and the damage it did to the entire community. Grog and petrol running were common. They'd buy alcohol or fuel from outside the APY Lands and bring it back in to sell. There wasn't much coming in from Western Australia. Most of it came from the Territory or from south of the APY Lands, from Coober Pedy way and places like that.

With every police jurisdiction that sits on the boundary with another, we'd interact. When someone commits a crime, a state border's not the protection they might think it to be. Yes, you might hear them say in the movies, 'I'm heading to safety across the state line.' That may happen in America, but in Australia there's the powers of a citizen's arrest, plus there's common law rights to pursue a felon across a border. So if someone's fleeing a murder, we don't need to be sworn in as a special constable to go across the border to apprehend them. Special constables were only sworn in for the less high-profile crimes, like common assault or traffic offences. The upshot there was that we were sworn in as special constables in the Northern Territory and we'd do the odd patrol up through Uluru to Yulara to link in with the Territory police. It was harder to link up with the Western Australians. Because their area was so huge, we didn't catch up with them all that often. They were stationed at Laverton and, to get to the border, they'd go on seven- or ten-day patrols over to Wingellina and Blackstone and those places. Of course we'd speak to them on the phone. You know, 'An offender's heading out that way, can you apprehend them.'

But you just had to treat it all with remote policing in mind, especially in relation to the limited resources we had at hand. We had two Aboriginal police aides — community constables as they're now known — out in each of the APY communities and each police officer from Marla was given a community to be the mentor of. Mine was Ernabella — Pukatja is its Indigenous name — and I'd work with the community constables out there. They were part of the team and we supported them the best we could. They'd call into Marla on the HF radio each morning. They wore the khaki uniform like we did. Only very rarely did we wear firearms out there, so of course they didn't. They had a police station and a police car, usually a Land Cruiser utility with a cage house enclosed. When we were out there on patrol, we'd work together; like if there were warrants out, they'd help us find the local malefactors. We'd then make an arrest and bail them and, when the court circuit went out there, we'd support the community constables in helping ensure the people would come to court.

Correctional Services was also in the APY Lands. Correctional Services is split into two: there's the jail side of it, then there's the community corrections side of it where you work off your fine, say for a non-payment of fines warrant. They try to use community corrections rather than incarceration. Correctional Services will tell you that keeping people gainfully engaged is far better than having them sitting around doing nothing in a prison cell. Their time spent in community corrections worked out to fifty dollars a day. So if you had a two hundred and fifty dollar fine, you'd arrange to work in whatever community you were from for five days to work off your debt.

Then I left the police force in the early 2000s. That was for various reasons; the major one being I had a young family and I had to consider their future educational opportunities. By that stage I'd worked in most of the communities in the far north of the state. Also, times were changing and I was more of a community police officer than any type of vicious law enforcer. I got heavily involved in every community I worked in. It was very rare that I wore a firearm. Now, of course, you have to wear one all the time.

And while I'd seen Australia at its worse, in relation to people and their behaviour and the horrors of fatal car accidents and things like that, probably the greatest memories of my years of policing was that I got to visit parts of Australia that the average Anglo-Saxon would never get to visit and possibly no one's ever been to. Most people wouldn't know that the highest mountain in South Australia is Mount Woodroffe, which is behind Ernabella Aboriginal Community. It's not Mount Lofty, in the Adelaide Hills, or St Mary Peak, up at

Wilpena Pound. In my day, the land was destocked so there was a lot of magnificent virgin outback country. I've been to places where I've seen animals, trees and plants you'd usually only find in books. I've seen waterholes of pristine beauty to which, due to the element of restriction, no one has access. I've seen waterfalls cascading down remote mountain ranges after rain. I've seen sunsets where I wished I had a camera. I've been on roads that are closed because of recent flooding where the land's a vast carpet of flowers. Just spectacular.

So yes, I finished up with the police on the Friday and started on the Monday with what's now known as the Outback Communities Authority. I just transferred over my police pension and long service leave and I moved into a job that paid more. We administer local government across the whole outback of South Australia. It was a pretty easy transition because I knew the area very well and I knew a lot of the people up there. Actually, we still use some of the people from when I was a policeman. I guess it was a promotion in some ways but, more importantly, I'm still doing what I love doing, which is working for and with the people of the outback.

# Policeman-the-Bastard

In 1978 I was transferred to the one-man police station out at Gascoyne Junction, in Western Australia. That one man was me and so I was officer-in-charge with the rank of senior constable. My patrol area covered about 46,500 square kilometres with a population of around two hundred, which included the Aborigines. So it was a pretty sparse and isolated existence. To give you some idea, Gascoyne Junction's a hundred and sixty-nine kilometres inland from Carnarvon and over seven hundred kilometres from Meekatharra, which was even further inland. It was mainly sheep country back in those days, with most of the stations being around a million acres. It took in the Kennedy Range. It also took in Mount Augustus, which is the biggest rock in the world; two and a half times larger than Ayers Rock — or Uluru as it's now known.

The actual township of Gascoyne Junction only consisted of the police station, a school, a shire office, the hotel and a few houses. There was a population of about thirty-five. That included my family, the teacher and his family and the people who owned the hotel. There was the shire clerk, Ian Ball — 'Eyeball' as he was known — and his wife. Then there were the shire workers, the road maintenance people and the like. The only other person in town at that stage was the Agriculture Protection Board fellow. He was in charge of all the doggers — the blokes who used to go out eradicating the dingoes — and he looked after the poisoning of weeds like mesquite. There's a bit of a hullabaloo about that these days because back then they were using an Agent Orange–type poison that may have caused cancer in people.

The shire office was a focal point in town as it also contained the telephone exchange and post office. Eyeball and his wife ran all that. The phone exchange was only open from 9 a.m. till midday. Then they'd have a lunch break and come back on from one till five. We had a telephone in the police residence, but it only worked occasionally. It was an old plug-in, wind-the-handle, party-line type where everyone along the line could listen in on your conversation. The police station had a separate phone. If you were making a business call it went to the shire office-cum-telephone exchange and they plugged you into the Geraldton exchange, which went on to Perth via the Mullewa exchange. At night, just in case of an emergency, a direct phone connection was left on between the hotel and the police station. Then if you wanted to make a private after-hours call out of Gascoyne Junction, there was a phone box outside the police station. So if we wanted to speak to family in Perth we'd have to go out into the phone box where you'd wind the handle and tell the telephone exchange girls at Mullewa who you were and who you wanted to connect to and they'd put the call through.

We only had the one child back then, a preschool-age daughter. My wife had previously been a school teacher and, with the school being right behind the police station, if the regular teacher went away, my wife would jump the fence and go over and be the relief teacher, and she'd take our daughter with her.

The house and the police station were in the same large yard. The police station was made out of brick and the house was an asbestos building on stumps. It only had the one air conditioner, so it was a hot bloody joint in summer. We had an old weather station on our block and, just for interest's sake, my wife used to take the daily temperatures and so forth. The highest temperature she read was 48.2 degrees centigrade, and that's pretty much the way it stayed for days on end. Then in the winter time, the cold winds would blow in off the desert and it'd be down to bloody freezing.

I had a Land Rover as a police vehicle to start with. It was a heap of crap. It wasn't air conditioned and, because the dirt roads and river crossings were so rough, the thing rattled and shook so much that the windows kept falling out. Then I'd been at Gascoyne for about two months when I got a message to go down to Perth to pick up a new police car. My superintendent was stationed in Geraldton, so I got in touch with him and got permission for my wife and daughter to come along as well. It was a shocking trip in that old Land Rover. We broke down twice. First the generator failed and we had to get towed into Northampton. Further on it broke down again and we got towed into Moora. By the time we reached Perth, it had taken us twenty-nine hours. The new police vehicle was a Toyota Land Cruiser ute; you know, the ones with the air conditioning under the dash, so the passenger gets frozen knees.

I really don't think the people down in Perth realised that Gascoyne Junction was one of the most isolated of all the state's police stations. Because, after I got the new vehicle, I put in a requisition for a vulcanising kit plus tyre levers and so forth for mending punctures, and I was told to take my tyres to the local Beaurepaires to get fixed. That would've been Carnarvon which, as I said, was a hundred and sixty-nine kilometres away. To prove the point, I climbed up the water tower and I took a photograph of the town. Then I drew it all out on a bit of paper and wrote in the mileages to all the big towns. A couple of weeks later, all the tyre-mending equipment arrived.

A similar thing happened after the old lawnmower blew up and I put in a requisition for a new one. They said, 'Get a quote from your local lawnmowing contractor.' So I got a quote from Geraldton and one from Carnarvon. They were both around thirty dollars for the mowing and near on a couple of hundred dollars to cover their travel. A lawnmower arrived the following week.

As for my patrols: having to regularly go away for days on end I got permission to take my wife and daughter with me. We'd stay on the sheep stations and, so that the powers-that-be could keep in touch with me, I used the Flying Doctor radio. I also had the police long-range radio, but that was terrible. When you talked on it, the noise it made sounded like pigeons in a loft. It'd go 'bloop, bloop, bloop'. And when I went out on these patrols I'd always take a toolbox with me. That's because the station owners, or 'squatters' as they were called, were always out working on the property and they never got around to doing much inside the house fence. So if the wives wanted things like cup hooks put in or doors fixed, I'd do all their odd jobs, which they were very grateful for.

These patrols were also a fantastic experience for my wife and daughter. So we got to know everyone and when they had shire meetings or whatever in Gascoyne, a lot of the station owners would either drive or fly in with their wives. So while the men were off doing whatever it was, their wives would come over home and have a good old chat to my wife. In fact, all these years later, we're still very good friends with a lot of people from the area.

In those days, with Gascoyne Junction being classed as 'remote', the maximum posting was for two years. They didn't want you to stay any longer. Maybe they thought you'd go stir crazy. I don't know. But it wasn't that good for families. If you had health issues, the Flying Doctor was the only connection, and if your wife was pregnant, she had to go to Carnarvon to have the baby. Carnarvon was also where I went to do the banking. That'd probably be once a month and it was dirt all the way. A lot of our groceries and gas and newspapers also came out from Carnarvon on the mail truck. You'd phone an order through and if it didn't rain, you got a mail truck every week. If it did rain, you didn't. Then we'd also order in bulk from Perth.

But as a policeman you were responsible for many things. If the Flying Doctor was needed, you went out and arranged to have the flares lit on the gravel airstrip. In those days, the flares were made from Sunshine milk tins with diesel-soaked sand and a wick in them. When you went on patrol, part of the job was to check on the welfare of the Aborigines out on the stations. You'd also issue driver's licences to them. Most times the licences were restricted to driving in the Shire of Upper Gascoyne only. If they wanted to go down to Meekatharra, to see their relatives, I could also issue them with a driver's licence that included the Shire of Meekatharra. I rarely did driving tests because in the Gascoyne and the Meekatharra shires there were no stop signs or crossings or whatever, so I usually just asked the station owner if they could drive. But if they were going to larger places like Carnarvon, where there were stop signs and pedestrian crossings and all of that, I'd give them a proper driving test then.

Some of the Aborigines had their own cars; 'motors' they called them. They had lots of different sayings; when you wanted to ask who the driver was, you'd say, 'Who was on the handle?' And you never wrote their Aboriginal name on the licence; it was always their white-feller name. That's because they thought that if you wrote their Aboriginal name down on a piece of paper and sent it away, they'd lose their name. It was just a belief of theirs and so it'd be Charlie Snowball. He's still alive up there actually. Ernest Edney's another one. Then there was the Dingo boys, Fridee Dingo and Billy Dingo. So I did all that and then I also went around and did a bit of a census of the Aborigines once a year, which was more difficult than you'd think because they moved about so much.

Another responsibility was the livestock waybills. If a station was carting stock you'd issue them with a waybill book on behalf of the Department of Agriculture. Then, if they were taking stock from A to B, they'd have to write down how many head they were carrying, where they were going and what their ear tags were. So I'd issue those and I'd have to, or supposedly have to, check on them too when the stock was being moved.

On the law-and-order side of things, there were never too many hassles. Most times, any problems were dealt with in an appropriate manner by the community. We had two major annual horse race meetings; the Landor and Junction races. They were three- to four-day events and people would come from everywhere. They were the great social gatherings of the year and, out at the track, we had a wooden electric pole cemented in the ground and if anyone got out of hand I'd just shackle them to the pole. Though, once again, that was pretty rare because the community usually sorted things out. Yes, they'd come over and tell me that something was up, but they'd mostly deal with it. You know, that they'd sent the person on their way or whatever — sent them packing. There was also a lot of mining exploration going on and if any of the miners were in town and caused trouble I'd just let their boss know and he'd sort it out.

But we just loved it. There was no TV so we read a lot of books. I'd been a stamp collector since I was a kid and I got to sit down and sort out all my stamps. We did a lot with our daughter. She learnt a lot up there too. We lived on goat meat. I'd learnt to kill and butcher my own meat. We made our own bread. It's also a very rich area for gemstones so I collected gemstones. It was good socially too. They'd bring movies out on the mail truck and we'd have movie nights. As far as sports went, the north mail run would play cricket out on the gravel airstrip against the south mail run. Then when the shearing teams came to town, we'd play cricket against them.

Yes, so we left in 1980 and the police station closed about three or four years ago when they built the big eight-million-dollar complex at the Aboriginal community out near Mount Augustus, which is something that sticks in everyone's craw. So I won't go there. So the place has changed an awful lot. And we really had some great identities back then too. There was an old Polish fellow, Harry. Harry got around in his Land Rover with his dog, Popeye. He'd go and camp out in the bush and build water tanks for the property owners from local stone. And when he had enough money, he'd come into the hotel and go on a bender.

He'd start off on beer and he'd end up on vodka. He'd make a real mess of himself and so they'd ring me and I'd go down and get old Harry. He'd be dead drunk and we'd load him and Popeye into his Land Rover, then we'd drive them out of town to a clay pan somewhere. I'd leave them there with sufficient water and a carton of beer. Next day Harry would wake up and realise that he was on his way out of town. He was never any trouble really, but that's just the way you dealt with him.

Then there were the three old pensioners who'd built separate fibro houses over the other side of the river, over the crossing. The town's called Gascoyne Junction because it's at the junction of the Lyons and the Gascoyne rivers and one time the river ran and the three pensioners needed fuel to run their lighting plants and so on. So I got an Aboriginal fella who lived near town and we three-quarter filled a forty-four-gallon drum with fuel and we drove upstream a bit, then we swam it across the river, down to these old pensioners.

They were bits of characters themselves. There was Bob Foy. Bob had apparently humped his bluey around the country as a kid. There was George Wansborough. George had worked on a shearing team as a cook or something. He'd had a stroke. He'd introduce me to everyone as 'Policeman-the-Bastard'. If my daughter went down the hotel with me to get a cool drink, he'd say to her, 'Your dad, Policeman-the-Bastard.' That was pretty much the extent of his vocabulary. The other feller was Billy Barr. Billy had been a shearer and he suffered extremely badly from arthritis.

But these three old pensioners, every day they'd drive across the river crossing in George's old HQ Holden station wagon and they'd go to the hotel and they'd have three beers each; a round each. Then they'd buy a carton of King Browns — the big bottles — and they'd go back over the river. And that was it for the day. They'd just sit down and drink the beer and talk. God knows what about.

# Policing 'The Coen'

There's this perception around that, back in our early days of settlement, the Native Police, as they were called, just went around shooting blackfellas for the white feller's greater cause. Now there's no question that that did happen. But there's more to it than that. There was retaliation from both sides. What you've got to realise is that those were the times when the government of the day was keen for the state to be developed and so white people were moving out into these outlying regions and, of course, the Aborigines were trying to protect their country.

That's why I wrote the book *Policing 'The Coen' 1885–2011*, which is an attempt to record historical incidents of policing in Far North Queensland, particularly around the Coen. The Coen refers to the Coen River, which is roughly halfway up Cape York Peninsula, seventy-five miles north of Musgrave. White settlement started to occur in the area as far back as the early 1880s when gold prospectors ventured north from the Palmer River goldfields. In those early days, the camps that the white prospectors set up were very small; mainly just for a few individuals. But even back then there were recorded incidents of Aborigines taking picks and shovels and axes out of the prospectors' camps, and the prospectors retaliating against them for that. But, to the Aborigines, these implements were far better for digging and chopping than what they'd been using.

A couple of years later, the Overland Telegraph Line came through. It started down at the Lynd River, which is just inland from Mareeba, and it ran right up through the centre of the peninsula to Thursday Island, then across overseas to

Indonesia and beyond. That was completed in 1887 and in the process of it being built, the Aborigines decided that the wire on the telegraph lines was excellent for spears. So they were pulling the wire off the telegraph line, and again there was retaliation for that as well.

But by the late 1800s–early 1900s, goldmining was dominant in that area and so the white population grew. As I said, it was mainly just a few individuals to start with. Then there might've been half a dozen miners come together to form a syndicate. In fact, at one stage there was a big goldmine right in the middle of Coen, called the Great Northern. Then of course there were a number of smaller mines scattered around the area, and it all worked well for a few years until they started to run out of gold. But during this time of prosperity, all these people required meat. So the cattle men followed on and a more substantial settlement grew, and it all caused a lot of friction between the blacks and the whites. Things got so bad that the commissioner of the time instructed the sub-inspector at Cooktown to proceed to the Coen and establish a Native Police presence there and to patrol up to the Archer River, which is about sixty miles north of Coen.

But as I was saying, let's put it in perspective because a lot of good work was done by those serving police officers at the time, much of which has not been presented to the present-day public. For example, take Queensland Police Commissioner Parry-Okeden. In the late 1800s, it was brought to his attention that there was a lot of friction between the Native Police and the Aborigines. This stemmed largely from the various small clans of Aborigines spearing cattle and horses for their own consumption. Of course, in the heat, the freshly killed meat would only last for a couple of days so they'd only eat what they could and leave the rest to rot.

So Police Commissioner Parry-Okeden, amongst others, particularly Sub-Inspector Lomond at Cooktown, attempted to stop this practice by having the police supervise the killing of a bullock at selected locations around Cape York. This was to happen on a given full moon and it was to allow as many of the Aboriginal clans as possible to come in together and partake in a feast of fresh meat. And it worked well. It stopped many of the spearings and it also helped appease the Aborigines in their attempts to thwart the spread of grazing throughout those outlying areas.

You may well ask why these events took place on a full moon. The answer there is simple: whilst the Aborigines did not have the knowhow nor the means of telling the date and the time, they most certainly knew when the full moon was going to be. To that end, word would go out, 'We're going to kill a bullock at Rokeby Station when there's a full moon.' Rokeby's about sixty-five miles north-west of Coen. Or, 'We're going to kill a bullock up near Moreton Telegraph Station on the next full moon.' Rokeby Station and Moreton Telegraph Station were just two points I know of that recorded the killing of a bullock for such an occasion, and I understand there was a number of others as well.

Just sticking with Police Commissioner Parry-Okeden for the moment: another example of where a lot of good work was done was in 1897 when he came up by boat from Brisbane and did a three-month packhorse and boat trip throughout Cape York Peninsula. With him he took Sub-Inspector Lomond from Cooktown and two Aboriginal trackers, or black troopers as they were called. Back in those days, there were a great many groups, each containing sixty to a hundred nomadic Aborigines, all spread throughout Cape York Peninsula. Along that journey Commissioner Parry-Okeden met with these numerous Aboriginal clans and, through interpreters, tried to explain the process of the settlement of the land. He spoke of how they — the blacks — should coexist with the white people that were coming into the country. He emphasised how the police were there to protect the Aborigines, just as long as they did the right thing. He also counselled the local Native Police in how to deal humanely with these issues.

In covering that vast distance, Commissioner Parry-Okeden and his party rode from Cooktown right up through the peninsula, then back out through Port Stewart by boat and up to Thursday Island. From Thursday Island he boated down the west coast of the peninsula where the party rowed up the Ducie River for some fifty miles. They then went south to Mapoon Mission, as it was then known back in those days. Then right down to Normanton, in the Gulf of Carpentaria before returning up through Thursday Island and eventually back to Brisbane.

So as I was saying, while the current perception is that we white fellers just rushed in and took the country from the Aborigines and treated them badly, such was not entirely the case. Because a lot of very good work was done by many a good, honest and committed serving police officer of that era; and that's what I was trying to get across in my book *Policing 'The Coen' 1885–2011*.

# Regret Jobs

I'm a Western Australian boy. Until I was six I spent a lot of time in the country. I grew up in the mid-west — Gascoyne area. My father was a truck driver and we followed him around — Mount Magnet, Meekatharra, Cue and up at Roebourne. I'm the youngest of four and, being as young as I was back then, I can't remember as much about those earlier times as my older siblings do. Then when my father left the family, Mum was stranded so we ended up in Perth and that's where I was living when I joined the police.

School was a bit of a disaster. Looking back now, I would've liked to have gone all the way through, but, to be honest, I just wasn't very good at it and, perhaps more importantly, I didn't have the interest in it. By that stage, my older siblings had married and left home so there was just me and Mum. Mum was about this high — tiny — but she was a very strong and independent woman and she made it clear, 'You're not leaving school until you get a job.'

'Okay,' I said and so I went to work with a mate who was a plasterer.

But, no, she said, 'That's not good enough. Get a proper job.'

I then got in touch with the R&I Bank, which is now Bankwest, and they said, 'Come in and do the test.' So I went to town. I arrived in the room and I found a spare desk and I put my pens and pencils down. Back in those days I smoked cigarettes, so I just ducked outside for a quick puff before the test. When I came back, a young lady had come along and she'd put my pens and pencils on the floor and she was sitting in my seat. At that age,

I was a bit nervous around young ladies, so I didn't want to confront her. But when I looked around, all the other seats had been taken so I just grabbed my stuff and walked out. And that was it. My banking career had ended before it had begun.

When I got outside, my first thought was, Shit, I'm in trouble here. What am I going to do now? Mum's gonna go crook.

By then I was up on Horseshoe Bridge in Perth and at the top of the bridge there was a city police station.

'Here's a go,' I said, so I walked inside and there was this old crusty sergeant behind the counter. I said, 'What've you gotta do to become a copper?'

He said, 'What the fuck would you wanna be a copper for?'

I said, 'Because my mum won't let me leave school if I don't get a proper job.'

'Okay,' he said and he grabbed a form, pushed it over and grumbled, 'fill this in.'

So I filled in the form and handed it back to this crusty old sergeant. He didn't seem too impressed about it, so my immediate thought was, I've obviously missed out here. I've got to do something. I can't go home to Mum empty-handed.

Back in those days, both the navy and army recruiting offices were down on Wellington Street, so I went down there and I filled out the forms to join them as well. When I got home, Mum asked how the test for the bank went. I lied and said, 'I don't think I did very well. They were very hard questions.' Then, like it was an afterthought, I added, 'But I've also applied for the police, the army and the navy.'

Well, the army and the navy never got back to me, but the cops did. You hear a lot of people say how they'd always wanted to be a cop since they were a little kid, but that certainly wasn't the case for me. I just needed a proper job to keep Mum satisfied.

I then joined the police as a cadet at the age of seventeen. As a cadet you just do office duties and things like that until you come of age. Then you go into the police academy. I went through the academy as an eighteen-year-old. Normally you'd have to wait till you're nineteen. But this was during the America's Cup era when they wanted to push a bunch of cops through in readiness for that huge event and they'd decided you could go through if you turned nineteen during the course. Which I did.

It was a seventeen-week course. The training was very regimented and gruelling. There was a big focus on the physical side so, no matter what shape you started out in, you came out rippling fit. We had a fairly brutal ex-navy instructor as our physical training instructor. I'll never forget him. He'd been at the academy for twenty years and the softest part about him was his teeth, so we were pretty disciplined and you certainly didn't answer back.

Anyway, I completed the course and ironically the first place I worked was at the city police station up on Horseshoe Bridge. So I ended up sitting on the opposite side of the counter from where I'd been handed the application forms by the crusty old sergeant who'd said, 'What the fuck would you wanna be a copper for?'

Then, yeah, I wandered around Perth for a while and when I became a detective I went down to Albany. Albany's a fantastic spot about two hundred and fifty miles south of Perth. It's a main regional centre. In the late '90s there were about thirty thousand people living there. The police district went east, out as far as Ravensthorpe, then north, all the way up to Brookton, which is on the doorstep of Perth. It's a pretty big area. We had about seventy cops in Albany itself and about another hundred and sixty spread throughout the smaller cop shops in the region. The countryside was just beautiful and the people were great and the work was really rewarding. This was before my wife and I had kids, so we had time to ourselves. We did a lot of squidding and we had a little boat. I love fishing, and we did a lot of wine appreciation. It was a very good time in our lives.

But I hit the ground running. What usually happens is that, when you arrive in a new place, first you go and check your house out, then you go and stay at a hotel for the night. Then the following day the removalist truck comes and so you unpack all your gear and get a few things into place before you start work. Anyhow, my wife and I, we'd just rolled into town. All my work clothes were still boxed away. Being Albany, it's freezing. I'm there in my tracksuit pants and ugg boots and the phone rings.

'How you going, mate? My name's Trevor Evans. I'm your boss. I don't know you from a bar of soap, but the other two detectives are out of town. We've got a homicide. I'll be around soon to pick you up.'

Apparently one bloke had stabbed another bloke to death. I thought, Well, what a welcome. I'd better get out of my ugg boots.

So I put on some shoes, then Trevor picked me up and we headed down to do this homicide investigation. A lot needs to be done in the first twenty-four to forty-eight hours of a homicide and, because there was only the two of us detectives, we had to split up and work with our uniformed colleagues. So things were very intense. Then after I'd put the body through to the morgue and all of that sort of stuff, I somehow ended up being stuck at the hospital by myself, along with the keys to the police vehicle. So I had a car but, with having just arrived in Albany, I didn't know my way around the place, so I had to ring up the cop shop to get directions back to the police station. And I could just imagine all the young uniformed coppers going, 'Oh yeah, we've got a good one here. Our new detective can't even find his way to work.'

That was my introduction to Albany. It was a great place. It was a busy place; always plenty to do. We did a lot of drug investigations and child abuse cases. There was also some family feuding between Indigenous folk within our district, which resulted in a few serious assaults. It was just the usual. Well, it's usual to us in the police force, though perhaps not so much for the general public.

But there's a few investigations that stick with you right through your life and they're the ones that you just couldn't solve. One was when I was investigating officer in a case where a bloke reported that his young wife had fallen off The Gap. Just like Sydney, in Albany there's a place called The Gap. It's a very rugged and treacherous piece of coastline and this feller told us that he and his young wife had been fishing out on a ledge and that he'd turned his back and when he turned around again, she was gone. Very early on in the investigation we were extremely suspicious. First, there's a massive drop of probably about two hundred feet and so you'd need a hell of a long fishing line if you were going to try to catch a fish from there. We then found out that his wife didn't like heights. What's more, she didn't even like fishing and, at that time, she didn't like him too much either.

Personally it was a really difficult investigation because the young lady had a lovely daughter and she had a really nice family. Her parents were of the staunch belief that the husband had played a role in her disappearance, as did we. We still think that. But we don't know. We've never been able to prove anything.

What we suspect was that he'd murdered his wife somewhere else and he'd also disposed of her body elsewhere. But we needed to check out his story thoroughly, so it turned into a massive search-and-rescue. We tried any number of things. We even had divers down in The Gap and all of that. But to no avail. We were unable to find the body. We weren't able to prove anything and the husband ended up committing suicide some six or seven years later by shooting himself. Whether that's connected, I don't know, but I'd suggest it probably is. That's my suspicion anyway. And not being able to bring that level of finality to a family and for them to still have their daughter missing is one of what I call my 'regret jobs'.

The thing is, there's a public expectation that we — the police — should be able to solve things; that we'll find the people who are culpable and we'll be able to bring them to justice and things will come to some sort of a resolution. Even if it is just finding a body. And we take that responsibility very seriously, because we also see how our job is to fix things and when you don't fix things, you feel like you've failed. And that's one of those occasions for me. So every time I hear that they've uncovered some human remains, especially if it's down that way, I think, Please, please let it be her. Let there be some resolution, for the family's sake.

# Scary

If you don't mind, out of respect, I won't mention where this happened nor give you any names or anything, but it was probably the most scary time I've experienced as a policeman. To put it into perspective, there was quite a high crime rate in this particular town; car theft, burglary, anti-social behaviour and all of that. Sometimes linked to that crime were the many kids that used to roam the streets. In fact, at night they thought they owned the place.

Now to quote the law under the Child Welfare Act, if you think a child is in need of protection, you can convey them to their home address. So in attempting to help make the local population feel more comfortable, that was our policy. We'd grab these kids off the streets, we'd take down their names and addresses, just in case, then we'd take them home and drop them off and say, 'You guys go inside. We don't want to see you out on the streets again.'

That's what we did and off they'd go inside. Mind you, eight times out of ten they'd just jump over the back fence and run off and we'd soon find them out on the streets again. So then we'd repeat the process, and that would happen anywhere up to five or six times a night. It was a big problem; a very big problem.

On this particular night, we were out on patrol when we came across a couple of kids roaming the streets. They would've been in their very early teens. At the time we were actually driving the boss's brand-new police-issue Commodore. It had only just arrived and he'd allowed us to use it for the night. Anyway, we picked up these two kids and we took them home.

As it happened, these two kids lived in a cul-de-sac, so we dropped them off then we waited in the street till they'd safely gone inside. That done, we went down to the end of the cul-de-sac and chucked a U-ie to head back out, not thinking any more about it. It was a completely simple job. But then, just as we're driving back down past the house where we'd dropped the kids off, about twenty-five people appeared and they started running towards us. Next thing, *bang*, a rock hit the side of our vehicle — the boss's new Commodore.

We later found out that the kids had run inside where there was some sort of a family gathering going on and they'd said, 'We've just been bashed up by the coppers. They're outside.'

As you'd expect a family to do, this family's reacted and they've come after us and they're angry. But we're thinking, What's going on here?

No sooner had we been hit by the rock than an eight-foot star picket's come spearing through the front windscreen of our vehicle. Do you know what a star picket is? It's one of those long metal fencing posts. I was driving. My offsider was in the passenger's seat. How it missed my offsider, I don't know. I still don't know to this day. No idea at all. So first it was the rock. Now it's the star picket.

I was pretty shaken but I just kept driving, with them chasing us. But, being the police we needed to know what had caused all this anger. So when we got to the end of the street we chucked another U-ie. That then had us facing back towards this advancing mob. It was dark; about 9 or 10 o'clock at night. Our vehicle's high beam is on. Where we were, the cul-de-sac led out onto a main link-road around the town and on the other side of us, as far as you could see, it was pretty much virgin bush. So we pulled up and we jumped out. 'Hey, what's going on?'

Then one of them came running up to us, swinging a star picket.

'Mate,' we called out, 'you're going to get locked up. Tell us what the problem is so we can sort it out.'

Still swinging the star picket, he shouted out, 'How dare you bash our kids!'

'Hang on. We didn't touch your kids. We just picked them up on the street and we dropped them off.'

'We don't believe you.'

By then there's more people coming out of their houses. There's now about forty people against just the two of us coppers. It's a stand-off and things weren't looking too good for us, so I jumped back into the boss's Commodore and I got on the police radio: 'Urgent. Urgent.' 'Urgent' is the call sign for the highest assistance required. When one of those comes through to the police station, the people who are on duty drop everything and come running. So we called 'urgent'.

We didn't have tasers back then. All we had were our extendable batons, pepper spray and guns. I think I had my baton out by then, as a warning. But people still came towards us, yelling and going on at us, star pickets swinging. I tried to call 'urgent' again on the police radio, but it didn't appear to be working, so we started backing away from our vehicle. As we did, these guys were moving in closer, shouting, 'We're gonna bloody kill you! How dare you touch our kids!'

By now we've moved probably thirty metres away from our car. We were across the road, just about into the bush. There's just the two of us. People are moving towards us. We're staying close in tight together, but we could still see the boss's Commodore in the background and I could just make out someone stabbing a star picket through the metal part of the door. I remember having the strange thought of, How am I going to explain to the boss how all this came about?

Anyhow, by now fifteen to twenty minutes had passed since my 'urgent' call and we still hadn't got backup. We're well away from the car so I can't even get to the radio now. It doesn't appear to be working anyway, so I pulled the mobile phone out of my pocket and I started trying to dial the station for backup. And I won't lie, I was shaking so much that I couldn't dial my phone. That's how scared I was.

As I said, I had my baton out to start off, but then I thought, Well, that's not going to do much against a star picket. We then tried pepper spray. We sprayed as many people as we could but, when one lot dropped back, others started coming through.

That's when I got my gun out. I think my partner already had his gun out by that stage. So there I was with my gun, ready to fire, and a lady pushed her way forward and she walked up to me and she placed her chest against my gun.

'Go on then. Do it,' she said.

Realising that that would've made things a whole lot worse, we backed off a bit further, all the time warning the mob to keep their distance. But still they kept coming; star pickets being swung at us with threats of, 'We're going to get you. It's payback. You hit our kids, we hit you.'

We've got our guns at the ready and we're warning them, 'Stay back. Stay back. We didn't touch your kids.'

Next thing, this police Land Cruiser troop carrier comes screaming around the corner, lights flashing, sirens blaring. As soon as the mob saw the second vehicle, they sort of started backing away from us.

We now know that just the one part of the 'urgent' transmission got through to the station and that three or four police vehicles had been sent out. Problem was, they didn't get the second part of the message and so they didn't know exactly where we were. Yes, they knew we'd picked up some kids; that we had them on board and we were heading to drop them off, possibly in a certain area.

Anyhow, subsequently, when all the backup arrived it turned into a running battle. And it continued into the night. Apparently, after me and my offsider were taken out of there, two or three more police cars were damaged and the boss's new Commodore had to be towed back to the station. In the end, I think that a dozen or so people ended up being charged.

The next morning, when the boss arrived at work, he saw his vehicle in the car park. So I didn't need to say anything. He knew that I was involved, and most probably had been driving, but to his credit he was more concerned about the night's events than all the damage that was done to his new police-issue Commodore.

A few days later, we sat down with the family to explain what had gone on. We said, 'Look, this's what happened. We didn't touch the kids. We just saw them in the street and we took them home and, what's more, it's happened several times before.'

'No,' they said. 'The kids said you hit 'em, so as far as we're concerned that's it; you hit 'em.'

We just couldn't get through to them. And it didn't stop there. Things didn't let up after that night. Every time I went to the shop or anywhere else around town they'd be there watching me and they'd say something; some sort of smart remark.

And that's what happens; sometimes when you think you're doing the right thing, that's how it ends up.

So, yeah, that would be pretty much the scariest encounter I've ever had as a police officer, and that was the first and only time I've had my gun out. Having seen what they'd done to the boss's car, I actually got to the point where I thought, If that guy with the star picket gets any closer …

And I probably would have.

Hindsight's a great thing, I know. Who knows what would've happened. But yeah, I probably would have. In my head I'd already made up my mind that if he'd gotten any closer that's what was going to happen.

# Sequel

My grandfather William 'Bill' Francis Johns was a policeman, an adventurer and a storyteller. My name is Greg Johns. I'm a sculptor. Part of this story I've pieced together from what my grandfather first began to tell me when I was about seven years of age. The rest I found out later on.

I grew up in the Adelaide suburb of Glenelg East and, as a young feller, we'd go and visit my grandfather and my grandmother Henrietta, or Hetty as she was called. My grandparents lived at Maylands, another suburb of Adelaide. By this time my grandfather would've probably been in his late seventies or just into his early eighties. He had like a small office out the back of their house — I guess you could call it his little hideaway — and it was where he kept his memorabilia. There were things like spent cannon shells from when he was in the Australian 9th Light Horse Regiment during the First World War, where he was involved in putting down the Egyptian uprising. He also had a large number of photographs from that time. When his back was turned, I used to sneak my mates into his office and I'd show them the image he had of a forty-four-gallon drum filled with decapitated heads that had been collected during the uprising. It used to really put the wind up them. But that was just one of the many interesting photographs he kept.

The little hideaway also had a lot of memorabilia from his police career; from his time in the outback and from his many adventures, up to his retirement. My grandfather joined the police force in South Australia along with his younger brother,

John 'Jack' Johns, in 1906. Back in those days, quite a few young constables did a five-year secondment up in the Northern Territory and so he was up there from late 1909 to early 1915.

There's been quite a number of stories told about my grandfather. As I said, his name was William Francis Johns and, with the William having been shortened to Bill, right back from his time in the Territory he gained the nickname of 'Mulga Bill', from the Banjo Paterson poem 'Mulga Bill's Bicycle'.

Anyhow, during his time in the north my grandfather gained the reputation of being the best shot in the Territory. And, as he told it, what very much enhanced his reputation was from the time he and another constable were out on patrol. They were on horseback and the other constable said to my grandfather, 'Bill, I've heard you're the best shot in the Northern Territory.'

'Oh, yeah,' my grandfather said, 'that could well be the case.'

'Then how about you show me just how good you are?'

At that time, they'd just passed by a large tree filled with white cockatoos and so my grandfather said, 'Yeah, I'll show you. I'll just throw my rifle over my shoulder and I'll shoot backwards without looking and I'll knock one of the cockatoos out of the tree.'

'Bet'cha can't,' said the constable.

'Yeah?' So then my grandfather threw the rifle back over his shoulder, pulled the trigger — *bang* — and a cockatoo fell to the ground, dead. Apparently the other constable was so amazed at the feat that he went on to tell the story all over the Northern Territory of how Mulga Bill Johns could shoot just as accurately backwards over his shoulder as he could forwards from his shoulder or even from his hip. Of course, my grandfather never let on that his shooting of the cockatoo was a complete accident, and so his reputation grew.

But the story I'm going to relate to you now is probably the best known one of all and it has been well documented by others as well. As I said, this was told to me, in part, by my grandfather when I was a young feller sitting in his little outside room — his little hideaway. It's about my grandfather and an Aboriginal man known as Neighbour.

Neighbour was from the Alawa people whose traditional lands were part of Nutwood Downs cattle station. Where the name of Neighbour came from I don't know. As with many of the Aborigines it was just a nickname he went by. At that stage, my grandfather was a mounted constable based in the north of the Northern Territory, over near the Gulf of Carpentaria, at Roper Bar. I'd say that his patrol area would've taken in the entire Roper region, including the then new Roper River Mission, or Ngukurr as it's now known in the Aboriginal language.

In early 1911 my grandfather was sent out to the Hodgson River area to arrest Neighbour and bring him back to face charges for stealing cattle. After my grandfather had arrested Neighbour, they headed back to Roper Bar. I don't actually remember him telling me that Neighbour was in chains, but I've since found out that he was. He had chains around his arms and he had a neck brace on.

On the way back, they got to the Wilton River. The Wilton was in flood. It was also crocodile-infested. My grandfather said to Neighbour, 'We have to cross the river,' so he loosened the chains from around Neighbour's arms — but he left the neck brace on — and they took to the water. They were swimming either side of my grandfather's horse; one arm on the saddle and using the other to swim with. Then, the horse panicked. It may have slipped on the bottom of the river, I'm not sure, but in doing so it went over onto its back and, as it did, it lashed out and it kicked my grandfather in the head.

The kick to the head knocked out my grandfather. There he was, stuck in the middle of the river, and he would've died. No doubt about it. But after Neighbour managed to scramble to the other side, he saw that my grandfather was in trouble. So he then wrapped the loosened chain over his shoulder and, with the neck brace still on, he swam back into the middle of the crocodile-infested and flooded river, where he managed to grab hold of my grandfather and pull him safely to the shore. Neighbour then brought my grandfather back to consciousness, rounded up the horse, and he rode sixty miles to the nearest white settlement to get help. Help eventually came and after my grandfather had recovered enough, the journey continued and my grandfather led Neighbour to the police station.

When the case came to court, my grandfather went in to bat for Neighbour.

'Look,' he said, 'I've done my duty. This is Neighbour, I've arrested him as required but there's no evidence against him.'

Anyway, Neighbour was freed and the story about him saving the life of my grandfather soon spread far and wide. When the Bishop of Melbourne heard about it, he referred it on to the Archbishop of Canterbury. Then in February 1911, King George the Fifth awarded Neighbour the Royal Albert Medal for bravery; the Royal Albert Medal being the civilian equivalent to the Victoria Cross.

The ceremony to award Neighbour with the medal was held at Government House in Darwin in December 1912. For the occasion, Neighbour wore a khaki police uniform. My grandfather believed that Neighbour was the only Northern Territorian, black or white, to have ever received the Royal Albert Medal. After the ceremony, Neighbour became an Aboriginal tracker at the Roper River police station and he also worked as a stockman at Nutwood Downs and Hodgson Downs cattle stations.

But the thing was, Neighbour was never allowed to keep the medal. The then Protector of Aborigines of the Northern Territory was under the opinion that there'd be people who'd try to make Neighbour part with it for their own good. That being so, it was left in the care of the Administrator of the Northern Territory, only to be worn by Neighbour on official occasions.

Three years down the track, there's a great sequel to this. This time Neighbour's up on a murder charge. An Aboriginal man went missing and was presumed dead, thought to have been thrown into the Roper River. By then Neighbour was living with the missing man's ex-wife. The evidence was circumstantial at best, but of course back in those days you didn't need too much evidence to arrest Aborigines and even less to convict them. So because Neighbour was living with the missing Aboriginal man's ex-wife, he was accused of the missing man's murder.

Now believe it or not, the amazing thing here was that the policeman who was sent out to bring Neighbour in on this murder charge, purely by coincidence, was my grandfather's brother, mounted constable John 'Jack' Johns. And he described in the reports I've read of how having to arrest the very person who'd saved his brother's life and then place him in chains and take him across the country to Darwin were the worst days of his life.

Neighbour then appeared in the Darwin court charged with this murder. If found guilty, he could've easily been hanged. So Neighbour appears in the dock dressed in a neat khaki police uniform with the Royal Albert Medal attached to his chest. Both my grandfather and his brother, Jack, spoke on behalf of Neighbour, as did many other luminaries, and after a short hearing Neighbour got off the murder charge. It's always been my assumption that, if it hadn't been for the Royal Albert Medal, things could've been far worse for Neighbour. So receiving that medal, I think you could say, saved his life.

Now there's also another story about Neighbour; a sequel to the sequel, if you will. In the 1940s, Neighbour was credited with helping save the lives of several Aborigines and whites when he helped ferry rations and supplies across the flooded Roper River to those who were stranded at the mission — Ngukurr.

Neighbour again proved himself to be a hero in many people's eyes, especially my grandfather's.

Anyhow, after my grandfather returned to South Australia in 1915, he kept in contact with Neighbour. He sent him food parcels and presents and, even though Neighbour couldn't read nor write, my grandfather wrote many letters to him under the assumption that someone literate would read them to him. And this went on for decades until Neighbour died in the early 1950s. He was about sixty by then and he was buried out on his traditional lands at Nutwood Downs station.

As for my grandfather, he continued police duty down here, in South Australia. He then joined the Australian Light Horse Regiment in 1917, just as it was on its way to Palestine. That's when he got involved in helping put down the Egyptian uprising. After the war he re-joined the police force and he worked his way up the ranks, ending up as Commissioner of the South Australian Police Force, which was a position he held from 1944 to 1949. He received the Order of the British Empire — OBE — in 1946 for outstanding service to the force. An interesting thing there is that he was the first person in South Australia to rise from the rank of constable and become Commissioner of Police. I think there's only been a couple of others in this state's history who have since done that, and one of those was my grandfather's brother, Jack.

So that's the story, pieced together from what my grandfather told to me and from what I've since heard. He died around 1970, when I was about seventeen, and you've got to put it in the context of the time. With my grandfather having been brought up in the Victorian era with all its biases and opinions I believe he grew through the experience. On many occasions I clearly remember him saying to people, 'I know blackfellas and they're very good people.' And he'd say it very, very strongly.

So to yet another sequel: for some inexplicable reason, in 2010 I was giving a lot of thought to the story about how Neighbour had saved my grandfather's life, and so I made a sculpture about the incident. Now let's not idealise over the whole thing because I think too many of our monuments lie and I like to tell the truth, warts and all. So to that end, my metal sculpture shows an abstract image of an Aboriginal man — meant to be Neighbour — with an iron brace around his neck and with a chain coming down. The reason I made the sculpture with Neighbour in chains is because it's definitely not the 'perfect' story, but it's a story that should be told. Then as a connection to the Aboriginal people's sense of country I sculpted part of his body with like a landscape profile.

Within the sculpture of Neighbour's head I've woven in a second head, that of a long-faced person representative of my grandfather. I constructed it that way because their two lives, that of my grandfather and that of Neighbour, became entwined through the event at the Wilton River and beyond. Then I've got a big hand that extends out from the body of the sculpture, which represents optimism. So hopefully it tells a bit more of a truthful story about Australia and some sort of coming together of blackfella and white-feller culture. That sculpture, *Monument to Mulga Bill and Neighbour*, is now in the Darwin library and quite often they bring young Aboriginal groups in and tell them the story surrounding the sculpture.

Of course there's a sequel to all that as well because, when I was making the sculpture, I had no idea that it was coming up to the hundredth anniversary of Neighbour having been awarded the Royal Albert Medal. Make of that what you will. But somehow the original medal had ended up in the National Gallery in Canberra and they were planning to make a presentation of the medal back to Neighbour's descendants.

Anyway, there was a bit in the local Adelaide *Advertiser* newspaper, as well as online, about me making the sculpture of the story surrounding my grandfather and Neighbour and I guess, in part, that's how they tracked me down. Initially Charlie King from Darwin emailed me. I didn't know it at that time, but Charlie's probably one of the ABC's best known presenters up there. Then in late 2010 he rang me and he explained what the presentation was all about and how it'd be great if I, as the grandson of the policeman who was saved by Neighbour, came up for the presentation. Charlie and I got on well and at the end of our chat, he said, 'So, Greg, are you going to come up for the medal being presented back?'

I said, 'Yes, absolutely.'

Then he said, 'Oh,' he said, 'first of all, I've got something to tell you.'

'What's that?'

He said, 'We share the same grandfather.'

'Oh,' I said, 'that's good. Ah, that's great. I didn't know about that one.'

Then he said, 'Oh, and the other thing is, Greg, I'm a blackfella.'

Charlie had been doing some research and he'd found out that, during the time my grandfather had been in the Territory, besides all the fabulous stories he told of his many adventures, he'd also managed to father children with two Aboriginal women. Hence our relationship.

So the handing back of the medal took place in the Northern Territory Library back in May 2011, with high-level government officials from all over the place, plus a whole bunch of Neighbour's descendants, who had travelled two or three days by car up from Roper River for the ceremony. There were also the descendants of the two Aboriginal women that my grandfather had had the children with. And though I was slightly nervous about how they would see things, I had no issue over the Aboriginality, none at all. And overall they were reasonably positive. So thanks to my grandfather, at last rough count, I now have somewhere between a hundred and eighty-five to two hundred and thirty Aboriginal relatives.

# Speeding

I grew up in Queensland at a place called Deception Bay, which is close to where I live now at Maroochydore. That was back in the 1940s. My father had a nine-hundred-acre property. He used to cut down the natural trees on the land to be used for stumps for those high-set Queensland-style houses, then we had a house cow and we also grew just enough vegies to help sustain us.

For my primary schooling I went to the Deception Bay State School. That was for the most part a one-teacher school. Then during the '51–'52 polio epidemic, my mother died. After that my father re-married and we moved in to Scarborough, on the Redcliffe Peninsula, and I finished my high schooling there.

But I'd always wanted to join the police force. Where that came from I have no idea. There could've been any number of reasons. In those days you had to be a single woman to be in the police force and it may have been because I didn't expect to get married and that, by joining the force, I knew I'd have a secure job for the rest of my life. Perhaps I'd read articles about policing somewhere and they captured my imagination, or it may have been after I'd heard about women like Eileen O'Donnell and Zara Dare who were the first 'appointed' policewomen in Queensland. That was back in the 1930s and even though they were 'appointed', they weren't actually 'sworn in', which meant they had no power of arrest. They were used more for escorting and searching female prisoners and so forth. Actually I was the one hundred and fifty-fifth woman to be 'sworn in' and the only reason I know that is because, in those days, women had a different registration number to the men.

So there's no one thing that I can put my finger on, but it's just wonderful to know what you want to be in life at such an early age. Many don't and many never find out. Still, to my benefit I was also fortunate enough to be able to do a lot of other things in life before going into the force. I joined when I was twenty-nine and by then us policewomen were getting the same rate of pay as the men. There was a lot of resentment about that because many of the males thought we only joined because of the pay. And it used to give me great satisfaction to tell them that I'd been earning more money outside of the force, in my previous job as a credit manager.

In my intake there were twenty-eight in the squad. About eight of those were women. I was the oldest in the intake and so I became the unofficial mouthpiece of the group. And in an odd sort of way we created history because we were the last intake at the old Police Depot on Petrie Terrace, in Brisbane, yet we were the first to finish off our training at the new academy out at Oxley. Though, mind you, when we first arrived at Oxley, there were no classrooms ready for us so we used to have our lessons in the lounge room.

In those days, for the first twelve months after being sworn in, you did three months here and three months there just to get a feel of the force and to experience other aspects of the job. My first three months was with mobile patrol, which is where you were in cars and you were directed to work. I was the first policewoman to be stationed at Newmarket Police Station and then at Holland Park Police Station. In between I did another stint back at the academy, which was in general administration.

I also did a stint in operations. That was when we had the 1974 floods. Back then, public servants answered the main switchboard during office hours, then after hours a police officer took over. I was actually working after hours on the main evacuation day of the floods. It was horrendous. The main switchboard lit up like a Christmas tree, so much so that I eventually pulled my headphones out and walked over to the sergeant.

'What are you doing?' he asked.

I said, 'Well, I'm not Superwoman.' I said, 'And even if I was, I've got no one to put all the calls through to.' The State Emergency Service was actually born out of those '74 floods. Before that we had to rely on the good will of the radio stations to broadcast messages, and the army to help evacuate people.

After that, I was fortunate enough to be transferred to Nambour, on the Sunshine Coast. That was in March 1974. Nambour was the police headquarters for the whole of the Sunshine Coast and the hinterland, and we had to work night duty on our own — that's both males and females. So if we were called to go out anywhere at night, we had to put the switchboard over to the senior sergeant, who had his residence behind the station, and he took charge of the station. And we didn't have triple-0 in those days either so, if we went out to attend an accident or anything and we needed the assistance of a tow truck or an ambulance or whatever, it was basically a case of hailing down a passing motorist and asking them to relay the message on. I think it was then that Apex, in their wisdom, eventually decided we needed triple-0.

Also, with being the headquarters for the whole area, any prisoners who hadn't already been taken through to Brisbane were held at the Nambour Police Station, and they had to be checked on every two hours by the duty officer. As far as I know I was the first policewoman to do night duty on my own and I well remember the time I had to look after Peter Vivian Wardrop. In fact I always say that every grey hair that grew out of my head came about because I had to look after Peter Vivian Wardrop.

Peter Vivian Wardrop was known as the Maroochydore Nail-bomber. He was involved in many things, drugs in particular, and our CIB detective-sergeant was like a fox terrier when it came to drugs. He just hounded Peter Vivian Wardrop, so much so that he developed an absolute hatred for the detective-sergeant. To that end, Peter Vivian Wardrop booby-trapped a cupboard in an abandoned house with gelignite surrounded by nails and, knowing full well the detective-sergeant would go out to investigate, he called the Nambour Police Station and said that there were drugs hidden in a cupboard on the premises.

In the meantime, two little sisters — a three-year-old and a two-year-old — got inside the house and the three-year-old opened the cupboard. The two-year-old didn't die but the three-year-old did. At that time, my brother was a police photographer and fingerprint man and he said it was just horrendous what happened to that little girl; just horrendous. Her name was Merrilyn Ruth Gartner. Funny how in the police force we always called people by their full name.

And then in 1977 I faced an armed gunman. That's why I was awarded the Queen's Gallantry Medal. I would've been constable first class by then. It was a domestic situation. It's a well-known fact in the force that most officers are injured during domestic situations, especially when alcohol and drugs are involved, because you just don't know how people will react in any given circumstance.

What happened was, before we got there the de facto had drunk half a bottle of whisky and he'd fired off something like eight bullets. The woman's children had run off to see if they could get an off-duty policeman. So we were called. There were four of us on duty that day: myself, my sergeant, my young constable and another officer. The situation was in Court Road, Nambour. There'd been problems there before which I'd attended to and so, when I heard the address, I said, 'Let me handle the situation.'

The couple lived in a low-set block of units which had a carport attached. When we arrived, I drove in and I parked the car in the driveway. The de facto was leaning over the bonnet of a car and I could see he had a gun — a .22 rifle. My junior officer and I got out of our vehicle and we walked towards him with our hands outstretched, to show him that we were unarmed. As we did, we repeatedly asked him to put down the gun, to which he repeatedly told us, in no uncertain terms, to go away. The woman recognised me and she was also trying to talk the gun off him.

We then closed in and we were able to disarm him, and I ran back to the police car and locked his rifle in the boot. It was one of those that had the straps attached. The straps had bullets in it. We also found that he had a canvas-webbing bag filled with boxes of bullets and so he could've kept us at bay forever. So then we were able to take him back to the station and we called the detectives in. I was okay up until then but when the detectives came and asked me to get the gun out of the boot of the car, they opened his rifle and there was already a bullet in the breach, ready to be fired; presumably at me. And I don't mind admitting it, that's when I really went to jelly. Of course in those days, we didn't have the luxury of backup or other units or any counselling or anything like that.

Anyhow, the de facto pleaded guilty and we were commended from the bench and as a result of that we were awarded the Queen's Gallantry Medal.

Then later on I left the police force; though that had nothing at all to do with the incident at Nambour. It happened when I served a speeding summons on a local cane farmer, and three years later we were married.

# Stan the Shearer

I got this story from a bloke who knew a bloke who knew a bloke's missus who was the sister-in-law of the copper in question; a certain Sergeant Ignatius Kelly. It's a good old-fashioned Aussie yarn, told in the true tradition. So do you want to hear it?

Okay then, here goes. Back a good while ago now, Sergeant Kelly did a stint out at Broken Hill, in the far west of New South Wales. Anyhow, this Sergeant Kelly had apparently once told the story of Stan the shearer.

Stan the shearer apparently spent a lot of time working around the West Darling area. And after he got his pay cheque at the completion of each round of sheds, Stan would call his motley pack of dogs into the back of his old Chevy buckboard and he'd head for Broken Hill and, in particular, to his favourite pub, Brady's Southern. Now, as it happened, Brady's Southern was located in Patton Street, right across the road from the police station.

Just about everyone knew when Stan was arriving in town because, as soon as he turned off Bonanza Street and into Patton, they'd hear his old Chevy spluttering, muttering and clanging down the road with this pack of mangy mutts in the back, barking and yapping at everything that moved and most things that didn't.

'Shard-up, yer bloody mongrels,' Stan would be yelling. But the dogs never took any notice.

'Stan's back in town,' would be the common remark around the neighbourhood.

Then once Stan had come to a grinding halt at the pub, he'd

step out of the buckboard, hunt the dogs into a wire compound at the back of the Southern, grab his bags, then walk through the back of the pub where he'd toss them into his usual room, the drunks' tank ... then he'd stride into the front bar.

'G'day,' he'd announce, like the returning prodigal, to which the regular three dowdy drinkers would wince and mutter, 'Shit, he's back.'

The only one who seemed anywhere near half excited about Stan's arrival was Bert, the publican, and that's because the next thing Stan would do was throw his shearing cheque down on the bar. 'Here, Bert,' he'd say, 'let me know when it's done,' and as Bert poured Stan the first of many more beers to come, he'd scoop up the cheque and stick it safely into his wallet. Actually I don't know how he'd do that; you know, pour a beer and stick a cheque in his wallet at the same time. He might've been ambidextrous or something. I don't know, but that's how I was told the story.

Anyhow, the thing is that while Bert was pouring Stan the beer and stashing the cheque away, he'd say, 'Now please, Stan, no trouble tonight, mate. Not like last time.'

'And the time before that,' would come the mutter from one of the three dowdy resident drinkers.

'And the time before that,' would sound another dowdy resident drinker.

'And the fuckin' time before that,' would chime in the third dowdy resident drinker.

'No worries, mate,' Stan would reply, wiping his wetted lips with his sheep-stained sleeve and shoving his empty glass forward for a refill, 'I promise ter be on me best behaviour. Honest,' to which the three dowdy resident drinkers would raise their eyes toward the pressed-tin ceiling of the pub, as if they'd heard all this a million times before. Which they had.

'I hope so, Stan,' Bert would say to no one in particular as he refilled Stan's glass.

Anyhow, this time around, as usual, Stan's promise came to nothing and later that night there's Stan, he's as full as a goog and rearing to have a stoush.

'Hey you,' he calls out to a burly miner known as Curly, 'do they call yer Curly 'cause yer so short?'

'Get stuffed, Stan,' retorts Curly at Stan's hint of his nickname deriving from short 'n curly.

'Get stuffed yerself,' slurs Stan.

'Here we go,' mutters the three dowdy resident drinkers in unison.

Anyhow, one thing then leads to another. Push leads to shove. Shove leads to shuffle, and then she's on. Stan and Curly are into it. Punches are thrown, left, right and almost centre, and the blue spills out of the front bar and onto the footpath.

By this stage, Sergeant Kelly's arrived on the scene. 'Righto, you two, that's enough. You, Curly, get home to yer missus 'n ten kids, 'n you, Stan, same as usual, you're coming with me,' and he pushes Stan in the direction of the police station.

'Thank Christ fer that,' mutter the three dowdy resident drinkers as they wander back into the pub to take up their well-worn bar stools.

'But, Sarge,' protests Stan, as he staggers across the road, 'how did yer know it was me what started the scrap?'

'Just a wild guess, I'd reckon, Stan; just a wild guess.'

Anyhow, early next morning Sergeant Kelly's at the cell door. 'Come on, Stan, wakey, wakey. Here's your usual: black tea with two sugars. The axe's in its normal place out beside the wood heap and I want the lot cut before you go and get those bloody dogs of yours and head out of town.'

Stan sits up, holding his head. His bloodshot eyes look like they've been run over by a grader. He has a couple of sips of tea, then he starts to pull on his boots.

'Look, Stan, how many times has this happened?' says Sergeant Kelly. 'Anyone'd think you'd have woke up to yerself after all these years, wouldn't they?'

'Yeah, yeah,' Stan replies as he shuffles outside to the wood heap. 'I guess I must be just one'a them slow learners, Sarge.'

'Well, this time, while you're back out in the shearing sheds, just have a good hard think about things, okay?'

'Yes, Sarge.'

Anyhow, a couple of months later the locals hear Stan's old Chevy coughing and spluttering down Patton Street, with his mob of mangy mutts barking at everything that moved and most things that didn't. Then as he passes the police station, Stan veers over to the wrong side of the road and, as he mounts the footpath, he nearly bowls over Sergeant Kelly. Amid the mayhem, Stan leans over into the back of his Chevy, grabs an axe and throws it over the back fence of the police station. Then he calls out, 'Sorry, Sarge. Almost gotcha,' before he continues on to his destination, Brady's Southern.

'That's it,' mutters the sergeant as he goes to grab his charge-sheet and head off to the pub.

As it happened, by the time Stan entered the front bar, Sergeant Kelly was already waiting for him; as were the three dowdy resident drinkers, full of expectation as to what excitement was about to unfold.

'What the bloody hell do you think you're doing, Stan, drivin' on the wrong side of the road, nearly bowlin' me over and throwin' an axe over my fence?'

'Well, Sarge,' Stan says, 'I've been thinking, like you said I should. See, you 'n me know exactly what's gonna happen, don't we? I'm gonna end up in me usual blue, right, 'n you're gonna drag me off ter the cell again, right, 'n the next morning yer gonna make me chop a pile of wood, right? So I thought this time I'd at least have a decent bloody axe.'

# Stunning

I was actually born in country Victoria. Then, when I was about three months old, we moved to the suburbs in Adelaide. My only country experience outside of that was when we'd go up to our shack on the Murray River at Mannum.

With regard to the police, I had no notion of joining the force. In fact I had a friend in school who wanted to be a police officer and I remember saying to him, 'What do you want to be a professional dobber for?' Ten years later, I joined the force and I've now been in the job seventeen years.

I was twenty-six when I joined, which was quite late. After school I worked in a bank for three years. Then I joined the navy. I was there for four years before I went backpacking around Europe, working in pubs and that. After I came back to Australia, I remember seeing a couple of articles about what the police were doing and that got me thinking, Gee, that'd be an interesting job. Perhaps there's a career path for me there.

So I was weighing up whether to join or not. One distinct advantage was that in the police you had shift work and so I'd be able to do things when other people were at work. Another advantage was that, unlike working in a bank, you don't know what you're going to do each day. Anything could turn up, and that seemed exciting. Then also, coming from a naval background like I did, I was comfortable within a ranked structure and I liked the uniformed camaraderie of a work team.

For training I went to the Fort Largs Academy at Taperoo; that's the old one with the asbestos buildings. Our group was the first to do the six-month course. Subjects covered things like victimology, sociology, though we didn't use those terms. It was more like, 'Okay, if you're stationed where there's a large Indigenous population you've got to remember these factors about their culture and how they'll impact on policing.' Or, 'If you're stationed in a suburb where the people are well off, this's how you handle crime in that area.' So every area you're stationed to has its own separate culture and perspective on life.

After graduation I worked in the city. I did look at country postings, and there were plenty of vacancies, but while I remained in the city the opportunities for promotion continued to present themselves and I would've been silly to knock them back. But then a vacancy came up out here on the west coast of South Australia, at Ceduna. I had the qualifications. I'd been doing a similar job for five years. I only needed to meet the key criteria of how to handle a placement like Ceduna. Luckily I'd experienced working with Indigenous community constables for the Aboriginal community in Port Adelaide.

What attracted me to Ceduna was that I'd already visited there three times. First was when I'd been on a backpacker's tour and I remembered just how stunning the scenery was all along the west coast. Later on, when one of my detective friends had been posted to Ceduna, I came over for a visit and I saw some very different features of the area and there was yet more of that same stunningness. Then one of the girls from my police work team at Henley Beach, she came out to Ceduna and when I visited her she took me to see even more stunning places. So I just thought, Hey, there's so much to explore and see over here, how can I miss out on an opportunity like this?

As it turned out, the policing side of things in Ceduna is very different from anywhere I've been. Very. Ceduna's the main regional station, then we have Penong and Yalata out west, Streaky Bay to the south, and Wirrulla and Minnipa to the east. At Ceduna we have around twenty-five police officers of which about one fifth are female. As for the township itself, the percentage of Aboriginal to white would be about fifty-fifty.

I work on two fronts: I'm responsible for my patrol team, who look after the more general side of policing, and I also supervise the Indigenous community constables — CC's as they're called. We currently have two female CC's here in Ceduna, one of which has just been awarded a twenty-year medal. Then there's just the one male CC out at Yalata Community. My job there is to make sure they're involved in activities that promote policing in a positive light so that the entire Aboriginal community can be confident of our support in a) resolving issues and b) preventing issues before they get out of hand.

Actually a lot of our work stems from Yalata Aboriginal Community. With Yalata having a no-liquor policy, there's always those who travel into Ceduna for the sole purpose of binge-drinking. Of course, not being town residents, they don't have a home here and so they end up having to rely on the services provided by places like the Sober-up Unit. Then there's also the Town Camp. That now has a 'no-drunk' policy because of all the problems it was causing. Apart from those two, there's various other campsites where they can bed down.

Another problem we faced was that, while they're out at Yalata, the Indigenous people still live culturally but then, after they've done cultural business — say, like initiations — they'll then come into town to celebrate. And unfortunately some of them have found themselves in trouble because they try to assert their newly initiated manhood, particularly on our female police officers.

To that end, when I first arrived in Ceduna we practised a 'Don't set them up to fail' ethos, which was an effective positive reinforcement method I'd used in the city. And we try our best to adhere to that.

But it's always a balancing act because, as in all towns like this, there is a good deal of racism and for effective policing we need to — we must — overcome that. A simple example there would be:

say I arrested a person who was trying to break into a house while the occupant was away. More often than not, when I go to get a statement from the occupant, their first question is, 'Were they black or white?'

And I'll reply, 'Look, what's your distinction here? Does it really matter if the person involved was black or white?'

So yes, unfortunately that sort of thing does go on and, in doing so, it does tend to create an 'us n' them' profile. That's perhaps more of a downside of things as far as policing here goes. But we're working on it. And I believe we're slowly making progress, because there are many people in this town — other than us — who really appreciate the value of policing as a positive influence and so they're also working hard alongside us at closing the gap.

As for special moments, you always get little surprises. There's a lad who's been with us for six months now, young Nick, and next Tuesday he's receiving the Police Bravery Medal. He'd kept it secret until we got an official email saying that he needed to be released for the special occasion.

We're like, 'Nick, what did you do?'

It turned out that it was a job he did back in Murray Bridge where he and his police partner went into a burning house to rescue a four-year-old child and they came out with a forty-one-year-old man. Unfortunately, the child did die but the thing was, he didn't realise just how important the Police Bravery Medal was until I got him to do some research on it. Even then he just went, 'Oh, okay. Wow.'

So that was a surprise, for us all.

Then as for other special moments; of course there's always the landscape. Always. It's that stunning scenery that drew me over here in the first place. Whenever we get someone new on our team, the first thing we do is to have a get-to-know-you barbecue. And it's not held at someone's house where there's loud music or a blaring television or where the mobile phones are always ringing. No, we'll all get in our four-wheel drives and we'll go out to somewhere like Davenport Creek where you've got the whole beach to yourself. There's no one else within cooee. There's just all that wonderful space, and we'll light a fire, put the hotplate over it, cook a meal, have a drink or two and everyone just sits around and talks.

# The Big Hit

Like I said, I'd been doing a bit of cattle duffing — stealing cattle — with the Casey boys up around the Queensland Gulf Country just so I could then afford to get over to New Zealand and set up with that Janet Wilson piece I'd met along the way. But I'd been going backwards, really. Then in the wet season of 1957 all that was about to change.

Actually, the story started a bit before then when someone saw me riding with split-bags across me saddle, going the back way along the Normanton–Croydon railway line, out to the Caseys' place, at Shady Lagoons. A split-bag's like a big chaff bag. See, if you can imagine, you sit on it and the sides hang down and you just cut the top, like that, and put your stores and things down there. Like, if you're going cattle duffing by yourself you'd usually take a split-bag because it saves taking a packhorse and then, instead of carrying your swag, you'd just carry a little blanket at the back.

Any rate, the local police sergeant, Sam Henry, he got wind of this so he thinks, Gee, this's pretty suspicious because, if I know Goldie, the only reason he'd be going along the rail line is so that he doesn't leave any tracks.

But the thing was, I hadn't been up to anything. You know, I'd just been in town getting supplies for this big, sort of, droving trip we were about to go on. And the only reason I was riding along the rail line was that it was too wet and boggy off the tracks. So I got on the ballast, where it's more solid under hoof. But Sam didn't know all that. He just naturally thought I'd been up to no good. And then, when Jimmy Casey turns up at the police station and fills out a waybill saying '300 head. Destination: Julia Creek. Travelling for sale', that really got old Sam suspicious.

Now in actual fact, we only had about a hundred and twenty head ready to travel. We'd got them from previous duffing trips. Oh yeah, they were unbranded cleanskins that we'd duffed and then we'd put our own brand on them. So they were legally ours ... Well, not legally, but with our brand on them no one else could put a claim on them, if you see what I mean.

But the real reason why Jimmy wrote down '300 head — Travelling for sale' was because, with the wet season coming on, mustering had finished and the stations had paid off all their men. So with hardly any men left on the stations, our chances of being seen were pretty slim. And so that left it pretty much open slather for us to pick up any cleanskins we came across along the way, just as long as we got our brand on them before the coppers came along. And also, it then wouldn't have mattered if we had less than three hundred head because all we'd say was, 'Oh gee, they rushed one night and we lost some in the bush.' For those that don't know, a 'rush' is the Australian term for what the Yanks call a stampede.

Now we'd already organised to sell whatever amount of cattle we ended up with to a buyer named 'Hungry' Dawson for ten pound ten a head. Hungry had a station on the Downs, the other side of Iffley. Beautiful fattening country it was too. Well, he'd been named 'Hungry' because of him being so mean and tight. One story goes that he went into the Gilliat Hotel and the feller behind the bar short-changed him. So they had a big blue over it. Then after the blue, Hungry went and offered to buy the pub off the publican, on the spot, on the guarantee he'd sell it back to the publican for the same amount of money the very next day.

'Why's that?' asks the publican.

'Because if I owned the place, I'd sack that mongrel so-and-so what short-changed me.'

Yeah, that's true. Oh, and that's right, another story about Hungry was: see, he used to have real bad arthritis in his back. Then someone told him to get a twelve-volt battery and to wire it up to his back and give himself a hit with it, and it'd cure his arthritis. And he did that for years and years and he swore by it. Even when the battery went flat he still reckoned it was doing him good. So yeah, that was Hungry Dawson.

Any rate, the Caseys and me, we set off from Shady Lagoons with this hundred and twenty head and along the way through Glenore station we start picking up cleanskins. And didn't we have a big hit. We picked them up from everywhere; from around Anabranch, then we went to The Lakes, Broadwater, then to Scrubby for a few days. Then there's an old cattle duffing yard that'd been on Glenore for years and years. I forget what it was called now but it was built with stakes in the ground and wire. Then from Glenore we went deep into Iffley Station country, to Vena Park which is an outstation of Iffley. And, oh mate, in the end we finished up with near enough to three hundred head or thereabouts.

But while all this is going on, Sam Henry the copper thinks, Okay, it's about time I went out and nabbed these fellers, cold.

Like, we didn't know any of this. So Sam's all organised to go out the next day but then the Norman River came up that night and he had to delay things. Of course, being the wet — and what a shocker it was — old Reg Quilty, the owner of Glenore, he's gone away to Sydney see, like he always did every wet. So Sam gets onto the new head stockman on Glenore, a feller named Arthur White, saying how the Caseys and me, we're in the area and up to no good and so they decide to jump in an aeroplane and go looking for us.

Now this Arthur White was known around Normanton as 'Whale Bone'. I don't know why that was but I once sold him a mare. But with him just having taken on the head stockman job, Arthur wasn't too clued up on where all the Glenore yards were.

So they then decide to fly out to Iffley Station to see the station manager there, a feller called Bill Young, who knew the area like the back of his hand. So when Sam Henry and Arthur White get to Iffley, they say to Bill Young, 'Have you seen the Caseys and Goldie yet?'

'No.'

So then they all jumped in a four-wheel drive and headed out to some high country. And that's where they come across the fresh tracks of around two hundred head. But that wasn't us, see. No. It turned out to be the Priestley brothers who were out there duffing. Oh no, we weren't the only ones duffing cattle. Not on your life. As I might've said, cattle duffing wasn't really considered thieving as such, because there was lots of other fellers duffing too, from all over the place. Everyone was at it, and some of them was good, like Jimmy Casey — and oh, he was real good — then there's other fellers who wasn't so good. And the Priestley brothers were on the 'wasn't so good' side of the fence.

There was three Priestley brothers: Dazzler, Seventy-Seven and Plaster, and they were all in their forties. From memory they had a little property just out of Croydon. I forget the name of the place just now. Now this's going to sound hard to believe but it's the gospel truth: see the Priestleys were notorious for getting lost. Notorious. Yeah, cattle duffers who always got lost. You wouldn't credit it, would you? But because they were forever getting lost, what they did was, whenever they went duffing, they'd take their cattle dog with them. Then, when they wanted to go home, they'd throw stones at the dog and it'd head for home with its tail between its legs and they'd follow the dog. Yeah, that's a fact. That's how they found their way home. Fair dinkum.

Oh, and that's right: one of them — Dazzler, or was it Plaster? — any rate, whoever it was, he had some sort of indent or something at the side of his lips, where his chin started, and so he used to forever dribble from the side of his chin. Anyhow, he'd be talking away and like, he's always reckoning about how he's going to shoot somebody. 'I'm gonna shoot that mongrel. I'm gonna shoot that other mongrel,' and there's all this dribble running down his chin. Then just as it's about to break away, he'd suck it all back up like one of them yo-yo things. Yeah, 'I'm gonna shoot that mongrel' — suck — and up it'd come. Yeah, I think it was Dazzler.

But any rate, unbeknown to us, the Priestleys had slipped into Iffley to give the place a bit of a tickle and they were lost out there somewhere. So then Sam Henry and Arthur White, after they'd seen all these cattle tracks, they jumped back into the aeroplane and they started out on a wide circle from the Iffley homestead, checking all the yards. But then the heavy rain come back in again and they couldn't see too much and so they had to give up.

The first we knew that Sam Henry was after us was when we'd left a yard on Glenore called Jumble Hole and we were heading over to Surveyors. Surveyors was a yard that had a crush. So that's where we were going to brand, cut and earmark what cleanskins we'd picked up along the way. And that's when we sees this aeroplane flying round. Well, we pretty much knew right away that it was someone looking for us, but we didn't know who. Not at that time. Anyway, it got Jimmy Casey all worried so he decided that we'd keep the cattle hidden in the thick timber all that day, then we'd walk them all that night till we got to Surveyors.

Any rate, as I said, a feller called Hungry Dawson was going to buy them off us for ten pound ten a head. But from Surveyors to Hungry's place was another eight days south, probably more. So we walked them again all the next night, across to Five Mile yard on Glenore, which is about five mile from the Wondoola Station boundary. Then, when we got to Five Mile, lo and behold, down she come again. More rain. Bucket loads. A good four inches fell, so now we're stuck good and proper because we can't get these cattle across the eighteen mile of black soil plain to Hungry Dawson's place.

Now, Jimmy Casey was the one what always done our deals so, being close to Wondoola, he went and saw Tom Wheelan, the manager there. Other than being the manager of Wondoola, Tom also owned a small station outside Julia Creek, called Glenmore. And Tom always had his eye out to buy cattle off all the duffers and that from around the Gulf and then he'd take them down to Glenmore to fatten them up, before selling them on. But see, Tom knew we were stuck with all these cattle, so he had us by the short and curlies and he only offered eight quid a head on delivery.

'Oh, okay, all right then,' says Jimmy.

So we starts walking them over to Wondoola. Next thing, Tom comes out to say how Sam Henry had rung him, asking if he'd seen us coming through. Of course, Tom's the bloke who's just agreed to buy these duffed cattle off us so he says to Sam Henry the copper, he says, 'No, Sam. Haven't seen hide nor hair of them.'

So Sam then says, 'Well, they're out there somewhere and knowing them, it's a dead cert they'll be duffing along the way.'

'Yeah, that'd be right,' says Tom.

'Tom,' Sam says, 'just let me know when they come through and I'll fly straight out and nab 'em.'

'Yes, Sam, all right. If I see 'em, you'll be the first to know.'

So Tom then arrives out where we are and he says, 'Look,' he says, 'Sam Henry's onta you so go wide around the station and take 'em up to the Twelve Mile yard because I don't want the blacks here seeing you with all these cattle.'

See, that's because the blackfellas are too honest. They'll spill their guts every time. Too right they will.

'Okay, Tom,' we say, and so we head out wide around to the Twelve Mile yard. That trip takes us another couple more days and when we get there Tom takes them over for eight quid a head, and old Sam Henry the copper, he's none the wiser about it all.

Yeah and so after we divvied up the spoils the Casey brothers give me a hundred and sixty quid. And that's the biggest lot of money I ever got over me three years of cattle duffing. I mean, really, if you worked it all out, over that time, I didn't even make wages. All I got out of it was the excitement. That's all. So I never made nowhere near enough to get to New Zealand. Any rate, by then that Janet Wilson piece had given up on me good and proper.

# The Captain's Lady — Ballad of Mary Ann Bugg

Mary Ann Bugg was a part-Aboriginal woman who was a former partner and accomplice of the bushranger Frederick Ward — Captain Thunderbolt. She was known as the 'Captain's Lady', and was Thunderbolt's eyes and ears. She kept watch for troopers, tended to their camps and stolen cattle, and cooked for Ward and his accomplices. Mary Ann was pregnant with their second child when they separated in late 1867. Their son was born in August the following year. It's doubted that Captain Thunderbolt ever knew that Mary had named their child after him — Frederick Ward Junior.

*Mary oh Mary, what have you done*
*You've married a man ... a legend to some*
*But he'll take you, he'll break you, he'll bring you undone*
*Spending each day at the point of a gun.*

Chorus:
*And it's high time you realised*
*You can't live your life with stars in your eyes*
*Yes it's high time you realised*
*You can't live your life with stars (in your eyes)*

*Mary oh Mary, take it from me*
*He'll take you to places you won't want to be*
*And he'll take you, he'll break you, you'll never be free*
*till he hangs from the gallows or from some gidgee tree*

Chorus:
*And it's high time you realised*
*You can't live your life with stars in your eyes*
*Yes it's high time you realised*
*You can't live your life with stars (in your eyes)*

Bridge:
*All lies will end when all hearts are broken*
*Out in the deep western skies*
*Love in the sense that love was awoken*
*From the time you set eyes ...*

*Mary oh Mary, where will you go*
*Now that he's gone to the devil below*
*He can't take you, he can't break you, but he'll never know*
*The child that is born has his namesake bestowed*

Chorus:
*And it's high time you realised*
*You can't live your life with stars in your eyes*
*Yes it's high time you realised*
*You can't live your life with stars (in your eyes)*

# The First Wife

I remember my first wife. I try not to, but I can't help it. She was the one I named the 'mad-knitter'. I tell you, mate, Madame Defarge, the crazy French woman from Charles Dickens's *A Tale of Two Cities*, didn't have a patch on her. If you might recall, Madame Defarge was the one who frantically knitted in front of the gallows while the French revolutionaries beheaded the royalist elite, or whoever they were. That was her — the first wife — down to a tee.

At the time of this incident we were rapidly heading towards our big split-up. We'd just been to a champagne-ie sort of breakfast do, over Deniliquin way, for the first wife's bloody quilting group and I was in a hurry to get back for the annual Finley Police and Citizens Charity Bowls Day. For those that don't know, Finley's in the New South Wales Riverina region, right down near the Murray River. Anyhow, I'd never missed the charity bowls day before and I was determined not to miss it now.

So we were driving home; the first wife's sitting there, knitting away like always — knit-one-pearl-one — when this motorcycle copper rides up beside me and he motions for me to pull over.

Obligingly I did. I ask the first wife to get my licence out of the glove box, which she did, and when the police officer arrives beside the car I wind down the window and pass it over to him. He takes a close look at the licence, then he takes a look at me, and he says, 'Sir, I clocked you going a hundred and twenty kilometres an hour in a hundred-kilometre-an-hour zone.'

I said, 'Gee, officer, are you sure? I had the cruise control set at just under a hundred.'

Not looking up from her knitting, my first wife says, 'Now, don't be silly, dear, you know that this car doesn't have cruise control.'

As I look up and see the police officer writing out the speeding ticket I lean over and say to the first wife, 'Can't you keep your mouth shut for just this once?'

Knit-one-pearl-one. She looks back at me and she says, a little louder than was necessary, 'You should be very thankful, dear, that that illegal radar detector of yours went off when it did or else you'd be done for going a lot faster than ... What was it, officer?'

'A hundred and twenty,' he says.

'Yes,' she says, 'you were certainly going a lot faster than a hundred and twenty, dear.'

Some sort of a smirk starts to spread itself over the police officer's face as he makes out a second ticket, this time for the illegal radar detector I'd only recently procured from 'Shifty' McNaughton, our local buy-anything-at-any-price supplier. So I look over at the first wife — knit-one-pearl-one — and say as quietly as possible, 'For Christ's sake, woman, keep your bloody mouth shut.'

At that moment the police officer frowns down through the window and remarks, 'And I notice that you're not wearing a seatbelt either, sir. I must remind you, there's also an automatic fine for that as well.'

I say, 'Well, you see, officer, I had it on, but I took it off when you pulled me over so that I could get my licence out of my back pocket.'

My first wife gives an audible smirk — knit-one-pearl-one — and before the police officer can take another breath, she pipes up and says, 'Now, dear, you know very well that you never wear your seatbelt when you're driving. I've told you any number of times about it but no, not you, you just refuse to wear it.'

I'd had enough, so I blurt out in no uncertain terms, 'Shut the fuck up, woman!'

The police officer interjects. 'Madam,' he says, 'does your husband always talk to you this way?'

Knit-one-pearl-one. She replies, 'Only when he's pissed.'

# The Plunkett Shield

As a police officer, one of the toughest things you have to face is having to deal with fatal accidents. Yes, over time you may become hardened to it, but you never become immune to it. Never.

My first bush posting was out in the Goldfields area of Western Australia where there was one particularly terrible stretch of road. People commuted back and forth from town to a mining site and it was fifty-one kilometres of hell. The thing was there was nothing wrong with the road; nothing wrong at all. It was all to do with the people factor. They'd go out early in the morning, work hard all day, they'd knock off work and they'd have a few drinks, then they'd drive back to town. Speed and stupidity.

One particular accident that really shook me was when two cars hit head-on. That time eight or nine people got killed. I was stationed at a place called Boulder by then. Boulder was two kilometres from the mine site and so we'd get all the fatals along that stretch of road. Unfortunately, two or three of those accidents I attended involved kids, and so you'd go out there and you'd do what you had to do, then you'd come back to the station and you'd have your debrief.

In those days we did debriefing differently to how it's done now. Whereas nowadays there's the availability of counsellors and all the rest of it. We had nothing like that. We used a very social side of debriefing where you'd sit down with your fellow police officers and you'd have a few beers and chat about this or that or the other. Sometimes you wouldn't even talk about the accident.

Then when you got home, you'd hopefully not have too much trouble adjusting to what you'd seen. But that didn't always work; sometimes you'd just lie in bed thinking, remembering, wondering if there might be anyone else still out there, wandering around the bush, wounded, injured or whatever. You'd probably dwell on that for a while. Then if you're lucky you might grab a bit of sleep before you had to turn up back at work at 4 o'clock in the afternoon. And that was it.

At another place I worked, we had thirteen fatals in twelve months. All bar one of those involved local people. Of course, with them being locals, if you didn't know them personally yourself, you most certainly knew someone who did. When things like that happen, after a while you start to feel a bit gutted.

But everyone reacts differently to tragedy. And while we have to deal with it on the spot, there's always those that then have to be notified. When I was working down the south-west of the state, I had an incident where I did a notification to a lady who was in her seventies. Her partner had been knocked off his pushbike and he'd been killed. For whatever reason, for me, the build-up to that notification was harder than many I'd previously done. I don't know. I can't explain it, because by then I'd been twenty-five years in the police force and so you'd assume I'd find it easier. But it wasn't. It was harder.

I remember knocking on the door. I was dressed in my uniform and when the lady came to the door, she took one look at me and the first thing she said was, 'Oh, he's had an accident, hasn't he?'

I said, 'Yes, he has and unfortunately he won't be home today.'

Then she invited me inside. She asked if I wanted a cup of tea.

'Yes, okay,' I said, so she busily made a cup of tea.

'A piece of cake?' she asked.

'Yes, thanks.' Then we sat down at a table out on the verandah and chatted for fifteen or twenty minutes; just flashes of memories along with some small talk.

When I offered her advice as to what to do next, she was attentive, thoughtful. 'Yes, yes, okay then. That's what I'll do. Thank you very much.'

As a policeman that's probably the thing that concerns you the most because, as I said, people's reactions to tragedy are always different, especially when it concerns very close friends or kin. So that one was particularly hard, and I still don't know why. But she was a lovely old woman and being in her seventies it makes you wonder how she'd cope and how she'd manage to continue on after having lost her long-time partner.

Yes, so now I'm in Kununurra, in the far north-east of Western Australia, over near the Northern Territory border. I'd already been up here before but this second time it was a permanent posting as senior sergeant, officer-in-charge. As for memories; when I came up here in 2002 I was still able to play football. In 2003 I coached the Ord River Magpies to a premiership in the East Kimberley Football League and we went back-to-back again in 2004. That was very, very special.

Probably the downside was when there was a fatal helicopter crash back in early November 2003. That took four lives, and unfortunately one of my football players was among the people killed. A group of ten from the Ord River District Co-op were on a heli-fishing trip out to Cape Domett, in the Cambridge Gulf. They'd split into two groups; one group was in a Jet Ranger, the other group was in a Robinson R44. It was a Saturday. The heat was terrible. By early morning it'd already reached 43 degrees centigrade. Then around 10 o'clock, they said, 'This's too hot, let's head back home.'

When that was agreed upon, someone said, 'Hey, we can't see too much out of the Jet Ranger, so how about we swap helicopters?'

'Yeah, okay,' they said. 'Fair enough.'

So with no thought they just swapped over the passengers. And they were having a great time. The pilots were happy and the loading didn't make any difference to the Jet Ranger. But the three passengers that changed over into the Robinson R44 were heavier than the ones that had flown out in it.

So they took off. The Jet Ranger went ahead and when they received a distress radio call, as the Jet Ranger's pilot turned his chopper around they saw a huge black plume of smoke coming up from the ground. It was a charred mess. There was nothing they could do right there and then so the pilot flew back to Kununurra, dropped his passengers off and alerted us.

The accident happened out on Carlton Hill Station, which was well over an hour's drive north from Kununurra, and at that time of the year the road was virtually inaccessible. We sent a crew out on the day and they eventually found their way in there. Then in the early hours of the following morning, a recovery crew went out and recovered the bodies of four people.

The official report said that the accident was due to a combination of heat and no air, plus the slight change of loading and a different stability set-up. Apparently they got to a point where they ran out of air in the rotor and they went down hard. The instant they hit the ground, the Robinson R44 exploded.

Then, because the boss and I plus an ex-army fellow and another experienced police officer had seen things in our past that had been extremely unpleasant, we decide to oversee the recovery side of things ourselves. Purposely we chose to do that. We thought it best not to expose any of our staff members who'd never witnessed the aftermath of a terrible accident such as this before. Yeah, and so that was it. But, another thing was, most of the fellows who died were well known and well liked so it really shocked the town, and the young bloke who was a member of my football team — Dave Plunkett — he was just twenty years of age; a champion young fellow.

That's probably the saddest part of my entire Kimberley experience, which has now spread over many years. And to be so closely connected to him. Actually, the day of his death coincided with our footy club's presentation night and when word about the accident got around, they rang me and they said, 'We'll have to cancel it.'

I said, 'No you won't. We'll have the night. Yes, it'll be subdued to start with, but Dave would've wanted us to go ahead because he was that sort of a man.'

So we went on with the presentation night. Only one of his team mates didn't attend and that was fine. But everyone else did and it was very subdued to start with. But after a while they all started to think, Well, Dave would've wanted us to be here and to enjoy it.

In the finish everyone had a pretty good night and it proved to be an important part of the initial grieving process. Then there were the funerals and the four of us who did the recovery attended every one of those. From doing that I suppose you could say we've all made lifelong friends. There are still people here in town that were connected to the accident and so the anniversary gets a bit hard because they try to find me, to reminisce. I still find that awkward.

Now, these days, each year we play for an award in Dave's honour. It's the game between Demons and Magpies and the winner receives the Plunkett Shield. But it doesn't get any easier. Like I said, you may become hardened to these things, but it's never easy. It's never easy, and that one was hard. It was tough, very tough.

# The Poetic Policeman

My father was a policeman, through and through. He joined the force in the mid-1920s, as a young recruit in the mounted police, and during his many years of service he covered just about all of Queensland. Though I venture to say that he was a little different than most, which was something that sometimes raised the ire of those above him, in particular the Queensland Police Commissioner, whom Dad bombarded with his poetry.

I've dug through Dad's records and I've come up with a couple of poems that may demonstrate this fact. The first was written in 1935 when Dad was stationed between Mackay and the Whitsundays, at a town called Calen. This was just prior to his being transferred to Laura, which is in the northern area of Cape York Peninsula. Apparently, up until this time the powers-that-be had never issued Dad with a firearm.

The poem goes:

*Ever since I joined the force*
*No firearm have I had.*
*In fact I haven't fired a shot*
*Since I was just a lad.*
*And around the pubs at closing time*
*This is what I hear,*
*'Come on boys, let's drink them up*
*Here comes the sergeant ... with his spear.'*
*So I now make requisition*
*For a brand new automatic*
*To stop the rumour going 'round*
*That I'm a bit erratic.*

So this was sent off to the Police Commissioner who was quoted as saying, 'Just who is this bloody nut who's always sending me poetry?'

Still and all, I believe that after the Police Commissioner received the poem, Dad was issued with a weapon.

The second poem was written much later on, in 1949, when Dad was stationed up in the Gulf of Carpentaria. I was born by then and from the tone of the piece it seems that, for the sake of Mum and us kids, Dad was keen to be transferred down to Marian, which is just west of Mackay.

It goes:

*Since I've been in the job I've covered quite an area.*
*Four years up on the Barcoo, three years in the Gulf of*
*Carpentaria.*
*I've been at Forest Hill, the home of spuds and pork.*
*Four years odd at Laura, way up near Cape York.*
*I've been along the Brisbane Valley, up Noosa and Blackbutt*
*way.*
*Two years on my own at Calen, twix Proserpine and Mackay.*
*Just on five years at Pentland. I've seen the Cape in flood.*
*I've been around the Islands and tramped through Bentinck*
*mud.*
*I'm transferred now to a place called Bollon.*
*It's somewhere on the map. I'm told it's on the Wallon.*
*It's pretty tough on wife and kids so for them it's my desire*
*To be transferred now to Marian ... Please let me know by*
*wire.*

Dad sent this off to Police Headquarters in Brisbane and received a wire back saying, 'You are transferred to Marian. Congratulations.'

# The Shirt off his Back

In 2012 I did a horse ride from just north of Brisbane, right over into the north-western corner of the Northern Territory. The original idea had been running around my head for about fifteen years, though as time passed I came to decide how someone should benefit from it. I was working in a hospital as a theatre assistant back then and I thought, Well, I may as well fly the flag for men's health. So I decided on the Prostate Cancer Foundation and because I'd spent some time in the bush I also included the Royal Flying Doctor Service.

My wife was supportive, though she did make it a prerequisite how I first had to pay the house off, which I did, then I had to paint it. I think her thinking was that, if disaster struck, at least the house would be painted and paid for. Anyhow, in the middle of all that I was diagnosed with non-Hodgkin's lymphoma. That was in 2008 and my first thought was, Shit, there goes my ride. But thankfully I jumped that hurdle.

The next years, up until 2012, were taken up trying to organise things. So much so that my wife said, 'Even when you're home, you're not home.' Because as soon as I got home from work I'd be on the computer and on the phone trying to sort out all the government red-tape to be able to collect money and also trying to get sponsors on board. I was actually hoping that a big mining company or something would come along and write out a handsome cheque. But that never happened; though I did get replies from Clive Palmer and Twiggy Forrest wishing me all the best in the venture.

Media coverage was another problem. I contacted all the likely television and radio shows and only got a couple of replies there. One said they'd like to help but they were already committed to doing something over at Disneyland, so they were a bit short. Another one told me how they get requests like mine all the time and, if I wanted to be interviewed, I should think outside of the square. I mean, all I wanted was a brief chat once a week about how we were going and to mention I was raising money for charity.

Anyway, it wasn't to be, and I still get annoyed about it. My wife says, 'Roger, let it go.' And yet they talk so much dribble on both radio and TV that you'd think they could've given us a little bit of airplay, wouldn't you? But, as they say, that's my axe to grind.

Anyhow, we eventually got sufficient people on board. We got a four-wheel-drive Navarro and some cash for fuel from Nissan Australia. Nathan Trailers built me a horse float. Unfortunately, they've since gone into liquidation. Both the Navarro and the horse float were sign-written with the charities we were supporting. ARB 4x4 came on board. My neighbour gave me five hundred dollars. One of the surgeons at work gave me a thousand dollars to cover food and expenses. Kilcoy IGA gave five hundred. Then Brian, my driver, and I would've put in around one thousand three hundred dollars each and I took three months' holiday on half pay.

Our destination was Bullo River Station. Bullo had been the property of Sara Henderson, the author. When I first approached Marlee, the woman who now owns the place, she said, 'Why did you choose us?'

I said, 'I've read all the books.'

'Well, you know all the gossip about us, then,' she said.

'I do,' I said.

On the first Monday in July 2012, we saddled up and set off. There was Brian, and I had a father and son ride with me as far as Chinchilla. I took three horses; two were brumbies from the RSPCA. We tried to travel up to forty kilometres a day. What we'd do was, each morning I'd ride off while Brian broke up camp. After he'd broken camp, Brian would pass me and go ahead and find a spot to set up again, then I'd arrive around 4 o'clock, depending on which horse I was riding.

We cruised pretty much up the highway, unless the locals suggested otherwise. They knew best, so it was good to follow their advice. We made sure that the only thing we left were our footprints. Brian tended to drive into someone's property and explain what we were doing and ask if we could camp in their front paddock. And, more often than not, before we knew it, they'd invite us in for a meal and offer us a bed.

We met up with one family out near Dalby who'd just arrived back from a camping trip. 'Oh,' they said, 'we'll cook for you.' So they invited their in-laws around and it was lamb shanks in the camp oven, fresh bread rolls, baked vegies, a couple of cold beers then sticky date pudding for dessert, which was a nice change from Brian's cooking, and I'm sure he wouldn't mind me saying that. Then to top it off we were offered a bed. In another place, we were going to camp in the shed but no, we got upgraded to the granny flat and we were fed a steak you could've just about put a saddle on. And when we left in the morning we were given fruit and vegies, four bales of hay and a hundred bucks, and invited to camp there again on our way back.

We went up through Kilcoy, across the Blackbutt Ranges to Cooyar, Dalby, Chinchilla, Miles, Roma, Mitchell. Then we followed the Landsborough Highway up through Longreach, then out to Mount Isa, Camooweal, then across the Barkly Highway to Tennant Creek, then up the Stuart Highway, across to Timber Creek, then on to Bullo Station. In all we covered around 3200 kilometres, give or take, during our three months on the road and we raised just under eighteen thousand dollars.

I guess it wasn't a lot of money, especially after it's been divided up between the two charities. But it didn't matter. We did it and the bush hospitality was fantastic. No, they mightn't have had a lot of cash to spare, but some of those people would've just about given you the shirt off their back. In fact, one bloke virtually did. Des was his name. He was a policeman. We met him just after we'd set up camp in a paddock south of McKinlay. McKinlay's only got a population of about twenty people. It's where part of the *Crocodile Dundee* movie was shot, at the Walkabout Creek pub.

Anyhow, Brian and I were sitting there having a cup of tea when this four-wheel-drive police vehicle pulls up. 'G'day, I'm Des,' he says. 'Have you blokes got anything to do with this paddock?'

I said, 'Well, no, we haven't, actually.' I thought he was going to move us on.

He said, 'Look, there's a bullock out up the road. Can you give me a hand to get it back in the paddock?'

I said, 'Yeah,' and so we stood out on the road while Des drove back to hunt up this bullock. The paddock only ran three strands of wire anyway and so the bullock just ducked in underneath the fence, back into the paddock. We then sat around and had a chat to Des. He'd only been there six months and his wife had just arrived a day or two beforehand. Anyhow, he said, 'If you're coming through McKinlay' — which we were — 'you can camp with us at the police station if you like.'

The next day, when we pulled in at the McKinlay police station, Des said, 'Have a shower, then we'll go to the pub and I'll buy you a beer.' So after Brian and I had cleaned up a bit we all went up to the Walkabout. Des puts his credit card on the bar and says, 'Okay, what're you drinking?'

I hadn't had much alcohol up until that time because, if you do, you tend to dehydrate too easily out on the road. So we had a beer, then a couple more, then a few more. When we got back to Des's place, he fired up the barbecue and we settled in for a couple more. Then, when the scotch came out, I said to Brian, 'Here, you can drink this. I'm done.'

But it was a great night; to the point where, when the alarm went off the next morning, I stayed in my swag longer than usual. I don't think I even had breakfast before we set off.

Later on that day we'd just set up a camp when Des turns up. He was coming back from over Julia Creek. He still looked a bit rugged so I reckon he was looking forward to getting home for a rest. He said, 'Don't forget to call in on your way back home.'

As it happened, on our way back home, we were just out of McKinlay when there was some sort of hiccup in the computer system of the Navarro, which caused it to get stuck in crawl mode. We could only go ten k's an hour. So when we reached McKinlay we stayed with Des and his wife for a couple of days while we sorted the problem out.

Anyhow, this particular night we were sitting around the fire. It was pretty cold and Des was wearing his police jacket.

'Gees,' he said, 'these bloody police jackets get too hot for me.'

I said, 'Well, how about you lend it to me then.'

'Okay,' he said and he tossed it over.

And I've still got it. It's sitting in my wardrobe. So if you get around to interviewing Des about police stories, tell him, if I ever come through McKinlay again, I'll drop it back to him.

# The Sundown Murders

Then there was the Sundown Murders. Oh, it was a nasty thing. That was in '57, just before Christmas. Hot as hell. It was out on the old Stuart Highway, up near the NT–South Australian border, about forty miles south of Kulgera. The Stuart Highway was pretty much an unsealed track back in those days. There was a lady named Thyra Bowman and her young daughter, Wendy, along with a family friend, Thomas Whelan, and they had a couple of family dogs with them. The Bowmans were driving down south, on their way to Adelaide in a Vanguard sedan, and they'd pulled up on the eastern side of the Stuart Highway to camp the night.

Another car, a black Plymouth DeSoto, was travelling north, towing a green two-wheel caravan. In the Plymouth was a bloke by the name of Raymond John Bailey, his wife and their young son, who was about four or five. Anyhow, they came along and set up camp about a quarter of a mile up the road from the Bowmans and Whelan. Then during the night this Bailey feller came down to the Bowmans' camp. He had a .22 rifle. As he neared the camp, the Bowmans' dogs started barking. I think one of them might've even bit him. But when Thomas Whelan sat up in his swag to see what the disturbance was, Bailey bashed him in the head and shot him in the back. Having shot Whelan, Bailey then bashed and shot Thyra Bowman and her young daughter, Wendy. He shot the dogs as well.

Because the Bowmans and Whelan were camped right on the side of the road, Bailey put the three bodies and the dead dogs into their vehicle, the Vanguard, and drove them out into the bush where he dumped them. He then drove the Vanguard back to the highway and left it there overnight. Early the next morning he went back and drove the Vanguard to a spot out near where he'd dumped the bodies. He left it under some trees there before he went back to his camp and he and his family continued north.

As had been previously planned, the Bowmans and Whelan were due in Adelaide on a certain date but, of course, they never arrived. Three days later, the police were notified. A huge search then got underway to find these three missing people. Quite a few police came up from Adelaide. I was officer-in-charge of Oodnadatta Police Station and by then I had my assistant, Bill Jacobs, with me, and we had the police come over from Finke. There were also a number of black trackers and the air force from Woomera was involved as well. Eight days later, we were notified that the Vanguard had been spotted by an RAAF Lincoln Bomber, under a clump of trees at the deserted Sundown Station.

When we reached the vehicle, there was no sign of the three missing people. Then a young feller by the name of Noel Coultard was riding around the bush on a motorbike and he came across the bodies of the three people and the two dogs, hidden under some blankets and canvas, about a mile or so from where the Vanguard had been found. Because it had been hot weather and they'd been there for quite a while, it was a hell of a mess.

Noel Coultard wasn't Aboriginal but, being the son of the owner of Kulgera Station, he was born and bred in that country so he could read tyre tracks as good as any black tracker. So he'd tracked the path of the Bowmans' Vanguard right to the spot where the bodies were. By then the Aboriginal trackers had found the place where the killer had parked his car, out on the Stuart Highway, and they told us that it was towing a two-wheel caravan.

First reports started coming through of how witnesses had seen a dark Ford Zephyr towing a green two-wheel caravan that was travelling north to Alice Springs at around the time of the slayings. The car was later sighted east of Tennant Creek. And then that was it. Nothing.

For a month or so, we were at a complete loss. We then had some luck. I just happened to meet an old feller out on the road who was heading north; a feller called Johnson. He was a land surveyor who travelled through that country quite a lot. I was coming down Welbourn Hill and we got to talking about things and I asked him, 'You weren't in the area around so-'n-so date, when all this happened, were you?'

'Yeah,' he said, 'I was coming up the road and I met this family in a black Plymouth DeSoto who were pulling a green two-wheel caravan. We had a cup of tea together and the feller said that he was heading up north to look for work.'

Then after they'd had their cup of tea, the feller opened the farm gate for Johnson and so he went on his way and the family went on their way up north. It was quite coincidental about the description of the caravan and also, to my mind, because they looked so similar, a dark-coloured Ford Zephyr could quite easily be confused for a black Plymouth DeSoto. So we sent out word to the Northern Territory Police to see whether they knew anything of a black Plymouth DeSoto, towing a green two-wheel caravan. Apparently someone said that they'd seen it in Tennant Creek and a bit later on the police located the DeSoto in Mount Isa.

There was an Adelaide detective up there with me who was leading the case, Charlie Hopkins, and by the time we flew over to Mount Isa they'd already arrested this Raymond John Bailey for the illegal possession of the DeSoto and also of a stolen rifle. So he was then charged and he was taken back to Adelaide. At first they wanted me to drive the DeSoto back. But to my mind it wasn't in too good a nick so I said, 'Well, I don't think it'd get there,' and so they then called the air force in and they loaded it up in one of their larger planes and they flew it back.

When they had the court case, even though Bailey tried to say that he wasn't guilty of the murders, forensics proved that the gun he owned was the same one that killed the Bowmans and Whelan.

Based on that evidence, Raymond John Bailey was found guilty of the murders of Thyra Bowman, her daughter, Wendy, and that of Thomas Whelan.

As far as I was concerned that was the right decision because after Bailey had been arrested in Mount Isa, I was in the police station with his wife when they brought him in to see her. I remember we were sitting there and she asked him, 'Did you kill those three people?'

'Yes,' he said, 'I did.'

She said, 'Why did you do it?'

And he just looked at her and he said, 'I don't know,' and that was it. He never said any more. He never ever actually said just why he did it. So as to the motive: who knows? Of course he could've been looking for money. But the lady he killed, Thyra Bowman, when we found her body she still had her money hidden down in her bra. So if he was looking for money, he missed that.

Then on the 24th June 1958, Raymond John Bailey became the second-last person to be hanged in South Australia. But, oh gee, when you look back on it, it was a terrible thing. I can tell you, we never camped on the side of the road again after that, and a lot of people still do.

# The Trailer

Well, I don't think I should give too many of my personal details due to the current police investigations, but my name is Bob and I live in the Sydney suburb of Petersham. As you can see, I'm middle-aged. I pride myself on being family orientated. I have a beautiful wife, Joyce, and two great pre-teenage kids, Samantha and Thomas. I've worked in railway maintenance ever since I left school at sixteen. I started out as an apprentice fitter and turner and I've worked my way up to foreman. So I guess you could say that I'm a very stable sort of bloke. In fact, Joyce often describes me as being 'the rock' in our relationship; most probably due to the fact that I'm the one who tends to remain calm during whatever crises may arise.

As far as the wider family go, my parents passed away quite a few years ago. Then Joyce and I had been caring for her parents up until Joyce's father, Stan, died a couple of years ago. That left Dot — Grandma or Gran, as we all called her — as the only remaining grandparent to the kids. But after Stan's untimely death, Gran's health rapidly went downhill, so much so that, with me still working and Joyce having her part-time job down at the chemist's, it got to the stage where she needed full-time care. That proved to be a very stressful time for us all; firstly of having to go through the process of finding somewhere decent for her to live, then more recently on the day we had to take her to Summer Hill Rest Home.

That was terrible. The poor old girl, we just about had to prise her out of her bedroom on the morning she left. It broke our hearts. That was one of those times when I really had to remain as calm as possible, just to help get us all through the day. Though between you and me, I did shed a tear later on, when nobody was around. Of course, then it took our dear Gran a good while to settle down in the facility. But she's a tough old girl and I think, deep down, she realised how we couldn't manage to look after her any more. So, in the end, things have worked out okay, I guess.

Anyway, enough of that.

Then it would've been in about March when Joyce started to receive emails with regard to her side of the family having a reunion during the September school holidays. It was to be held out the west of New South Wales at Joyce's home town of Wilcannia. Initially I wasn't that keen on going. A few years back we'd gone to one of their so-called family get-togethers and it'd nearly ended up in an all-in brawl. But seeing how Joyce had always been keen for the kids to keep in touch with her side of the family — something I'm fully supportive of — I felt obliged to take them.

At first we were hoping we could get away without Grandma knowing. But after one of the kids, Samantha I think it was, let slip about the reunion, there was no way known that we were going to go out to Wilcannia without her. Actually, I really had my doubts about her going on such a trip. I said, 'But, Gran, don't you think you're a bit too frail to go on such a long trip?'

'I'll be all right. No need to worry about me,' she replied, ever the trooper.

But there was a glimmer of hope in as much as we only had a small two-door Cortina and I'd worked out that, by the time I fitted Joyce and the kids in, plus all the goods and chattels we needed for the two-week trip, there'd be no room for Grandma. So on our next visit I mentioned it to Grandma. I said. 'Look, Gran, I'm afraid there may not be enough room in the car for you.'

That's when she mentioned I should hire the trailer. She'd kind of snookered me there. So the day before we set off I got a tow bar fitted to the Cortina and then I hired a small trailer from a friend of a friend of a friend who charged like a wounded bull.

'Fifty bucks a week plus another five for the tarpaulin, and if you want a spare tyre that'll be another twenty-five bucks.'

With time running short, I agreed. 'Yeah, all right then,' I said and early the following morning Joyce and I packed our goods and chattels into the trailer and the car boot, the kids into the back of the car, and off we went to pick up Grandma from Summer Hill Rest Home.

Of course, by the time we arrived, she'd already packed and had been waiting in the foyer for at least an hour. So into the back of the Cortina she got, in between Samantha and Thomas, and off we went, up Parramatta Road, onto the Great Western Highway, through St Marys and on to Penrith. Then while we were winding our way up the eastern slopes of the Blue Mountains, I just happened to glance in the rear-vision mirror and notice that Gran wasn't looking too well.

'You okay in the back there, Gran?' I called out above the excited noise of the kids.

'Yes, I'm okay,' she said. 'I'll be fine as fine as Larry, just as soon as we get over the mountains.'

Though by the time we'd zig-zagged down the western side of the Great Divide and into Lithgow, it was clear that she wasn't too well at all. Even Joyce had begun to worry. Luckily the kids hadn't noticed that anything was awry and they just continued to niggle each other, as young kids do. Still, when we reached Bathurst I suggested we take a travel break and enjoy a nice picnic lunch. Which everyone agreed to. But after I'd laid down the picnic blanket and Joyce had taken out the Thermos and the curried egg sandwiches she'd prepared earlier that morning, Gran decided to stay in the car. 'I'm all right,' she said, 'No need to worry. Just need to catch my breath.'

It was then that I suggested to Joyce how it may be best if we stay over in a motel at Dubbo that night, just to allow Grandma a bit of extra time to recover from the ordeal of crossing the Blue Mountains.

So we did. Later that afternoon I found a small, reasonably priced hotel on the western outskirts of Dubbo and we settled in; one family room and a single room for Grandma, just so she could get some peace and quiet. Then after a take-away Chinese meal — of which Gran ate very little — she decided to turn in early. The kids turned on the telly, Joyce turned on her laptop and I began to silently wonder if bringing Grandma with us on such a long trip was really the wisest thing to have done. You know, perhaps I should've put my foot down harder.

By morning, Grandma was looking a little better. When I say 'a little better', that's all she was, because she still had a pale-grey look about her and, for some strange reason, her memory wasn't as sharp as it usually was. It was like, overnight, she seemed to have forgotten the names of most of the wider family members. I asked if she wanted me to take her to see a doctor but, no. She'd come on this trip to get back to family and nothing was going to stop her. 'I'll be all right. Don't worry about me.'

'Okay,' I said and I plugged onward to Nyngan. At Nyngan I turned the Cortina onto the Barrier Highway and we headed toward Cobar. Then, you wouldn't believe it, ten kilometres out of Cobar, the back left tyre on the trailer blew — *bang*. And so, while the kids got out and had a run around the bush and Joyce and Grandma sat in the car discussing the possibilities of us all dying out in the vast wilderness of the Barrier Highway, I took the tarpaulin off, unpacked the trailer, got out the spare tyre, loosened the wheel nuts, jacked the trailer up, took the flat tyre off, put the new tyre on and released the jack. When that was all done I repacked the trailer, making sure that I'd tied the tarpaulin back down nice and tight.

'Okay, everyone,' I said. 'Let's head off and we'll grab a bite to eat in Cobar while I sort out a new tyre.'

Which we did.

By the time we'd left Cobar, it was getting well on to mid-afternoon and Grandma was looking quite poorly. Joyce in particular was extremely concerned, though whenever she asked Grandma if she was feeling okay, it was the usual reply of, 'I'm all right. Don't worry about me. Not long to go now, anyway.'

And so we left it at that.

Now I don't know if you've ever driven west on the Barrier Highway late in the afternoon; if you have the option, I'd suggest you don't. The setting sun just glares straight into your eyes, which makes for very uncomfortable driving. Still, as I squinted into the sunset, I took some solace in the fact that at least we were close to our destination, and what's more things had settled down in the car. Joyce's head was now lolling about between sleep and awakeness. The kids had dropped off, as had Grandma, and for the first time on the journey I was able to relax into my own thoughts.

That's until there came an almighty scream from the back of the car. It was Samantha. 'Grandma's dead!' Then, almost simultaneously, Thomas started screaming, 'Grandma's dead!' and when I glanced in the rear-vision mirror there was Grandma, eyes and mouth wide open ... and she was dead.

I immediately pulled the Cortina over onto the verge of the road. I needed time to think. If ever there was a crisis, this was it, and I had to try to remain calm.

Joyce was of no help. She'd shot out of the car along with the kids and they'd joined in a sobbing chorus of, 'Grandma's dead. Poor Grandma. What are we going to do now?'

I then came up with an idea. 'Okay,' I said, 'everyone settle down. We're nearly there. Less than a hundred k's to go, so how about everyone just get back in the car and we'll sort out Grandma when we get into Wilcannia.'

That didn't go down too well. Not at all. No way were the kids going to sit in the back of the car with their dead grandma stuck between them. I looked to Joyce for some sort of support, but she'd turned into a bawling wreck.

That's when I came up with another plan. 'Okay,' I said,

'here's what we'll do then.' And I explained how I was going take all our stuff out of the trailer and then I'd put Grandma in it, cover her over with the tarpaulin and hide the trailer in the bush. When we got to Wilcannia, I'd go straight to the police and sort things out from there.

Nobody had a better idea so that's what I did. I unloaded the trailer and put all our goods and chattels down beside the road. Once that was done, I carefully lifted Grandma out of the back of the Cortina, placed her in the trailer and secured the tarpaulin down nice and tight. I then drove the trailer down a small track, into the bush, uncoupled it, covered it over with some tree branches, just in case, and I left it there and drove the Cortina back out to the road. As a marker to where I'd left the trailer, I made a small mound of rocks on the roadside. After enticing Joyce and the kids back into the car, I stacked in all the gear that had been in the trailer and off we went.

When we arrived at Wilcannia, I dropped off Joyce and the kids at one of the relatives' places and I drove around to the police station. When I explained to the sergeant what had happened, he suggested that, because it was just on dark, it'd be best if we go out at the crack of dawn the following morning and sort out the situation.

Which we did. Just on sunrise the police van arrived outside Joyce's relatives' place. The sergeant had brought along his Aboriginal police aide, 'Just in case,' and so I jumped into my Cortina and the police followed me back out along the Barrier Highway. When we arrived at the small mound of rocks, I led the police along the track, the short way through the bush, to where I'd left the trailer. When we arrived, the tree branches I'd laid over the trailer were still there, but the trailer wasn't.

It'd disappeared. Vanished. I just couldn't believe it. Nor could the police sergeant. Then after the Aboriginal police aide had had a bit of a look around, he said, 'Trailer's been nicked, Sarge. Someone's stole it.'

# Visa

My wife, Yvonne, and I grew up in Liverpool in the UK. Even though we only lived a couple of miles from each other, we never really met till twenty years ago. We've both done various jobs. Yvonne worked for British Telecom. We did a lot of retail stuff. I was a joiner for three years and I was a part-time police officer with the special constabulary. That's like a volunteer reserve.

As a special constable I'd done just about everything. I'd even run stations on my own. But just taking that final hurdle and applying for a full-time job in Liverpool's main constabulary of Merseyside was difficult. Yes, I passed all the tests. I was up top on the physicals. I had the knowledge and all of that. But then you had to go through a series of interviews, and I'm hopeless at talking about myself, just hopeless. Then when I was thirty-three, the Metropolitan Police of London had a big recruitment drive and we thought, Let's give it a go. If it happens, it happens.

Normally it takes about eighteen months to get accepted into the police, but four and a half months later it was, 'Come and have a test. Come and have an interview. Come and have the physical.' And it was like, 'Oh, okay.' So I went down and did my eighteen weeks' residential training in Hendon.

After I'd graduated, my family came down to London to live. But because my mum had been our babysitter so that Yvonne could go to work back in Liverpool, it was, 'Hey, we now haven't got a babysitter for our five-year-old son. We haven't got a circle of friends. We haven't got this. We haven't got that.' But when our son started school they gave Yvonne an hour here, an hour there, helping out in the classroom. Then she did a course here, a course there, and after about three years she finally became a teacher.

One of my initial postings with the Metropolitan Police was at Forest Gate, which was in the traditional East End of London. That was a massive cultural shock. It's where the likes of Jack the Ripper had once plied his 'trade' and where the Kray twins, Ron and Reggie, had based their organised crime network during the '50s and '60s. By the time I arrived it'd become a hugely diverse community with around forty or fifty per cent minority groups. Before long that had risen to sixty or seventy per cent. Initially it was mostly Asian and Indian, then an African group drifted in, followed by a large influx of Eastern Europeans. That tipped the balance to around eighty per cent and by then your traditional white Englishman was in the vast minority.

So I did three years on the beat, followed by three years in traffic, covering the whole of north-east London, then I went back as a sergeant to run a community team along the lines of safer neighbourhoods. I had ten staff. I had four police officers and six community support officers, who are similar to our Australian community constables. We covered two wards, which had near on six thousand people living in a one by two mile pocket of land. If you've ever watched *Coronation Street* on television, it was exactly like that; there were rows and rows of back-to-back terrace houses.

But then the career progression in the UK started to dry up. Promotion was getting harder and harder and there were minimal roles for me as a sergeant. And also, after thirteen years of policing in London, we wanted a quieter, less stressful life. Just in the area I was working we had seven hundred and fifty police officers and in a twenty-four-hour period, our unit could receive up to a thousand calls. They could be anything from 'There's a noisy neighbour' to 'There's been a murder' or 'There's been a robbery' or 'There's been a fight'.

And the traffic was horrendous. It'd take me a good hour to drive the seven miles to work. And the amount of times Yvonne and I would be going out somewhere and I'd be called back to work because something was happening; I was never off duty. There was always the expectation that you'd be available to step in at short notice.

Anyway, when the opportunity came up to have a bit of an adventure and come over here to Australia, we jumped at it. It didn't matter that I'd have to take a promotional step backwards to constable. I could always work my way back up. Initially I applied for Western Australia, but that's when they were at the end of their big recruitment drive. We'd put in a lot of effort there, so that was a real blow. Then two years later we applied for South Australia, and that's when all the trouble started.

I came over by myself in the January. SAPOL — South Australia Police — acknowledged prior service to some degree but, because I hadn't been in a firearms unit in the UK, I did a week of firearms training. And even though I was an advanced pursuit driver and police motorcyclist with the Met back in the UK — which, mind you, was renowned as being the best in the world — that wasn't recognised here in Australia so I had to do a week of driving training. Following that was eight weeks of the transitional law. Well, basically a theft is a theft, a drunk's a drunk and a fight's a fight, but the administrative side of things was completely different. You can say, 'I'm arresting you for stealing,' but then what forms do you fill in? What computer package does it go on? What do you need to do after that? So I had to be brought up to date there.

Anyhow, when Yvonne came out for a brief visit to Adelaide, even just looking around, we said, 'Yes, it's nice, but it's busy. We want to get away from all the cars and traffic lights.' So when I got back to the UK we researched all the rural stations in South Australia and when I saw Ceduna was available, it was like, 'Great, let's try going outback.'

So then, just as we did two years previously with the Western Australian Police, we started going through the whole process again. We excelled in everything. We had everything we needed. I'd been offered a position at Ceduna. Yvonne was a qualified teacher in the UK and was keen to retrain once we got out here. Our daughter, even though she's autistic, could provide references over a five-year progression of employment and our son had decided to stay with his older brother in Manchester and go to Salford University. We'd even said our goodbyes to our friends and the rest of our family. So all was set. Then we get an email from the Immigration Department saying, 'Due to your daughter's circumstance we are unable to offer her a visa.'

We were gutted. They went on to say how she may well become a burden on healthcare and social services in Australia. Mind you, this was despite her having proof of previous employment and that she was largely self-reliant and that she rarely sought medical assistance. Then they're like, 'Well, if you pay one thousand five hundred pounds and have an independent report done by a psychologist, we'll reconsider the situation.'

So we did; we paid the money and when the report came back it actually read that our daughter would become self-sufficient and she'd eventually be able to live on her own. But no, they still wouldn't take her. No visa. They wouldn't even consider it.

What made matters worse was that the immigration people were so apologetic. They were saying, 'Sorry, we appreciate your situation. But that's the way it is. Our hands are tied.' Then they offered us temporary residencies with the assurance they'd try to sort something out after we'd arrived here. That wasn't of any help because the law states that you have to be a permanent resident of Australia before you can join the police force. So we were stuck between a rock and a hard place. I mean, even the

South Australian Police Assistant Commissioner contacted me to say how sorry he was that he couldn't offer me a position, not until I had permanent residence status.

Anyhow, I was sitting there one night, back in the UK, stewing over all this and I thought, Well, this's a complete mess. We're not going to Australia. We've explored every avenue of appeal. We've even spoken to the UK Prime Minister. We'd already spoken to the Australian Minister for Immigration and he was like, 'I'm awfully sorry, but there's nothing I can do about it.'

Then I thought, Blow it, and I wrote a four-page letter and I sent it to twenty different Australian-based news agencies and within a day it exploded. We were on the internet. We were on the radio. We were in the newspapers. The Adelaide *Advertiser* ran with the original story and apparently, within an hour of publication, their website received over four hundred comments condemning the Immigration Department over the matter. Of course, with us still being in the UK, we didn't have a clue as to the huge fuss my letter had made.

Then one morning at half past five, the phone rings and I'm like, 'Hello?'

'It's the head of SAPOL recruiting here.'

'Yes?'

'We're pleased to say we have an offer of employment.'

I'm like, 'Please explain? We haven't even got our visas.'

He said, 'Check your emails and have a look at the internet.'

So we did and it was like, Oops. There was even a personal letter from the Immigration Minister along the lines of how he could do something about it after all, but that he could only intervene and facilitate entry for me and my family if we were all on Australian soil.

Well, Yvonne was in tears. So was I. Everything was resolved.

So I came over here to Ceduna first, without my family and I was astounded. It was exactly what we were after. It was like, 'Good, it hasn't got any of that. Great, it's got loads of that.

Yes, there's a few little problems here and there, but they're minuscule within the greater context, and it only takes me two minutes to drive to work.'

Then when Yvonne came out to have a look around, as we were driving in from Ceduna Airport, she noticed how everyone was waving at us and she was like, 'What? Do you know all these people?'

I said, 'No, I don't. Everyone around here waves at each other.'

She just couldn't believe it. I mean, even if you smiled at somebody in London it'd be, 'What? What's the matter with you?'

And oh, she loved it so much that she cried at the airport. She just did not want to go back and finalise a few things before her and our daughter came over. Then when Yvonne did get back to the UK, we were chatting on Skype and she said, 'Our son's got something to tell you.' This is the one who was living with his older brother in Manchester and had a placement at Salford University.

I was like, 'Oh, not more trouble. This's the last thing I need. What's gone wrong now?'

He gets on and the first thing he says is, 'I want to come to Australia too.'

So he's over here as well and we've all just sort of fallen into the place. Every day we embrace it. Even though our son's unsure of what he's eventually going to do, he's already got a job in a local supermarket. My wife has employment. And the irony of the whole thing is that, other than me, our daughter was the first one in the family to get a job. Well, she's actually got two jobs. She's a cleaner at the school and she works in the op-shop. And they can't get enough of her.

## Wife-to-be

Groote Eylandt? Groote's on the western side of the Gulf of Carpentaria. It's the largest island in the Gulf and it's about six hundred and fifty kilometres east of Darwin, as the crow flies. It comes under the jurisdiction of the Northern Territory Police. I was stationed there a couple of times. First as a relief for a fellow who'd gone on holidays for a couple of months. The second time was in a permanent position and I was there for two and a half years. In fact, that's where I got married to my wife-that-now-is; up there on Groote Eylandt, by a Catholic priest from Nhulunbuy, if my memory serves me correctly.

There's the two major communities on Groote; Angurugu Community, which was where the police were based. That's on the north-western side on the island. Then there's the Umbakumba Community, which was about twenty kilometres over on the eastern side of the island. We had about five or six of us coppers stationed at Angurugu and the worst part was when we'd get called over to Umbakumba of a night-time. Usually it'd be to arrest someone who was running around drunk, threatening people with a spear and what have you. That was pretty scary. In fact, I remember driving out to Umbakumba one night and thinking, Wonder what's going to happen? Hope I survive.

Though the other police, the ones who'd had more experience than me, taught me how to handle a situation like that. The idea was to get them in your headlights — on high beam — so that it momentarily blinds them. Then while they're temporarily blinded you drive as close up against them as possible so they haven't got the room to throw the spear at you. Then, as quick as a flash, you jump out of your vehicle, grab them and take them in fast, before they get the chance to spear you. That's how it was done.

I had a couple of experiences like that during my first time on Groote, and it put the wind up me. Like I said I was there for a couple of months on relief, then I went down to Tennant Creek. I was in Tennant for a year and I actually enjoyed it, which may surprise you. There were about twenty of us coppers. It was pretty good policing and I had a good social life as well, as my wife-that-now-is is always keen to remind me. Though, of course, we weren't married back then. It's just where we first met, down in Tennant Creek.

It was quite funny actually. A copper friend of mine from Alice Springs had taken a couple of months off and he'd decided to have a bit of a look around the place. He was driving from Alice Springs to Tennant Creek, on his way up to Darwin, when he came across two female hitchhikers. One of them turned out to be my wife-to-be. She's Canadian, and my mate picked them up. At that time I was living in the barracks at Tennant, and so when they got into town they all bunked down there. Anyhow, my wife-to-be's first memory of me was of this pissed fellow staggering home, with a sheila under his arm. No, definitely not the best of first impressions.

Anyway, my mate then took the two girls up to Darwin and I didn't think any more of it. Well, I actually didn't remember too much about it in the first place, to be honest. Not long after that I got asked to go out to Avon Downs to do a relief for four months.

Avon Downs is out on the Barkly Highway, going towards Camooweal. It's about thirty kilometres from the Northern Territory–Queensland border. It was pretty quiet. There was no actual settlement or anything there. It was just a one-man station. But there's a little creek there where you could go down and catch a few yellow belly and every now and then someone would pull in and say, 'We're coming in to the Territory. We want to register our firearms,' or to register their cars, motorbikes and sometimes their trucks. I'd be on hand to do that. There was also a pretty big district to look after so I'd go around to all the different cattle stations and do their registrations and what have you. Then very occasionally you'd have to deal with highway accidents. But over all there wasn't that much to do. I mean, they even used the lockup as an airing room to hang cow carcasses.

Anyhow, while I was out at Avon Downs, my mate and the two girls went and did their separate things in Darwin. Then somehow they caught up again and my mate said, 'Hey, I'm going over to Queensland now. If you want to come along, you're welcome. Come or go, do whatever you want to.' I think he had some property over near Toowoomba or something.

'All right,' they said, 'we'll go over to Queensland with you.'

So they did and along the way, of course, they stopped off at Avon Downs. My mate hadn't told the girls that I was out there and I can still remember my wife-to-be's first remark when she saw me: 'Oh no, not you again.'

But this time I wasn't drunk and I didn't have a woman under my arm and the yellow belly were biting and luckily one of the property owners had given me a carcass to hang in the lockup. I had plenty of food and so they decided to stay on for a few days and I guess that's what started us thinking. Following that they all went over into Queensland. They did a bit of travelling around there and on their way back through they all stayed over at Avon Downs again and, as they say in the classics, one thing led to another.

Though being Canadian on a tourist visa, it then came time for my wife-to-be to leave the country. So she did, and after a few weeks of letter writing I got up the courage to phone her from a public telephone booth and, with heart pounding, I asked her to marry me. Which was a proposal that she accepted, thankfully.

Then before she'd returned to Australia, that's when the permanent vacancy came up out on Groote Eylandt. I applied for the position and got it and when my wife-to-be arrived back in Australia, that's when we were married; up there on Groote Eylandt. Yes, and so that's how my wife-to-be became my wife-that-is and here we are, now thirty-six years on, and we're still married. We've had five kids and we've currently got seven grandkids.

There's a bit of romance for you.

# Wild West

When the explorer Charles Sturt passed through the north-west of New South Wales in the late 1820s, he described the area as 'uninhabitable'. A few years later, in 1835, the surveyor-explorer Sir Thomas Mitchell arrived on his expedition to explore the path of the Darling River. And even Mitchell had his difficulties. Apart from dealing with the tough environment, there were also tensions with the local Aboriginal people, so much so that Mitchell built the stockade of Fort Bourke to protect his men. It was around this small structure that the first settlements of Bourke began.

Then followed another problem: just how to gain access to the goods and supplies that were needed to establish the settlement? Then in the late 1850s, after having come up the Darling River from the bottom end of the Murray River, Captain William Randell arrived in his riverboat the *Gemini*. Once that feat had been accomplished, Bourke began to grow.

One of the original settler-pioneers to the area was Vincent Dowling. He came overland with just over a thousand head of cattle and established a station on the banks of the Darling. Other settlers — squatters — soon followed. In many ways, this growth also signalled the demise of the local Aborigines' traditional way of life, as these early settlers had them working on their station properties. There were no wages as such. They would've only received things like tobacco and sugar, tea and flour, just for their keep.

As in most fledgling settlements throughout Australia, one of the first buildings to be erected in Bourke was a pub, the Old Fort Hotel. John Kelly, a friend of Dowling's, built that in the early 1860s. Then of course, as the small township sprang up, along came a vast array of characters; from do-gooders, to business people, to dreamers, gamblers and, of course, you had your fair share of larrikins and criminals. And it's those sorts of Wild West-type stories that are of interest to me because, when you take a closer look, I can tell you, the Australian bush certainly doesn't lack any colour.

One such story comes from the early days of the riverboats. Actually, I think it might've even involved William Randell. Randell often took on board a lay preacher; someone who'd be available to play hymns on his boat's harmonium and give sermons to the passengers and crew along the way. On one such trip to Bourke, Randell happened to meet a Presbyterian lay preacher whom he invited to accompany him on the *Gemini* all the way back down to the bottom end of the river system. The story goes that the preacher turned out to be none other than Frank Gardiner, the notorious bushranger. In a desperate attempt to avoid the authorities, he'd robbed someone of their clerical garb then posed himself as a lay preacher. As you might imagine, it would've been an interesting twist to have had Frank Gardiner standing up there on deck, extolling the virtues of a good Christian life along the lines of 'thou shalt not steal' and 'thou shalt not kill' while he made his escape down the river.

But in those early days, organised law enforcement had only just started to gain control out in the more centrally populated places like Dubbo. In doing so, a lot of the criminals, such as Frank Gardiner, were moving further west, beyond police reach. So around Bourke and other such far-flung places it was like the Wild West. If there'd been a crime out on one of the station properties, say, horse stealing or cattle duffing, the locals would form their own posse and head off in pursuit of the perpetrators.

From what I've read, one of the first court cases to be held in Bourke was that of a hardened criminal from Norfolk Island.

He'd been arrested for bushranging by John Kelly and a few of his mates. With there being no jail in Bourke, when they brought this fellow in, they had to tie him up in the pub's kitchen. Vincent Dowling was then nominated as magistrate and the Norfolk Islander was tried there and then, in the kitchen.

Another interesting character from those early days was Oscar Hughan. Hughan was an educated Englishman who, as a young man, had gone to Boston, America, where he'd apparently done some acting and had written stories and some poetry. He's said to have known Henry Longfellow and a few of the other well-known American poets. Eventually Hughan came to Australia and he ended up living in Bourke, where rumour has it that he'd sometimes be seen galloping around town, dressed in a red coat and blowing a bugle as if he was hunting the hounds. But very early on Hughan was writing dispatches to America about his time in Bourke and that's when his stories began to appear in American newspapers; about horse and cattle thieving and how the blacks were spearing the cattle.

To my mind, Hughan's writing style was a touch cynical, a bit flourishing and a bit tongue-in-cheek. The other day I was reading a story he'd written about a police officer who was bringing a criminal in from the bush. As it happened, this criminal had a wooden leg and at night he was made to take his wooden leg off so that he wouldn't escape while the policeman got some sleep.

So, as you can imagine, there was a fairly lawless chunk of country out west back then and so, when the lawmen did start arriving, they faced huge challenges. They had to be hard, tough individuals; firstly because there was very little structure to support them. Then, with having such huge tracts of land to police, they often had to spend a lot of time out bush on their own. To make their job even more difficult, as had been the case with the likes of Ned Kelly, there were patches of settlers who were pro-bushrangers. To some, these criminals were quite heroic figures and, in keeping with that image, many of them tended to choose romantic names like Captain Thunderbolt, Thomas 'The Angel' Hobson and Captain Starlight.

In reality, they weren't that romantic at all. Most of them were just thugs and thieves and it was already tough enough for the settlers to try to scratch out a living in the driest part of the state without having someone gallop in and steal your stock or your supplies. They even held up hawkers; by now there were quite a few travelling salesmen going from property to property, from town to town, trying to make a decent living, and they'd steal from them too. Then, of course, if these crooks came into town, they'd soon be up to no good there as well. So the effort to bring law to the west was a monumental task and to my mind it's those men who were the real heroes of the west. Into this mix you can add Sergeant Andrew Cleary.

Cleary was an Irishman who I believe trained as a police trooper in Sydney. When he arrived in Bourke in the mid-1860s, the area he had to police was the size of England. But over time, he became greatly respected. He was a hard, tough, yet fair individual. He had that bit of flourish; that bit of style. I guess you could liken him to a Wyatt Earp-type character in as much as he gained the reputation of being the man who always got his man.

There were already a few stories floating around about Cleary before he arrived in Bourke. One involved a bushranger down around Coonamble way. For weeks Cleary had tracked him across country. Then one evening he came across him camped on the other side of the Castlereagh River. Cleary laid low that night and at the crack of dawn the following morning he swam across the Castlereagh and apprehended the bushranger while he was still in his swag.

Another story went along the lines of how he'd chased a gang down towards Warren. This time he had a constable with him, plus some black trackers, and he caught up with the gang while they were at a pub. The police rushed them. There was apparently quite a gunfight and, when one of the gang tried to ride off, Cleary single-handedly jumped the bloke, dragged him off his horse and wrestled him to the ground.

Yet another story was that, when Captain Thunderbolt was wreaking havoc throughout the area, Cleary had chased him all the way up to the New South Wales–Queensland border to Hungerford, where he got away. The second time he caught up with Thunderbolt, the bushranger was camped on a lake over near Brewarrina. When they galloped into his camp, Thunderbolt was off like a shot, leaving his wife, Mary Ann Bugg, behind. She was jailed for six months as an accomplice bushranger but, due to a judicial technicality, they eventually let her go. But it was because of Cleary's unerring harassment that Thunderbolt decided to move out of the area. So I suppose, in some sort of way, that was a victory for Cleary, and in the end Thunderbolt was shot and killed by police further east, towards Uralla.

But the main story I wanted to tell began sixty miles north of Bourke, at the little settlement of Enngonia. Just as a point of explanation; remember when I mentioned how many of these bushrangers took on romantic names? Well, there were something like three different Captain Starlights; Harry Readford being amongst them. When Thomas Alexander Browne, the magistrate-cum-writer from Dubbo, wrote his book *Robbery Under Arms* — under the pseudonym of Rolf Boldrewood — he took different elements of those three bushrangers and created his own version of Captain Starlight to be written into the book.

Anyhow, this guy called Frank Pearson was one of the three who took on the name of Captain Starlight. Though, mind you, Pearson also went under a number of various other aliases including Doctor Pearson. He was an educated man; a bit like Breaker Morant and the like who were troubled boys from decent English families who'd either been sent out or had willingly come to Australia in an attempt to make something of their lives.

In November 1868, this Captain Starlight, along with his accomplice, Charles Rutherford, alias William Bedford, had stolen horses and gear from Belalie Station. Constable John McCabe and a fellow constable, Hugh McManus, were after them. Earlier that day they'd ridden into Enngonia where they'd stopped at a tiny one-room pub called the Shearer's Inn. While they were inside the inn, Starlight and Rutherford happened to ride into town. They dismounted and hitched their horses and, when they walked into the pub, there's the police standing there. A shootout ensued. McCabe was seriously wounded in the chest, and Starlight and Rutherford escaped and galloped off. After the shooting, a posse of locals set out to chase them. They tracked them along the Warrego River but, with no sign of Starlight and Rutherford, they eventually gave up.

Unfortunately, Constable John McCabe died a few weeks later from the injuries he'd received. Starlight and Rutherford were next seen down near Tilpa, on the Darling River. The history books have it that they then split up and, while Rutherford went south, robbing from station properties as he went, Starlight came back up the Darling, robbing from station properties as he went too.

When Cleary heard that Starlight was coming up-river, he set off on horseback, looking for him. There'd been word of a notable robbery near Louth, at Gundabooka Station, where apparently Starlight had taken over the homestead, got hold of the brandy, and he'd made everyone drink to his health; 'Now drink a toast to Captain Starlight,' and that sort of stuff.

Starlight had then ridden off towards Mount Gundabooka. This was just before Christmas 1868. When Cleary arrived, a couple of station hands told him how they'd sighted Starlight in a hut near the base of Mount Gundabooka. Gundabooka's quite a steep range; rugged country too, very dry. Cleary, along with a couple of constables and a black tracker, then tracked Starlight and on Christmas Day they went up the mountain and found Starlight hiding in a cave.

Due to a lack of water, Starlight was apparently crazy with thirst and, because he'd been using his pants as a pillow, they caught him with his pants down, literally. So they dragged him out of the cave and hauled him off. Starlight later said that he'd had a bead — a sight — on Cleary, but he didn't shoot because, having already shot one policeman, he wasn't game to push his luck any further.

The odd thing about all this is that, while Cleary was escorting Starlight back to Bourke, the two men formed a friendship. Cleary later said that Starlight was one of the nicest men he'd ever met. Starlight likewise responded by describing Cleary as being a good man.

Anyway, Cleary had to then take Starlight from Bourke to Dubbo and from there Starlight was taken to Bathurst to stand trial.

In those days, if you shot a policeman you'd usually be hanged, if not given a life sentence. But for some reason, and I'm not sure why, Starlight only received a fourteen-year jail term. Some think that, because he was an educated man, he may well have had influence or friends in high places. I don't know, but that's all he got — fourteen years.

In another twist to the story, while Starlight was in Darlinghurst Jail, he converted to Catholicism and he began painting pictures. To my knowledge, he's the only bushranger-artist I've heard of. Actually, if you go to St. Vincent's College in Potts Point, in the school library there, they've got a folder of Starlight's paintings. We've even got a couple here in the Back o' Bourke Centre. They're quite a motley collection of paintings — average at best — and mostly of flowers. Though interestingly enough, in amongst them there's a sketch of a policeman at Bourke, which is obviously Cleary because he'd visited Starlight in jail a couple of times, simply as a friend.

As for Cleary, I believe that his health eventually broke. As you might imagine, being a police officer out west would've been both physically and mentally draining. There was a lot of hard riding, hard living and it would've been pretty intense work because, if you're on the trail of a criminal, you'd have to be forever alert — on your toes — and so sleep wouldn't have come easily. I've found a couple of articles about Cleary where it's said that he ended up dying in Sydney quietly, peacefully.

I don't think the same could be said for Starlight. After he got out of jail, he disappeared for a while. Eventually he was tracked up in Queensland where he'd gone back to his old ways of assumed identities and fraudulent activity. Then he was last heard of over in Western Australia. But he was a troubled soul. I doubt if he would've ever really settled down. I say that because, in amongst his paintings, I remember there was one of an English flower called *Heart's Ease* and underneath it he'd written the words, 'I wish I had some.'